THE SPIRITUAL LEGACY OF
ARCHBISHOP FULTON J. SHEEN

REV. CHARLES P. CONNOR, PhD

ST PAULS

Library of Congress Cataloging-in-Publication Data

Connor, Charles P. (Charles Patrick)
   The spiritual legacy of Archbishop Fulton J. Sheen / by Charles P. Connor.
      p. cm.
   Includes bibliographical references (p.   ).
   ISBN 978-0-8189-1311-2
   1. Sheen, Fulton J. (Fulton John), 1895-1979. 2. Theology. 3. Catholic Church—
Doctrines.   I. Title.
   BX4705.S612C66 2009
   282.092—dc22
                                          2009040618

Produced and designed in the United States of America by the
Fathers and Brothers of the Society of St. Paul,
2187 Victory Boulevard, Staten Island, New York 10314-6603
as part of their communications apostolate.

ISBN-10: 0-8189-1311-8
ISBN 13: 978-0-8189-1311-2

Printing Information:

Current Printing – first digit   1   2   3   4   5   6   7   8   9   1 0

Year of Current Printing – first year shown

2010   2011   2012   2013   2014   2015   2016   2017   2018   2019

The author wishes to express his sincere gratitude to
Marilouise Agnone Ruane
without whose assistance this Manuscript
would not have become a reality.

TABLE OF CONTENTS

PREFACE
by HIS EXCELLENCY TIMOTHY M. DOLAN,
Archbishop of New York

"Never has anyone succeeded in effectively presenting the timeless and seemingly alien truths of Catholicism to a skeptical American audience as Fulton J. Sheen," observed the great historian of the Catholic Church in the United States, John Tracy Ellis.

That's as true today as it was three decades ago when I heard Monsignor Ellis say it in a lecture at The Catholic University of America.

Ed Sullivan, Milton Berle, Jackie Gleason… the great personalities of TV of over half-a-century ago are now part of nostalgia, admired, yes, but seen as frozen in an era-no-more.

Not Fulton J. Sheen! Interest in him is higher than ever. As one now privileged to offer Mass daily in Saint Patrick's Cathedral, over the crypt where he awaits the resurrection of the dead, I am amazed at the number of those who come in search of him.

And the cause for his beatification advances!

But what actually did he say? We recall the sound bites and smile as we are moved still by the re-runs of *Life Is Worth Living*, but was there a consistency, a focused philosophy to his thoughts, writing, preaching, and lecturing?

Ask no longer. Read Father Connor's work. It's not so much a biography – look to Thomas Reeves for that – as much as a concert of the major themes emerging from sixty years of public speaking and publication.

You'll see the central, unchanging emphasis: a life empty without God; the futility of systems – e.g., Marxism and Fascism – ignoring God; the gentle wisdom of the Bible and the Church; the infinite influence of the One born in Bethlehem and executed on Calvary; the tender power of the Mother at His crib and at the foot of the cross; the enduring presence of this Christ in the Eucharist; the centrality of the cross; our duty to the poor.

It's all here. Yes, Fulton Sheen repeats a lot. Like Beethoven said, "We've all only got one symphony in us." But we never seem to tire of him saying it over-and-over again. He's like that faithful steward who brings forth the old and the new from the storeroom.

And Father Connor has given us a wonderful key to that cellar.

Already a fan of Sheen? You'll be more fond of him than ever after reading this book. Heard of Sheen, curious about him, but unfamiliar with his teaching? This is a good place to start.

And I'm confident that you'll nod in agreement with John Tracy Ellis.

> ✠*Timothy M. Dolan*
> Archbishop of New York
> December 9, 2009
> *Feast of Saint Juan Diego*
> *Thirtieth Anniversary of*
> *Fulton J. Sheen's Death*

INTRODUCTION

by FATHER ANDREW APOSTOLI, CFR

*Vice-Postulator for the Cause of
the Canonization of Archbishop Fulton J. Sheen*

In the 1950's the name Bishop Fulton J. Sheen was known to millions. He was the first and perhaps is still the greatest media evangelist in the United States. He had been on radio for 20 years as the voice of *The Catholic Hour*, speaking to an estimated listening audience of 4 million people every Sunday. As a TV evangelist he far surpassed those numbers with a viewing audience estimated at 30 million people every Tuesday night. His presentations on his television series, *Life Is Worth Living*, merited him an Emmy award in 1952 as the *Most Outstanding Personality on Television*. He had a molding effect on the religious formation and education of millions of Catholics and non-Catholics as well.

People were drawn to him. Both by nature and grace he was a remarkable speaker. The very popular Protestant evangelist, Billy Graham, once referred to Bishop Sheen as the "great communicator." What made the bishop's message so appealing? A number of factors contributed to his effective mission. First, he was endowed with a great intelligence. He achieved some of the highest academic accomplishments by any American churchman. He was the first American to be invited to work for the *Agrégé* degree (a kind of "super doctorate") from the University of Louvain in Belgium. He was awarded the degree with "outstanding distinction." He was also the first American ever to win the *Cardinal Mercier In-*

ternational Prize for Philosophy. Then add to this his experience of 24 years teaching philosophy and religion at Catholic University in Washington, D.C. His teaching style was characterized by an exceptional ability to present some of the deepest teachings of our Faith in a language that an ordinary Catholic layperson could easily grasp. This was reinforced by his deep convictions regarding the truths that he taught. To quote a phrase he himself once used, he was "a salesman who believed in his product." It certainly showed through, and it is even now still apparent to those who watch reruns of his TV programs, hear his tapes or read his books. A final quality that enriched his legacy was his obviously deep spiritual commitment to live by the very mysteries of Faith he talked about. He used to say that he drew his strength and insights from his many daily hours spent in prayerful communion with Jesus in the Most Blessed Sacrament.

Many people, even today, still remember Archbishop Sheen simply as a media personality. Despite the impact he made in the 1950's and 1960's, circumstances caused him to be somewhat forgotten in the years immediately after his death. However, with the opening of his Cause for Canonization on September 14, 2002, there has been a resurgence of interest in Archbishop Sheen and his writings and talks as well. He has made a "comeback" that is influencing a new generation of Catholics and non-Catholics alike. People are treasuring the depth, beauty and spiritual richness of his guidance.

The present book, *The Spiritual Legacy of Archbishop Fulton J. Sheen* by Father Charles P. Connor, Ph.D., is certainly a great contribution to the Archbishop's renewed popularity. Without doubt, it is a vast treasury of the Servant of God's wonderful teachings on the spiritual life. With his own scholarly ability, his clear presentations and his deep heartfelt convictions and love of the Lord, Father Connor's presentation will touch many minds and hearts. It will add to the spiritual growth and renewal of all who will read this newest addition to the legacy of the late Archbishop.

Introduction

Father Connor has drawn from many sources in the writings and other presentations of the Archbishop. He has done a great service in drawing together such a large number of themes that touch various aspects of Christian living. His scholarship saves us the task of having to read through the Archbishop's 65 books or listening to all his tapes.

Father Connor starts with the themes of God, life and creation, and then moves on to the mystery of the Incarnation. He then presents a variety of practical topics on living the Christian life including temptation and sin, conversion, the mystery of suffering and the importance of prayer. He offers great insights into several of the Sacraments of the Church: the Eucharist, Confession, the Priesthood and Marriage. Of course, he presents one of the late Archbishop's favorite themes, that of the Blessed Virgin Mary whom the Archbishop often called "the woman I love." Father Connor reveals the Archbishop's insights into the place of Our Lady in God's plan of salvation as well as his deep personal affection for the Mother of God.

This book is not a theological textbook. That would not have been Archbishop Sheen's approach. It would run the risk of being dry, lifeless and unchallenging. But Father Connor's wonderful skill is to show these teachings in a living movement through the journey of the Archbishop's life. It is my joy to recommend this book to everyone who loves God and loves His faithful servant, Archbishop Fulton J. Sheen. No one will be disappointed in their reading!

As the Archbishop would say: "God love you!"

Father Andrew Apostoli, CFR
Vice-Postulator for the Cause of
Archbishop Fulton J. Sheen
Memorial of Our Lady of the Rosary
October 7, 2009

Chapter One

THE LIFE OF ALL LIVING

"How life changes its meaning when we see the love of the flesh as the reflection of the Eternal Light shot through the prism of time," Archbishop Fulton Sheen once wrote. "They who would separate the earthly sound from the heavenly harp can have no music; they who believe that love is only the body's breath soon find love breathes its last and they have made a covenant with death. But they who see in all earthly beauty that faint copy of Divine loveliness… these will, even on earth, learn that Love was made flesh and dwelled amongst us."[1] This view that all earthly love reflects the initiative of the Divine Lover in heaven, forms the basis of Archbishop Sheen's writings on the Heavenly Father; God is constantly in search of us, and the entire purpose of our earthly lives must be to grow in our love for Him. *The Life of All Living*, a work published while he was a young Professor of Philosophy at the Catholic University of America in Washington, D.C. in 1929, seems, in its title, to reflect much of the author's meditation on this theme.

Grounded as he was in Thomistic Philosophy from his graduate years at the Catholic University of Louvain in Belgium, Sheen never seemed interested in dwelling at length on Thomas' proofs for God's existence, since

> No one is born an atheist or a skeptic, one who doubts the possibility of ever discovering truth. These attitudes are made less by the way one thinks than by the way one lives. If we do not live as we think, we soon begin to think as we live. We suit our philosophy to our actions....[2]

Hence all of our spiritual lives in this world are to be a pursuit of the God who loves us, a rekindling, as it were, of the flames of faith given us at Baptism. Sheen was very quick to note that the mysteries of God could not be perceived by reason, but only by revelation, although

> Reason can... once in possession of these truths, offer persuasions to show that they are not only not contrary to reason, or destructive of nature, but eminently suited to a scientific temper of mind and the perfection of all that is best in human nature.[3]

As a result, the young priest set himself to a task he described as an "analogical description of revealed Truths in terms of biology... a Supernatural Biology – a treatise on Divine Life."[4] This was a novel approach in the late 1920's, and followed his earlier tract *God and Intelligence in Modern Philosophy*, which won him the *Agrégé en Philosophie* at Louvain just a few years earlier. Though written essentially for scholars, it was introduced by the Catholic convert and author G.K. Chesterton, and established Sheen's credentials in the academic world. *The Life of All Living* would do the same in the world of spirituality.

To arrive at the life of God, the soul's ultimate goal, one must climb the hierarchy of order; all life is characterized by some sort of activity, and science describes it as an imminent activity. Saint Thomas Aquinas further stressed that the greater the imminent activity, the higher the form of life. This law appeared to be so universally true, it could be proven at all levels, plants, animals, man, even the angelic orders. In the plant order could be found the power of locomotion, or growth; in the animal order this was also true, but sense perception must be added as well; in man, however, something entirely new emerges

> ...we find in man a new kind of immanence... the internal activity of thinking and willing. The life-principle in man is the source of a new kind of activity not hitherto found in the whole realm of creation, an activity which, because of its very superiority marks him as the lord and master of creation, and that is the internal power of thinking and willing. Man can reproduce his kind, he can nourish himself – in this he is like the plants and vegetables. Man has also the power of locomotion and the power of seeing, tasting, touching, smelling and hearing – in this he is like the animal. But nothing else is like him in his capacity for knowledge and love, for thinking and willing. In man, for the first time in the long search for perfect life, do we find a being which retains the fruit of imminent activity within itself.[5]

Life is viewed as a pyramid, an ascension from the lowest forms of life to the very throne of God, who is spirit and perfect life. The Heavenly Father is described by Sheen as one whose first act is to think, not one thought following on another, but all at once. In other words, God does not think of one person one moment and of another the next, rather, all is known to Him always. Nor does one thought die while another is born – His thought process is totally different from ours, since human thoughts follow in a sequential order.

In several of his works, Sheen used the example of flying over a cemetery and seeing many family graves in succession, taking note of the various dates of death of each member in generational order. In the Divine Mind, such is not the case; all are known to the Creator in one, uninterrupted thought.

Sheen saw the thinking and loving capacities found in man as clear reflections of the Divine. The first "thought" of God was the generation of His Son, the Word, just as any earthly son is the product of generation from his father. Our capacity to love was a mere mirroring of the love between Father and Son, namely, the Holy Spirit. Developed in clear, logical style, with the highest degree of doctrinal orthodoxy, and described as the top of a pyramid, the only place where the fullest and most perfect life was to be found, the author was just as quick to bow to the mystery. "How all this is done, I know not," he admitted, "but I do believe on the testimony of God revealing."[6] Our souls, the principle of spiritual animation found in us all, were, therefore, microcosmic examples of supernatural life. The fact that we too know and love proved that the seeds of perfect life and perfect love are to be found in us all.

> Life is not a push from below but a gift from above; it is an imperfect representation of divine Life. There is no spontaneous generation in this world, either naturally or supernaturally. Life must come from Life. When we return to It we live, when we depart from It we die – and that Life – The Divine LIFE – the only Life, the Life which all seek, many without knowing it, is the Life of God, the Life wherein all life rests....[7]

Fecundity is a term less used than in past decades. It is defined as fruitfulness, a capacity for abundant production. In the 1920's, Fulton Sheen applied this biological term to the spiritual life by observing that it is the nature of life to be enthusiastic, "for all life tends to diffuse and communicate itself, and even to overflow its perfection, in order that others might share its joy of living."[8] He noted that both the Greeks and the scholastic philosophers believed all life tended to diffuse itself, and that a strong case was to be made for the application of this principle to the chemical, plant, animal and rational orders. Once again, this tendency in the various steps of human development was but a manifestation of a "Divine Fecundity," the process of God going out of Himself; most especially in His pursuit of the creatures He so loves.

> What is the nature of this Divine Fecundity? If everything that is good diffuses itself, what is the nature of the diffusion of Perfect Goodness? It is twofold: internal and external. Internal diffusion is revealed to us in the Blessed Trinity. God ... is fecund. From all eternity He engenders His Word, and the Word, because generated, is called a Son.... And since love in its real meaning is the attraction of those who communicate in life, it follows that there is a subsisting love between the Father and Son, and this subsisting love which is distinct from both, though not separate, is the Holy Spirit.
>
> This diffusion of Infinite Life in the communion of the true and the good does not exhaust the fecundity of God. There are yet other kinds of diffusion which are free and external, and which depend upon the free choice of Almighty God. God has no need of these external manifestations. He has no need of space for His sojourn, for His life is immense. He has no need of time in which to exist, for His existence is eternal.[9]

Nonetheless, these external manifestations of God are continuous, though not all at once. God does not unveil the totality of His majesty to His creatures all at once; rather, "He merely gives His creatures little glimpses and reserves the full vision for heaven."[10] The first way God revealed Himself was the creation of the world; He did it, said Sheen, for the same reason we find it difficult to keep secrets, because it was good. Using the example of a man placing his hand on some clay and the product subsequently bearing the imprint of his hand, God, the Triune God, created the world, and that creation bears the imprint of His Divine handiwork. Nowhere can that handiwork be better seen than in His Incarnate Son. In a description Sheen was to use often in his writings, he beautifully captures God's primordial self-revelation. He who is born without a mother in heaven is born without a father on earth.

> He who made His Mother is born of His Mother. He who made all flesh is born of flesh. "The bird that built the nest is hatched therein." Maker of the sun, under the sun; Moulder of the earth, on the earth; Ineffably Wise, a little infant. Filling the world, lying in a manger; Ruling the stars, suckling a breast; the Mirth of heaven weeps; God becomes man; Creator a creature; Rich becomes poor; Divinity incarnate; Majesty subjugated; Liberty captive; Eternity time; Master a servant; Truth accused; Judge judged; Justice condemned; Lord scourged; Power bound with ropes; King crowned with thorns; Salvation wounded; Life dead; "the Eternal Word is dumb." Marvel of marvels! Union of unions! Three mysterious unions in one: Divinity and humanity; Virginity and fecundity; Faith and the heart of man. And though we shall live on through eternity, eternity will not be long enough for us to understand the mystery of that "Child who was a father and of the mother who was a child."[11]

God's presence in His Divine Son is the most perfect manifestation in this world of the perfect life found in the Blessed Trinity. The next question is how to discover that perfect life in our own lives. Once again, the answer was described in scientific terms. There were two fundamental laws of life Sheen developed in *The Life of All Living*: the law of expansion and that of mortification. Of the two, the latter directly concerns itself with access to the higher life of God for the creature, and is summed up in a very famous Sheen adage, "Unless we die to a lower life, we shall never rise to a higher one." Following the order of nature, before mineral life can enter into plant life, before plant life can enter into animal life, each life must die to itself.

> Before the plant can live in the animal it must be torn up from its roots and pass, in a certain sense, through the jaws of death; before the animal can enter into the life of man it must pass through fire and water which constitute its Gethsemane and its Calvary. Each thing must die to itself, it must immolate itself if it is to have its life perfected. Nothing is "born" to a higher life unless it be born "from above." If the plant could speak it would say to the mineral: "Unless you are born again you cannot enter into my kingdom." If the animal could speak it would say to the plants and to the minerals: "Unless you are born again you cannot enter into my kingdom." These elevations bear a remote and imperfect analogy to our own life. Yet Christ can speak for He is the Word; He can say to man, "Unless a man be born again of water and the Holy Spirit, he cannot enter into the Kingdom of God."[12]

Our souls are the spiritualizing force of our body, and as long as the soul dominates the body, such regeneration is indeed possible. But, as early as the 1920's, Sheen was saying there are two possible directions a man can take:

> Either he must adapt his life to dogmas, or he must adapt dogmas to his life…. If our life is not regulated in accordance with the Gospel, then the thought of Hell is a very uncomfortable kind of thought. To ease my conscience, I must deny it. I must suit a dogma to my mode of life.[13]

Far from entering into the perfect life of God, hell is the very absence of God for all eternity, and is a possibility, given the misuse of our free will. In a lengthy course of instruction on the Catholic faith, prepared for inquirers as well as cradle Catholics, Bishop Sheen noted that no sooner had we read in Scripture of the creation of the world, than we also read of chaos entering in – unexplainably so. For the believer, Original Sin, the first deliberate act of disobedience against God, committed by our first parents, was and always will be passed on to their progeny – indeed, even after the purifying waters of Baptism, the residue remains, for we are all victims of concupiscence, the natural attraction to sin and evil. This misdirection of our free will shall always account for man's movement in an opposite direction. While some men will live their lives in a constant pursuit of the Divine, others will consider themselves divine, and their own ego supreme. Herein lies the age old, unending dilemma. Yet, despite man's obstinacy, his Creator is continually in pursuit.

Rebellion could take a variety of forms: agnosticism, atheism, the death of God, all creaturely escapes from God's ever search-ing love. Sheen's response to these various forms of denial was always based on a keen perception of each argument, and his reply invariably won over many, and brought numerous souls to God. Agnosticism was much discussed in the 1930's when Sheen wrote *Old Errors and New Labels*, a study of contemporary errors in the light of history. It is interesting how he situates the problem.

> Only about ten percent of the people think for them-selves. Columnists and headline writers think for the greater percent of the remainder. Those who are left are the agnostics, who think agnosticism is an answer to the riddle of life. Agnosticism is not an answer. It is not even a question.[14]

Agnosticism was of two kinds: a doubt about things above

or a doubt about things below. Of the two, Sheen saw the first as far more dangerous, since it led a person to despair. The second, which he termed Christian agnosticism, could be very helpful since any serious doubt about things below us can often provide hope that our thoughts and actions are headed in the right direction. The material world he called the vestibule of creation; the world of science and reason, the sanctuary of creation; and the world of mystery and revelation, the Holy of Holies. These three might be viewed as a temple, each part unlocked by a specific key. The first was opened by the five senses; the second by reason, and the third by the "delicate key of faith." Modern agnosticism or skepticism cast significant doubt on this third and most sacrosanct area of the temple, but such doubt, said Sheen, was really an obstacle to true progress and hindered any sort of true growth. If one agreed, the next step was how to arrive at a "full-orbed vision of faith."

> By no other means than by following what seems to be the most natural thing in the world – that restful act of winking – winking at reason, pulling down its shutters for a brief moment; in other words, doubting that reason can and does know all things knowable.... It is during that first terrible moment of doubt about reason, that plaintive admission of healthy skepticism, "Help thou my unbelief," that God sends His gifts of Faith and Grace. Never once does this outlook on knowledge ask us to pluck out our eyes, or to extinguish the light of our reason. It asks us to use that first, to use it hard, to investigate Divine claims, but not to believe that reason can give the answer to all life's riddles. After a study, then a wink, then a doubt about the finality of reason, then a suspicion that there is a higher light, and then, aided by Grace, the ascent to Faith.[15]

Atheism was quite another matter; in fact, Sheen always thought the concept a contradiction in terms. He used the argument that certain things are so basically fundamental, that to deny them is to assert their very existence. He would repeat many times throughout his career that if I deny I exist, I am merely asserting my existence – because I have to exist before I can deny my existence. Likewise, why would there be anti-prohibition laws in the United States if there were nothing to prohibit? Or anti-cigarette laws if there were no cigarettes? If, therefore, there is no God, as atheists claim, how can we admit to the existence of atheism?

Doesn't atheism imply there is something to "atheate"? Nonetheless, such arguments would not dissuade those intent on denying God's existence. In Sheen's younger years, he wrote that there were two ways of being an atheist – to simply say there is no God; or to hold that we need a new idea of God, that He is "Space-Time or the ideal tendency in things." Some decades later, he forcefully reiterated the two types of atheism:

> There are simple persons who have read a smattering of science and concede, probably, there is no God; but the other type of atheist is militant, such as the communist. They really do not deny the existence of God, they challenge God. It is the reality of God that saves them from insanity. It is the reality of God that gives them a real object against which they may vent their hate.[16]

Of the two sorts, the young Father Sheen had an interesting encounter with the second. For several years as a graduate student in Europe, he did pastoral work at Saint Patrick's Church in Soho Square, London. He would go there over Christmas holidays, and in the summer when classes were not in session. To this day the venerable landmark may be visited. Still a thriving parish near Covent Garden, the structure has changed little since the day the young priest walked in the rear door and found a lady, prior to the start of Mass, lecturing the congregation with her own brand of atheism. "There is no God," she boldly asserted. "There is too much evil in the world – science has proven there is no God." She related that each evening she went out to Hyde Park and preached against God, in addition to circulating pamphlets throughout England defending the atheistic position. In the midst of this harangue, Father Sheen approached her and told her how delighted he was to hear her so forcefully proclaiming she believed in God. "You silly fool, I do not!" was her reply. Sheen responded that he believed her to say just the opposite, and then used this illustration: suppose he were to travel through England circulating pamphlets that protested belief in twenty-footed ghosts; suppose, further, he went out to Hyde Park preaching the same. She readily agreed that she would consider him crazy for doing such. He then asked her why she was not equally crazy for speaking against the existence of God. She could not grasp the parallel, so he explained that his protest against twenty-footed ghosts was directed against a figment of the imagination, whereas hers, against the existence of God, involved a concept she personally hated. She was fighting against something as real as "the thrust of a sword or an embrace," but a twenty-foot ghost could never inspire someone to such militancy. Only the existence of an omnipotent, all searching judge of our souls could drive one to such a reaction. "I hate you," was her reply. In front of the congregation, and with this outburst, Father Sheen gladly retorted, "Now you've given the answer." Atheism, then, is not a doctrine, it is a cry of hatred in the human heart.

By the late 1960's, in the post war, post atomic age, in which political dissent, assassinations, the sexual revolution and theological crises within Catholicism were all part of the world scene, Bishop Sheen, by now Ordinary of the Diocese of Rochester, New York, penned *Footprints in a Darkened Forest*, trying to capture the mood of the modern age, and in particular, the mood of modern atheism. He once again distinguished between an intellectual atheism in which the name of God was relegated to earlier civilizations, and a hatred of God, characteristic of modern man's desire to fashion God in his own image, should he so much as desire His existence. It was extremely important, Sheen said, to look beyond the words of modern atheism to the underlying motives. If such duality still existed in late 20th century atheistic thought, and if the "God Is Dead" movement was symptomatic of much of it, what, or who replaced the Creator?

> No one ever gives up God without substituting an idol. There must always be a Golden Calf, and the reasons given for adoring it are as irrational as the one that Aaron gave: "I put gold in the furnace and it came out a golden Calf." In the 18th century, the "calf" was Nature; in the 19th century, it was Humanity; in the 20th century, it is the Ego. Now it is each man making himself the god-man. Thus the question "Do you believe in God?" ... is now "Do you believe in your ego?" Do you believe that you are your own creator, your own savior, that you transcend all your darkness and fears and dreads, and that there is something greater in you than your own importance and littleness?[17]

More sobering, perhaps, than the notion of the death of God, is that of His absence – symptomatic as well of the late 20th century. Bishop Sheen concentrated much on the thought of the German philosopher Friedrich Nietzsche (1844-1900) who introduced the world to the death of God. Nietzsche, the son of a Protestant minister, as a young man, was much in love with God, though his faith waned in later life and ultimately seemed to disappear. He once wrote to his sister attesting that atheists went through their own sort of hell. Much of the "how" of life could be endured if one knew the "why," but atheists did not know a why. "The very eternality of the individual is but a damnation," he once said and, as Bishop Sheen observed,

> Nietzsche... was one who really chose to believe that God was dead, in order to make room for his ego....

Nietzsche himself became mad. One day seated at his piano, he stopped touching the keys with his fingers and began thumping them with his elbows, shouting and shrieking against the person of Christ.[18]

He seemed, in Sheen's mind, very typical of a century in which God had become absent from the lives of so many. Hell begins here, he often wrote, and it could be proven in the lives of those who had given up the Life of All Living. An even greater price was to be paid by nations who had allowed their religious fervor to decline, since they became prey for the godless political movements the 20th century knew so well. Bishop Sheen wrote extensively on the subject of Communism throughout his career. He taught courses on it at the Catholic University of America and it formed some of the topical material for his Catholic Hour radio broadcasts in the 1930's and 1940's, as well as his Emmy award winning television series *Life Is Worth Living* in the 1950's. He approached his topic from many angles, but continually returned to the same theme: the absence of God gave rise to godless thought.

Religious belief is so essential to the heart that once it is cast aside, some false form is called in to fill the void. Unless the house is tenanted with goodness, seven devils worse than the first come in to dwell there. When minds abandon their concern about final destiny, they substitute for the mystery of what happens after death, the mystery of how someone was murdered. But mystery there must be. At the end of the 20th century we find ourselves living in an era of superstition in which minds believe everything as fanatics and quacks become shrines of worship and objects of adoration. Whence came the millions to accept the superstition of Nazism, Fascism and Communism if it were not from an emptiness of soul brought about by a loss of faith?

The essence of political superstition is the identification of the political and the sacred, as the essence of economic superstition is the Communist identification of the laboring class and Messianism. It was the great boast of the 18th century that "God" and "the supernatural" would be exorcised by an exposure to light. But what happened with the rejection of religious faith was the upsurge of political superstitions which came very close to making the world a madhouse.[19]

Modern man, therefore, uprooted as he has allowed himself to become, is lonely. Loneliness is the essence of the absence of God. And because of this loneliness, movements such as Communism had great appeal. Bishop Sheen not only said the absence of God characterized the modern age, but this period followed directly on one in which God was so very present to humanity. He predicted that we might be living in a period between a death and resurrection, with a rebirth ahead of us. The loneliness of humanity can, at times, be broken through, and if this be true, why can the same not occur for humanity as a whole? One example was to be found in the life of a convert Bishop Sheen was instrumental in bringing into the church, Doctor Douglas Hyde, onetime editor of the *Communist Daily Worker* of London. He and his wife were seated at home one evening, listening to a radio address by Molotov. During the course of the talk, Mrs. Hyde openly challenged what was being said to her husband, stating her belief that Molotov was not truly a man of peace, but rather filled with inner violence, and committed to such a principle in dealing with others. Hyde warned his wife that what she was saying, even in the privacy of their home, could be very dangerous. She expressed little remorse or fear over her words, and, after more of the same, Hyde insisted that if she kept it up, he would have no choice but to report her to party officials. She replied, "Report me." Shocked by her response, and carefully listening to the content of her objections to Molotov, he told her she was talking like someone who could possibly become a Catholic. "I am," she said, to which Dr. Hyde replied, "Shake! – So am I." Such was clear proof of a Divine inner penetration into the lives of two individuals, a husband and wife, living as intimately as a married couple would, and yet, neither was aware of the working of grace in the other. It was also proof that no matter what form rebellion against God takes in our lives, how long it has persisted, or how deeply it has taken root, the "Hound of Heaven" is always in pursuit, and once His grace arouses human receptivity, unbelievable transformations may take place.

God has His own ways of getting into souls, Sheen wrote, and when humanity is reduced to personalities, there are basically only two: those who have found God and love Him, and those who are still searching for Him. The difficulty in the 20th century is that much of humanity is no longer impressed with the physical ordering of the universe and the natural thoughts of the creator who fashioned it, as much as they are with anxieties within themselves. Traditional proofs for the existence of God no longer appeal to man, not because they have lost any of their power of persuasion, but because today's human mind is not trained "to obey the laws of human logic in the search for truth." This disordered tendency, so prevalent in modern times, has always been present, in varying degrees, in souls. In his work *Lift Up Your Heart*, Bishop Sheen used two examples of the groping, searching individual, interiorly unhappy, and in search of the Life of All Living. The first was the story of the Samaritan woman at the well. She went out in the midday heat to draw water – most unusual that time of day in that part of the world. Obviously the woman was an adulteress, and the other women would not want to associate with her at the well in the cooler hours of the morning or evening. At that strange hour, this sinner encountered absolute goodness and purity in the person of Christ, and they are brought together by a common factor – thirst, the desire for a drink of cool water. Our Lord deals with her where she is at that moment, and when

He begins to disturb her conscience, she attempts to change the subject, asking Him on which hill it is proper to worship. Christ's reply that the Kingdom of God is within her allows the focus of the discussion to continue, until the woman is brought around to the fact that Our Lord is a prophet, and far more – by the end of the dialogue, she is convinced of His Messiahship.

The second example the author used came from the missionary journeys of Saint Paul – this time to Athens, where he found an altar which contained an inscription "To an Unknown God." Paul began with the Greeks where they currently were, and assured them that the unknown God they were searching for was the God he had come to preach to them.

> In this spirit, the true lover of God may well say to the people of this century: "I perceive that you are religious people, for walking through your streets, I find more than one statue to the unknown God. You, too, are looking for a God whom you know not. I see a statue to Marx – who promises the brotherhood of man, but who cannot give it, because he denies the fatherhood of any God. I see a statue to Freud – who offers peace of mind, but who cannot give it, because he denies all belief in God and all need for redemption from sin."[20]

There were two ways man could experience the God for whom he was searching, or, as Sheen put it, two trap doors through which God could enter the human heart: our love of goodness, and our melancholy and despair. Our happiness in all God has created can lead us to a greater appreciation of, need for, and love of Him. Also, our misery and unhappiness might equally be a source of coming to Him, since life's experiences teach us that nothing earthly can fulfill our longings and desires.

Bishop Sheen's life was filled with numerous examples of individuals who experienced what he often called the "Divine

Invasion," and he never ceased relating these fascinating stories in his preaching and writing. One had to do with Madame Citroen, a woman who ran a boarding house where the young Father Sheen lived one summer while studying French at the Sorbonne in Paris. He had been resident in the home no more than one week when the woman came to him with a problem. Since she spoke only French, and he understood little of it at this early juncture, he enlisted the help of some American school teachers also boarding there, whose command of French was quite good. Madame Citroen proceeded to tell the priest that some years earlier her husband had abandoned her and her small daughter. The girl grew up and became "a moral wreck on the streets of Paris." She then pulled out of her pocket a container of poison which she told the priest she intended to take that night. She had ceased all belief in God, and had cursed Him intensely. If God did exist, and if He were loving, He would never have allowed her to fall into this predicament. Sheen told Madame Citroen he felt he could help her, and asked her to postpone her decision for nine days – a novena as it were. He claimed never to have prayed so hard over a nine day period in his life, and, in the end, the woman received a great grace. Several years later, while traveling through France, Sheen enjoyed the hospitality of Madame, Monsieur and Mademoiselle Citroen at their home, not in Paris, but in another city. He later enquired of the parish priest if the Citroen family were practicing Catholics. The priest not only assured him they were, but added how edifying it was to see such people who had had the faith all their lives! The pastor had not known the background, but Sheen did, and no doubt gave thanks to the Divine Invader.

Yet another incident many years later Sheen was fond of relating had to do with a phone call he received from a woman asking him to visit her brother who was dying in a nearby hospital. The man had led an evil life, and had been responsible for corrupting the morals of countless young people. He had asked some twenty priests to leave his room, and Sheen presumed he would have no more luck than the previous clerical visitors had had. Nonetheless, he complied, and began a series of visits with the man whom he never identified, but simply gave the name William. He went to the hospital every night for forty nights, and early on would simply open the door, stick in his head and greet the patient with, "Good evening, William." After some time had elapsed, Sheen found himself at the bedside, and eventually the conversations were lasting fifteen to twenty minutes. At no time did he ever mention the subject of religion – conversations were simply the sort of small talk one might imagine at sickbeds. On the fortieth evening, Sheen finally said to him, "William, you're going to die tonight." And William responded affirmatively. "Don't you want to make your peace with God before you die?" William replied quite firmly that he did not, and asked Sheen to leave. The priest replied that he had not come alone; rather, he had brought the Lord with him in the sacrament of Viaticum (in addition he had brought the Holy Oil to anoint him). William replied that he wanted the Lord to get out as well. Sheen then knelt down by the bedside and prayed intensely for this man who was dying an excruciating death of cancer of the face. He promised the Lord that if the man showed any sign of repentance, he would build a chapel for poor Black Catholics in Alabama. Before he left, the priest whispered into the ear of the dying man, "William, before you die, won't you please say, 'My Jesus, Mercy'?" William replied he would not, and more forcefully than before, insisted that Sheen leave. The priest told the nurse on duty that he would be happy to come down to the hospital at any hour of the night if the patient showed any sign of remorse whatsoever, or if he specifically asked for the ministration of a priest. At approximately four o'clock in the morning he received a phone call from the nurse telling him William had died. "How did he die?" asked Sheen. The nurse told him (without herself knowing what had transpired) that shortly after the priest had left the room, the man began saying,

"'My Jesus, Mercy,'" and he never stopped saying it until he died. The moral of this story was that there is a price tag on every soul in the world, and even in our rebellion, the Hound of Heaven continues His pursuit.

Another invasion of the Lord in the midst of great despair centered once again around Saint Patrick's Church in Soho Square, London, one cold January morning. Father Sheen had just opened the front door of the church prior to the early morning Mass, and a young woman, totally emaciated, obviously sleeping there all night, fell in. She looked up, greeted Sheen with, "Good Morning, Father," and when he heard the title Father, he assumed she was a Catholic. She told him she had been, but had fallen away from any active practice of the faith. She pointed to a billboard high atop the Cross and Blackwell Jam Building on the opposite side of Soho Square and informed him she was the leading lady in the musical being advertised. He invited her into the rectory for a cup of coffee, and after they had visited for awhile, he asked if she would like to return in the afternoon to continue the conversation. She said she would, provided he did not ask her to go to Confession. He agreed, but she pressed him further till he more than assured her he would not ask her to go to Confession. That afternoon, after they had talked a good while, he asked her if she would like to see some original paintings in the church, and as they were walking down the side aisle, he "pushed" her into a confessional. He had kept his promise, he had not asked her to go to Confession! She later became a nun in a cloistered convent of Perpetual Adoration in London, and led a truly saintly life.

The English mystic poet who much inspired Bishop Sheen, and whose poem, "Hound of Heaven," he oft quoted was Francis Thompson. A one time medical student, he became a dope addict as a young man, and would often sleep out under the produce wagons found in London's Covent Garden. Early on, he began writing poetry, and submitted some of it to Wilfrid Meynell, editor of *Merry England*, leaving his only forwarding address: Mr.

Francis Thompson, Charing Cross Post Office, London.

When Meynell discovered him, he and his family befriended him, sought out a cure for his addiction, placed him in the care of the Norbertines at their Abbey at Storrington, and allowed him to renew his literary and spiritual vitality. The "Hound of Heaven" was perhaps his most famous poem. It was found in his coat pocket following his death, and within one year, had sold fifty thousand copies. Soon it was being studied as far away as Tokyo, in the Japanese language. It was a work suiting the modern mood well, and in it, the poet describes the many ways he fled God in his own life. He lived only forty-eight years, and was buried in Saint Mary's Cemetery, Kensal Green, London. A good insight into his belief that only one who has allowed his ego to be penetrated by grace can receive the Hound of Heaven's advances is to be found in the epithet on his tombstone

Francis Thompson
1859 – 1907
"Look for Me in the Nurseries of Heaven"

Edifying as it is to read these stories of spiritual heroism, Bishop Sheen was much preoccupied with how everyone can be open to God's loving embrace. He suggested two ways in particular: helping one's neighbor, and remaining open to encounters with the Divine that will come to us from without. As was so often his custom, he offered practical examples of both. Helping our neighbor was exemplified in the story of the Indian who traveled to Tibet to do missionary work in that largely non-Christian country.

Journeying through the terrain with the aid of a Tibetan guide, they became very tired and extremely cold at the foothills of the Himalayas, and stopped for a brief rest. In the ensuing silence, the missionary thought he could hear a faint cry for help in a nearby ravine. He told the guide he was going on foot to see if he could help the needy person, and the guide told him he was crazy – he would freeze to death if he attempted to stay out any longer than necessary. Nonetheless, he started out, eventually found the frozen man, helped him up, and the two continued on, the missionary quite energized by the errand of mercy. When they arrived at the spot where he had left the guide, they found him frozen to death. He likely would have survived had mercy overtaken him as it did the missionary.

A contact with God from without could be illustrated by the conversion story of Clare Booth Luce, who, as a young woman, had lost her eighteen-year-old daughter in an automobile accident. She was bitter, and had no faith whatever. This future Congresswoman and United States Ambassador to Italy came to Bishop Sheen to talk about God. He began by saying he would speak of God for five minutes, then she could have forty-five to speak for or against Him. Sheen had been talking no more than two minutes when she jumped up from her chair, stuck her finger under his nose and said "Listen, if God is so good, why did He take my daughter?" Her instructor replied, "In order that you might be here learning something about the purpose and meaning of life." Many people have tried to know, love, and serve Him who loves us so much, others spend much of their lives searching for Him, and still others have, for whatever reason, rejected Him. Still

> The amazing thing is that God who sees the series of our years gone by, as well as the marks we have left upon our character, still loves us…. He sees us with a Father's eye and loves us, wanderers though we may be, with a Father's heart.[21]

It is, then, this Divine Lover, the Life of All Living, who endlessly pursues us during our earthly sojourn, and, if we are to be separated from Him for all eternity, it would never be His doing; it would be the misuse of our free will. "Man could not be independent of God," Fulton Sheen wrote, "any more than a ray of sunlight could be independent of the sun."[22] He illustrated with the example of an inventor of a machine that shortened human labor and greatly benefited mankind. That inventor would receive patent rights on his invention in perpetuity, and would be legally protected from the encroachments of those who might try to duplicate his invention for their own purposes. In much the same way, we are God's invention, and He has certain rights or claims on us – namely our intellect and our will. And in the exercise of these for love of Him, and for His greater honor and glory, we achieve liberty and freedom in their truest sense. God has as much right to these faculties of ours as an author has to the royalties on his books.

No matter what historical period we speak of, human beings will always have the same three fundamental desires: for life, for truth, and for love. Life is the final gift we surrender, the one we hold onto as long as possible; desire for truth burns within each of us, in the midst of the artificiality surrounding us; and the desire to love and be loved is intrinsic to our human nature. We all possess elements of each, but we do not possess them in their fullness – we always have a longing for more. Also, life is short, and quickly fleeting. In the course of the years given us, we will never be able to grasp life, truth, or love to the highest and most perfect degree. What, therefore, is left for us to do?

> I must go out to a Life that is not mingled with its shadow death, out to a Truth that is not mingled with its shadow error, out to a Love which is not mingled with its shadow hate. I must go out to that which is Pure Life, Pure Truth, and Pure Love – which is God.[23]

And, said Fulton Sheen many decades ago, if we would "sound the depths of God," we must go to our own very human experiences, all of which are a very dim echo, a distant reflection of God. If we look closely at so much with which we are familiar, we will perceive very clearly the Life of All Living.

> If the possession of life thrills and exalts us; if the conquest or discovery of a new truth lifts us up to heights of intellectual joy; if the human heart in its noblest reaches and purest affections has the power to cast us into an ecstasy of delight, then what must be the great Heart of Hearts! If a human heart can increase the joy of living, then what must be the great Heart of God! If the spark is so bright, oh, what must be the flame!![24]

Chapter Two

THE INCARNATE SON OF GOD

Jesus Christ, the Incarnate Son of God, is the Eternal High Priest, to whom all other priests are uniquely configured. A man ordained to the priesthood of Jesus Christ is, to use philosophical terms, ontologically changed – changed in his very being by the indelible character given him at priestly ordination. Fulton Sheen was one such man; to him, the person of Christ was his very grounding, the reason for his earthly being, and the center of his existence. In October, 1979, following a warm embrace in the sanctuary of Saint Patrick's Cathedral, New York City, Pope John Paul II told the elderly Archbishop how well he had spoken and written of the Lord Jesus throughout his life. Nothing said it better. Nothing could have expressed the Church's official approval of the career of this truly charismatic, and at the same time extraordinarily holy man. What, specifically did John Paul mean? How had Sheen written on this topic?

Our Lord's life and work could best be understood by starting with the yearnings of the pre-Christian world. During the 1950's, in the course of his immensely popular television series, *Life Is Worth Living*, Sheen devoted one telecast to this topic. The world was weary, looking for answers, for solutions to its difficulties, in short, looking for a messiah, though not always consciously aware of it. Such was traceable one thousand years of pre-Christian history, looking at the Greeks, the Eastern world and the Hebrews.

The Greeks produced Homer, who in turn produced the *Iliad* and the *Odyssey*; in the former, Homer concentrates on Hector, one of the greatest of Trojan heroes, a king who was made great in defeat; in the latter, the story of Penelope was told, a woman whose glory shown forth amid sadness and tragedy. Relying on the English classical scholar and Catholic convert Christopher Hollis, Sheen emphasized the puzzlement of many Greek philosophers over the concept of victory in defeat, or honor in suffering.

> There was really no answer given to this problem until the day of Calvary, when a defeated man hanging on a Cross ultimately became the conqueror, and a Mater Dolorosa at the foot of the Cross became the Queen of Christendom.[1]

Five centuries later, a great Greek dramatist Aeschylus wrote *Prometheus Bound*. The main character is bound to a rock for the crime of stealing fire from heaven, and in the course of his bondage, an eagle swarms down and devours his entrails, a symbol of modernity starved for truth, for ultimate answers, for lasting peace. One of the other characters in the book, Hermes, is compelled to address Prometheus, telling him not to expect any sort of end to this misery until some god appears and vicariously takes upon himself the sins of humanity.

Ancient Hindu cultures were not unaware of the same type of thought. These peoples would often sacrifice lambs to Ekiam, one of their gods, asking the question in prayer form, "When will the savior come? ... When will the redeemer be among us?" Confucius continued this theme in his writing, believing that someone who would know all things, and control them, must someday come. Buddha, who lived more than five hundred years before Christ, said he was not the first Buddha to live on the earth, nor would he be the last. One was coming who would not die, who would possess full truth, and usher in a kingdom where that truth would prevail. People would know him, Buddha contended, because his name would mean love.

Roman civilization produced many examples of yearning, beginning with the orator Cicero, and his prediction that a king would come whom humanity must recognize in order to be saved. Suetonius and Tacitus each proclaimed as much, to the consternation of the Roman Senate who, centuries before events surrounding the Holy Innocents, passed a law depriving all male children of the right to life. Anxiety reached fever pitch, though the statute was never enacted because of the large number of Senators' wives expecting children.

Horace wrote of a "Golden World" he hoped his readers could escape to, leaving behind the "hopeless horrors of reality." On a far more positive, and very beautiful note, the *Fourth Eclogue* of Virgil, written to honor Caesar Augustus, predicted a new generation sent down from heaven, a child yet unborn, who would recognize his mother with a smile. The messianic content of this poem has never been lost on believers, and it surely was not lost on Bishop Sheen.

The Bishop next considered the Hebrew civilization, destroyed by the King of Babylon in 586 B.C. In the course of the siege, the Babylonians took Daniel, one of the wisest of the Jews, into captivity. No sooner had this happened, than the King had an unexplainable dream that he asked Daniel to interpret. As he listened to the King's description, Daniel said the dream was an omen of the destruction of numerous worldly kingdoms, a destructive cord that would not be repaired until the coming of the messiah. In convincing fashion, Sheen traced for his television audience the various conquests of the pagan world, one after another, until the rise of the Roman Empire onto the world stage. After describing how Rome became supreme, the next step was the census of the entire world decreed by Caesar Augustus. No area or citizen could escape it, since the Emperor had before him a rather telling map, titled "Orbis Terrarum – Imperium Romanum," equating the entire world with the then known empire. In his characteristic prose style, the Bishop described the world situation:

> From the western ocean to the Persian plains, from the frozen north to the edge of the southern desert, the list went out from his hand to every sweating governor and satrap and tetrarch and king. The world is to be brought to unity. The human race had only one capital: Rome; one master: Caesar; one language: Latin. Morally the world was one in its sin and corruption; materially it was one for it had reached the highest peak of organization and unity. There are no longer Medes or Persians, no longer Scythians or barbarians, no longer Greeks or Babylonians. There are only Romans; there are only men. Nations were not awaiting a king, but rather mankind was awaiting a king.[2]

Little did the "bookkeeper of the Tiber"[3] realize he was fulfilling the ancient prophecy that the Messiah was to be born in Bethlehem. Such was fulfilled when a carpenter in Nazareth read of the census and set out to fulfill the dictums of its law, along with his wife who was with child. It would appear from this narrative that history convincingly proves the coming of Christ and who He was. This, however, is far from the truth. One needs a much stronger apologetic to convince a rational world, especially those attracted to other founders of religions, their philosophies, and even their personalities. One had to "line up the claimants," as it were, and this Bishop Sheen did as part of the introductory material he offered in a lengthy course of instruction for potential converts. It was true there were similarities in many world religions; there are natural truths that the mind can grasp, and since a number of these general principles are found in many world religions, people conclude there is little, if any difference. To counter this, Sheen used an argument from the world of art. We may be in an art gallery admiring a wide variety of paintings, and, upon examination, see many similar strokes or colors in these paintings. Just because this is so, we are not led to conclude it was the same artist who painted each one. In the same way, though there are similarities in many of the world's religious movements, we cannot from that conclude God brought them all into existence as part of His Divine plan. Rather, God chose to reveal Himself in history, and to present truths that are above the power of human reason. To convey them, He sent His only Son into the world at a given moment in time. The founder of no other world religion is as necessary for that religion as Christ is for Christianity, nor is it possible for a believer to enter into the same kind of relationship with any other religious founder as the Christian enters into with Christ. Buddhism does not require one to fall in love with Buddha; only that an adherent become an "enlightened one" and follow the founder's teachings. Confucius did not demand such intimacy, nor did Mohammed. Moses did not command people to put their faith in him; rather he was simply one of the instruments through whom God made covenant with His people. In Christianity, Sheen forcefully stressed, one must totally put on the heart, mind, and will of the founder, and let oneself be totally assimilated into the Christ life.

> The argument from prophecy is really very simple. Just ask yourself if any founder of a world religion, or any innovator of a modern religion, was ever pre-announced. His own mother could not have pre-announced five years before his exact birth. No one knew that Buddha, Confucius, or Mohammed were coming. But all through the centuries there was some dim expectation that Christ was coming.[4]

Those whom Sheen was preparing for reception into the Church were given a summary of the Old Testament covenants God made with Noah, with Abraham, and with Moses. He cited one Jewish scholar who later became a Christian, in noting there were four hundred fifty-six prophecies that circulated throughout the ancient east prior to Our Lord's coming, predicting the event in one form or other. With all of this, Herod's lack of surprise at the birth of Christ is understandable; he had heard too many prophecies that the King was coming, He who would be ruler of all mankind. Hence, the decree went out that all male children under the age of two were to be killed. Bishop Sheen, in much of his preaching, often made reference to this event, and asked the rhetorical question: Had the Czar of Russia ever done the same in order to kill Joseph Stalin? or the President of Germany in order to obliterate Adolf Hitler? Obviously not, since neither were predicted on the stage of history. Christ Himself would confirm these predictions when, at the age of about thirty, He went into the Synagogue of Nazareth, was handed the scroll on which the prophecy of Isaiah was written, and told the Jews that on that very day Isaiah's prophecy had been fulfilled in their midst.

In God's designated time His Son came, being born in an obscure stable because there was no room in the place where travelers lodged. Sheen's commentary on this has become memorable:

> The inn is the gathering place of public opinion, the focal point of the world's moods, the rendezvous of the worldly, the rallying place of the popular and the successful. But the stable is the place for the outcasts, the ignored, the forgotten. The world might have expected the Son of God to be born – if He was to be born at all – in an inn. A stable would have been the last place in the world where one would have looked for Him. Divinity is always where one least expects to find it.[5]

Our Lord became incarnate in time and history, according to His Father's preordained plan, and we refer to His coming among us, His Incarnation as Christmas. In an essay written some dozen years before his death, Sheen further explained its significance.

> Christmas is the enfleshment of the eternal Person of God; the beginning in time of the human nature of Him Who is without beginning or end. When I go to a blackboard and write the word "Love," the idea of love does not begin to exist at that moment; it already had existence in my mind for years. What actually happens is that "Love is made chalk and dwells on the blackboard." So, too, when Christ took upon Himself a manhood from the womb of His Mother Mary the "eternal Word was made flesh and dwelt amongst us." That is why Jesus only once in His life said that He was born, but He immediately added that He "came into the world." This is the way He always expressed His eternal Person – as "coming into the world," because He had eternal pre-existence. He who created the world is born in the world; He who made time is measured by it.[6]

Bishop Sheen often reminded his listeners and readers that Christ was the only one who came into the world to die. All human beings come into this world to live; death is an interruption of life, much as Socrates' life was interrupted when he was forced to drink hemlock, or any other well known mortal who completes his or her earthly sojourn. But Christ's death was imminent – the shadow of the Cross was always before Him. He was God's Son, sent expressly to do His Father's bidding. But how can we be sure of this? How are we to put our faith in Him?

The miracles Our Lord worked during His public life were great proof. There are thirty-five of them mentioned in Scripture, three having to do with raising from the dead, nine with nature, and twenty-three with healing. The point of these miracles must be grasped by believing hearts.

> He worked them as signs to convince men of the fact that He who came to work these miracles was the One who was promised. He never worked a miracle to amaze a multitude. He never worked a miracle to satisfy His hunger or thirst. He never worked a miracle to obtain a living. He never received money for the things He accomplished. He refused to convert the stones of the wilderness into bread to satisfy His own hunger or to cause water to gush out of a rock to slake His thirst; instead, He asked a woman to let down her bucket to give Him a drink.[7]

It was pre-announced that the Messiah would work miracles, and Saint John, in his Gospel, seems to consider them absolutely consistent with Christ's divinity. They were of an entirely different sort from those found in the Old Testament, since the latter were worked by God in answer to the prayers of His people and His prophets. There was nothing secretive about them; rather, they were performed in public places, with many people present who could later verify them. Our Lord's miracles, said Sheen, were inseparable from His Person. If they were to be removed from the Scriptures (much as the 18th century Deist Thomas Jefferson did when he wrote his own version of the New Testament, removing from it all mention of the miraculous), the identity of Christ would be destroyed, as would the credibility of Scripture itself.

Without a doubt, the most spectacular of His miracles was His Resurrection, the very basis of Christian hope. We have five distinct accounts of the story, four from the evangelists, and a fifth from Saint Paul who had spoken to Peter and James about three years after his conversion, and who also maintained friendships with a number of the Apostles. For Sheen, the events surrounding the Resurrection were very straightforward:

The fact is our Blessed Lord died on the Cross, was buried in a hundred pounds of spices as was the custom, and a watch, or a guard, was set. In the history of the world only one tomb has ever had a rock rolled before it and a soldier set as guard to prevent a dead man from rising; and that was the tomb of Christ on the evening of Good Friday.[8]

No teacher of Catholic doctrine, including Fulton Sheen, would be so naive as to discount objections to these miraculous happenings. He presented the two major arguments from modern skepticism; that the apostles had contrived the story, that is, lied, and that the same men, in their disappointment following Christ's death and burial, had only imagined they had seen Him; they were hallucinating in their grief. To the first, he raised the question, what chance would there have been of persuading the world of the truth of the Resurrection if it had never happened? The Apostles had not only preached, but suffered as a result of their preaching – people do not do such things for events that never occurred. As to the second, that they were deluded men, Sheen noted that the Apostles surely knew the difference between a trance and reality – the appearances of the Risen Christ to them took place in the common, everyday circumstances of life, and there could be no mistaking what they saw. The most astounding thing about the Resurrection was that no one, most of all His closest followers, believed it would happen; this is precisely why the women went with spices on Easter morning to anoint the body. Also, visions do not occur to different persons at the same time; they are a person's private dream, and no two persons dream the same dream simultaneously. Further, a vision could never have rolled away a stone and taken a body from within a tomb. And if the Body of Christ had never left the tomb, how would it be possible for these "deluded" souls to imagine a vision of an empty tomb? One almost gets the feeling Bishop Sheen was compelled to respond to skepticism out of necessity; his primary concern was the teaching of the faith, especially the deepest spiritual implications to be derived from its great truths. In Our Lord's rising from the dead, much was answered.

> The Cross had asked the questions; the Resurrection had answered them. The Cross had asked the question: How far can power go in the world? The Resurrection answered: Power ends in its own destruction, for those who slew the foe lost the day. The Cross had asked: Why does God permit evil and sin to nail Justice to a tree? The Resurrection answered: That sin, having done its worst, might exhaust itself and thus be overcome by Love that is stronger than either sin or death. Thus there emerges the Easter lesson that the power of evil and the chaos of any one moment can be defied and conquered, for the basis of our hope is not in any construct of any human power, but in the power of God who has given to the evil of this earth its one mortal wound – an open tomb, a gaping sepulcher, an empty grave. If the story of Christ ended with that cry of abandonment on the Cross, then what hope have we that bruised Goodness and crucified Justice will ever rise triumphant over the massed wickedness of men?[9]

With the Paschal Mystery, we have the inauguration of the New Covenant, which Sheen quickly compared to its forerunner. Mount Sinai was a principal scene of the first, Calvary of the second; in the first covenant, God dealt exclusively with one nation, in the new covenant, He deals with all humanity. Justification was by the law in the old; it is by grace in the new. In the old, the emphasis was on carrying out what God had commanded; in the new, it involves the total transformation into Christ. The hopes of the old were fulfilled in the new, while the longing of human hearts in the first instance found their realization in the second.

God is in search of humanity in the new dispensation; just the opposite was true in Old Testament times. The covenant ratified in the death and resurrection of Christ was the key opening the locked door. The New Covenant, wrought by Jesus Christ, the God-Man, in whom the hypostatic union of human and divine natures combined in one Divine Person, brought the Old Covenant to perfect fruition.

The question of the two natures in Our Lord's Divine Person occupied much of Sheen's thinking on God's Incarnate Son, and the way he wanted to describe Him to those planning to embrace the fullness of faith. He wanted them to understand the infinite debt that had been incurred by humanity's sin. The problem was the finiteness of human beings and their inability to repay such a debt. The principle Sheen used was a practical one: Honor is in the one honoring; the Pope would receive a greater honor being visited by the President of the United States than by an individual citizen. The other side of the proposition is that sin is measured by the one sinned against. If the President of the United States had been sinned against by a lesser political figure, it could be said that a Governor would commit a graver sin against the Chief Executive than the Mayor of a city would. All of us have sinned against God who is infinite, therefore our sin and guilt is infinite. To further explain, Sheen took the example of a clock whose mainspring was broken; to return the clock to working order, the mainspring must be supplied from outside, and the new mainspring must be placed within the clock. Men could not redeem themselves any more than a clock can repair itself. If man is ever to be redeemed, such redemption must come from without, and be applied to the inner being of every member of humanity. Finally, the illustration of a pencil was used; the pencil has a nature of its own, but must be acted upon for any results to ensue. If I take my hand, reach down and pick up the pencil, I have united my hand, which has its own nature, with the nature of the pencil – both natures are united in my person. The same could be applied to Our Lord's

Divine Person with its union of the divine and human natures. God emptied Himself and assumed our humanity, so much did He love us.

> He is a God who took His own medicine. He made man free. Man abused freedom and brought upon himself all the ills to which he is heir. God came down and took upon Himself a human nature so that He might feel every kind of torture of the human soul and every twisted pain of a human body.[10]

What Sheen was describing was the physical, psychic and moral transference Our Lord made His own in the Crucifixion. Physically, He assumed all our pains, sufferings, emotions, fears, trials, tribulations, and the like. Psychically, He knew all the loneliness of humanity, mental illness, all the psychoses and neuroses that are part of the human condition, all the darkness associated with atheism, all the doubts and skepticisms of the modern world, all the anger of those who curse and blaspheme Him and His Church. Morally, He took each and every sin of the world as if it were His own. Is it any wonder Bishop Sheen often remarked that none of us need to wait until we die to have a biography written of our lives? Such has already been produced – in autobiographical form. All we need do is look at the Crucifix, and there we find written the entire story of our earthly lives.

Many would accept this reality and make it the center of their existence; others would not. Sheen compared this to a world renowned Doctor who discovered a cure that would help millions, and made that cure readily available. Many would seek the remedy, but others would question – how could they be certain that it was an authentic cure? Humanity was much the same.

> If the sin of Adam had so many repercussions in every human being who has lived, shall we deny the Incarnation of Our Blessed Lord has had a greater repercus-

sion? Can the sin of one man have greater effects and disorder in human nature than the Incarnation of the Son of God has in ordering all humanity? Thus, I say everybody in the world is implicitly Christian. They may not make themselves explicitly Christian, but that is not the fault of Christ. He took their humanity upon Himself.[11]

The statement was proven true in a number of instances in Bishop Sheen's life. On one occasion, he was passing through an airport of a large city en route to another destination. He was stopped by a young Jewish boy who began telling him many of his personal travails. The Bishop patiently listened, and after some time took from out his pocket a small crucifix and placed it in the boy's hand, telling him that Moses, at God's command, had placed a serpent in the bark of a tree, so that all who gazed upon it would be cured of physical maladies. In the same way, if this young man were to gaze upon the sight of the crucified, he would experience great calm and inner peace. Some days later, the Bishop was passing through the same airport on his return trip, only to hear the same young man calling to him, and enthusiastically waving the crucifix.

On another occasion, Sheen received a telephone call from a Jewish jeweler in New York whom he had known for years. The gentleman informed him that that afternoon a group of Catholic sisters had come into his shop with a box containing a large number of silver crucifixes they were disposing of. They had given up the religious habit, including its crucifix, telling the Jew it separated them from the world, and they were particularly interested in how much money he would give them for the silver in the crucifixes. The jeweler asked Bishop Sheen if he could use the crucifixes, and then further queried, "What's wrong with your Church? – I thought the crucifix meant something to you." Sheen proceeded to tell him some of the ills besetting the Church, and within a few months time, he received him into the Church!

Still another episode involved Sheen's convert Clare Booth Luce, and her husband Henry, who described himself as a Presbyterian of sorts. Luce was the son of Protestant missionaries, but the religious fervor had not rubbed off. One day, Bishop Sheen was riding in the car with Henry and his wife, and Henry declared that he could never accept the divinity of Christ – as far as he was concerned, He was just like anyone else of His time, a common Jew. With her razor-sharp mind, Clare retorted, "But only on His mother's side!" The wit was not lost on Sheen. Many years later, in his apartment on East 77th Street in Manhattan, he recounted the incident to Malcolm Muggeridge, the famous British author, editor, journalist, producer, and soon-to-be-convert to Catholicism. He said that he had used Clare's retort, but in a very different context, one which proved the universal effects of Calvary:

> ...there was a young Jew who used to come to see me when I was at death's door, and for no reason at all, I hadn't known him before. But every day that he missed he apologized and said, "I had trouble with my wife." I thought it was domestic trouble: it was not. He said, "She has cancer." And he said, "We've been to the Doctor and we're preparing for an operation." And I said, "Sid, I want to give you something." And I gave him a little crucifix. I put it in his hand. I said, "I'm giving you an image of a Jew on His mother's side." And I said, "If you can ever develop any affection for this Jew on His mother's side, some day you will find out who His father was." And the next day he came back in the evening and said, "I went into the examination – the last examination before the operation." He said, "I almost crushed that crucifix, I held it so closely." And he said, "She has no cancer." And now he has the crucifix – he's sick again in the hospital – and he has it by his bed.[12]

Archbishop Sheen was nearing the end of his life when he recounted that story, and reference to his being at "death's door" was to one of the many trips he made to Lenox Hill Hospital in New York for the treatment of a heart ailment that ultimately claimed his life. These incidents recall well the implicit Christianity of every soul in the world, and account, in some measure for the tremendous effect Sheen had on the conversion story of countless individuals, many of whom he had never met.

With the completion of His death and resurrection, the work of the Father's Incarnate Son was not finished. He would soon ascend into heaven, send the gift of the Holy Spirit to His Church, and through that same Spirit, commence the work of His Mystical Body on earth. Sheen introduced the topic of the Ascension historically:

> Moses had fasted forty days before giving the Law, Elias had fasted forty days before the restoration of the Law, and now for forty days the Risen Savior laid the pillars of the Church and the new Law of the Gospel. The "forties" were about to end and the Apostles were bidden to awaken the fiftieth day, which was the day of jubilee.[13]

The Ascension of Christ into heaven was not to be thought of as some sort of locomotive action, where He would pass beyond the furthest star and enter the kingdom. Our Lord likewise had a descent from heaven, which did not mean physical descent, but a "drawing aside of the veil in which divinity was revealed to humanity."[14] When we profess our faith in the creed in both these events, we are stating our belief in the humiliation and the exaltation He experienced; humiliation in His emptying Himself to become a man, and exaltation in returning to His Father. We speak of Christ being at the right hand of the Father, which does not convey geographic locale; but rather a sharing in the Father's glory, it is Christ acting as mediator between His Father and humanity. Christ's presence in heaven following His Ascension has a twofold meaning for all of us on earth; there is a human nature like ours in heaven – a reminder of what our human natures are destined to share in; and also, we have a High Priest in the heavenly kingdom who is able to sympathize with our weakness, because, as Scripture points out, He was tempted in every way we are, yet never sinned.

> The end and purpose of God coming to this earth was to bring us to perfect union with the Father. How could He do this? By showing our flesh is not a barrier to divine intimacy, by taking it up to heaven itself, by showing those who pass through trials, sufferings, misunderstandings, whatever they be in this life, that they will have their body glorified. By sharing in Christ's cross, we share in His glory. The goal of all humanity is in some way reached in the ascension.[15]

When, on one occasion, Our Lord told Caiaphas that he would one day see the Son of Man seated at the right hand of power, He had His Ascension clearly in view; He returned to the Father not only with His Divinity, but also with His human nature. While on this earth, Christ's human nature was as deeply affected as any of our natures might be by the sight of beauty, the sight of sorrow or affliction, the sight of happiness, etc. All of this is now present in heaven. Sheen made the point that, figuratively speaking, we could say the Ascended Lord is continually showing His scars to His heavenly Father, asking Him to forgive the sins and transgressions of humanity because of the sufferings He endured, the reparation He made through His death. This is Christ's mediatorial role, exercised for us at all times.

Christ also made certain we would not be left orphans. On the feast of Pentecost, the birthday of the Church, He sent the

Spirit of Himself and His Father, their Holy Spirit, in the form of tongues of fire, on the Apostles, the Blessed Mother, and others gathered in that same Upper Room where He had celebrated His Last Supper with the apostolic company. In introducing the topic of Pentecost, Sheen encouraged his hearers to ponder these questions: "Would it have been better to have lived in the days of Our Lord? Have we missed a great deal not being contemporaries of Christ? Have we actually lost something? Is the modern age at a disadvantage being so far removed from Him?"

Given the gift of the Holy Spirit, the answer is an unqualified "No." At the time of Christ, there were those who accepted Him, those who were indifferent, and those who rejected Him and His teaching. The presence of the Spirit of Christ is simply another form of the same presence, just as the Eucharistic Christ in our tabernacles is yet another form, the closest form by which we can come to Him on this earth. If we are of the sort to reject Him and the teaching of His Church in the twenty-first century, we would likely have been among the doubters, or even scoffers who were His contemporaries! If, on the other hand, we are among the lovers of Christ in the modern age, the Holy Spirit can work wonders for us.

> As the telescope does not reveal itself, but the stars beyond, so the Holy Spirit does not reveal Himself, but Christ. Just think how we are able in this age of ours to communicate with distant parts of the earth thanks to electric or light waves. Why can't Our Lord, who dwells in heaven, be within whispering distance of us through His Holy Spirit?[16]

One of the great works of the Holy Spirit Bishop Sheen stressed was the consciousness of sin that He implants within us. The world, no matter what age we are living in, will try to convince us of quite the opposite, and in the most persuasive manner imaginable. It is made to look so very attractive, so very accept-able, that we are almost inclined to feel the problem lies within ourselves for not accepting and adapting to the ways of modernity. It is the gentle workings of the Spirit, ever so clearly disturbing our consciences, that persuades us of the truth. The Spirit not only shows us the horror of sin, but gives us a keen appreciation for what the suffering and dying Christ wrought for humanity. Returning again to his theme of the Cross as the autobiography of each of us, Sheen became more explicit:

> We can see our lives there: our pride in the crown of thorns, our avarice in the nailing of hands, our flight from grace in the pinioned feet, our rebellious loves in the pierced side, and our disrespect to the body and the flesh hanging from Him like purple rags. The blood is the ink and His skin is the parchment and our sins constitute the writing. Every sinner who has the spirit of Christ always thinks of sin in relationship to the Cruci-fixion. Then our Blessed Lord becomes our hope.[17]

The Church that He established is yet another form of His presence among us, namely, His Mystical Body. Until the coming of the Spirit fifty days after the Resurrection, the Apostles, said Sheen, were like the elements in a chemical laboratory. Science is able to describe one hundred percent of the chemicals that go into and make up the human body, but science is unable to produce a human being, because it lacks the principle of unity, the soul. In much the same way, without the Holy Spirit, the apostles would have been unable to give the Church Christ's divine life; they needed the Spirit's gift of Christ's unifying principle. Once they had received it, they were able to spread the Gospel message throughout the then known world. Each of them, save John the Evangelist, died a martyr's death so much was that Spirit at work within them. The Church they formed was the prolongation of

Christ in time. That is why we refer to it not as His physical, but as His Mystical, Body in this world. The story of Saint Paul's conversion on the road to Damascus is one of the most forceful proofs of this doctrine of our faith to be found in Scripture. All believers are familiar with the details of his being thrown from his horse, but the content of the theophany that followed is the most revealing part; a voice from heaven asked Paul why he was persecuting Him. Notice Our Lord did not say, "Why are you persecuting my Church?" He said, "Why are you persecuting me?"

> If someone stepped on the foot, would not the head complain because it is part of the body? Our Lord was now saying that in striking His Body Paul was striking Him. When the Body of Christ was being persecuted it was Christ the invisible head who arose to speak and to protest. The Mystical Body of Christ, therefore, no more stands between Christ and an individual than His physical body stood between Magdalen and His forgiveness, or His hand stood between the little children and His blessing. It was through His human body that He came to men in His individual life; it is through His Mystical Body or His Church that He comes to men in His mystical corporate life.[18]

Bishop Sheen described with great clarity the four marks of the Church; One, Holy, Catholic and Apostolic. The Church is One because it was unified by the life-giving gift of Pentecost; it is Holy in its members, and especially in its freedom from heresy and schism; it "expands and redeems humanity without regard to race or culture" and is therefore Catholic; and it is Apostolic in its origin from Christ, and not from a mere man who was separated from Him by decades or centuries.

Thus the Christ who "emptied" Himself in the Incarnation now had His "fullness" on Pentecost. The kenosis or humiliation is one fact of His Being; the pleroma or His continued life in His Bride, Spouse, Mystical Body or Church is the other. As the emptying of the light and heat of the sun cries out for the filling of the earth with its radiant energy, so the downward course of His love finds its completion in what Saint Paul calls His "fullness" – the Church.[19]

If Sheen was anything, he was a realist. In speaking of the Church, he never gave so glorified a picture that he might be perceived as living in a fantasy world. He never attempted to gloss over the problems, the scandals, the human errors and sinfulness to be found in Christ's Body on earth. In his 1979 conversation with Malcolm Muggeridge, long before the sexual scandals of the twenty-first century were upon us he noted

> ...what is hard for the Church to get over in this world is the incarnation of principles. The principle of the Hypostatic Union, that Christ has a body, and that body is made up of cells; it's made up of a soul, a head visible and a head invisible. And the body can suffer an awful lot. That is to say, as Christ's body suffered physically, so His Church, His Mystical Body suffers morally; its scandals, its weakness, its worldliness. It must have been very difficult for the Apostles ever to have looked at Christ not answering the challenge to "come down and we will believe." To think that He through whose fingers tumbled planets and worlds could be held by a nail, and yet, this is His body, and all that He would preserve of it really would be the scars. He kept those so that what all men see about the Church today, to generalize, is this suffering side, this mystical side that is not very edifying.[20]

The very important point was that one did not maintain a

myopic view of the Body of Christ, but looked at the entire picture. In describing the Church as the prolongation of the Incarnation, Sheen traced the story to the Old Testament People of God, the *qahal* in Hebrew. This relationship with His chosen people was sustained in His choosing the twelve apostles, men who were perhaps connected to the twelve tribes of Israel. He gathered these closest collaborators around Him to revivify Israel, to bring all her promises, prophecies and sacrifices to fruition in the New Israel. When Our Lord used the word *qahal*, He did so in a personal sense, my *qahal*, my family, as it were. The relationship He would create and build was not one of law as the old dispensation had often been interpreted, but one of love. Just as Moses often sprinkled blood on the people as a sign of the covenant they had entered into with God, Bishop Sheen said that "there will not be the sprinkling of the blood of goats, bullocks and sheep, but He will give His own blood." This new covenant, Our Lord predicted, would grow and spread throughout the world; it would grow not in the sense that a physical plant is built up by the work of brick and mortar, but growth would be like that of a cell which has been shot through with divine life.

Such was the Father's Incarnate Son in much of the spiritual literature produced by Fulton Sheen. Once Incarnate, the Divine Son was to spend thirty years obeying, three years teaching, and three hours redeeming. His earthly life is passed over quickly in the Creed because, Sheen said, the only thing important about an earthly life is whether we are doing the will of God. For the Son, that was His only purpose; for Christians, it is molding themselves in the Son's likeness. The Incarnation continues in the Church Christ established, and in its members. Through several decades of the 20th century, Bishop Sheen was one of those members, quite actively so. How many he brought to the Incarnate Son through his efforts will never be known this side of eternity.

Chapter Three

TEMPTATION AND SIN

On one of his many visits to Paris, the young Father Fulton Sheen went into a hotel near the *Opera Comique* to have dinner. There was an Englishman in the Dining Room playing the piano, and playing it well. After he had finished one of his numbers, Father Sheen approached him and invited him to join him for dinner. The man expressed some doubts, since he had never spoken with a Catholic priest before. Sheen put his mind at ease by telling him priests were just like anyone else; "Stick me with a pin, I'll jump too," was the retort he would recount in his sermons to priests years later. The man did join him, and began to tell part of his story. One year earlier, at a nearby table in the same dining room, the pianist had spotted a young woman trying to break a lump of sugar into a cup of coffee. He went over to assist her, and she began to tell him about her husband who abused her. The Englishman invited her to come live with him, she did. Now he had grown weary of her. A number of similar liaisons had earlier ended in the same fashion after about a year's duration, but this one was a bit different. The young woman in question had left the English-man a note that if he did not remain with her to celebrate the first anniversary of their living together, she would commit suicide by throwing herself into the Seine. The piano player then asked the priest if he would be justified in continuing the relationship to avert her plan for ending her life. Sheen said, "Absolutely no: one must not do evil so that good will come of it; and furthermore, she will not commit suicide."

When dinner was concluded, the priest informed his friend that he was heading to Montmartre. The Englishman, quite shocked, told Sheen he was just beginning to think him a good man, only to hear that he was headed to that hellhole of Paris. The priest informed him that there was a great deal more on the hill of Montmartre than dives and dens; there was a great Basilica to the Sacred Heart, where hundreds of people thought nothing of spending the night in adoration of Our Lord in the Blessed Sacrament. He told the Englishman he intended to go to the famed shrine for the entire night – he was welcome to join him or not, as he chose. He came along, and made not the slightest attempt to leave the entire night. The sun rose over Paris, Father Sheen offered an early morning Mass, and the two departed, making a mutual agreement to meet again at night to continue their conversation; all the while, Father Sheen hoping he could win this soul for Christ.

That evening, when Sheen arrived at the designated meeting place at the hotel, he entered the lobby only to find his English friend in company with a very attractive woman. The gentleman told Father Sheen they had just met this afternoon, and had struck up a friendship. Sheen replied that the man must make a choice; either the two of them would have dinner, or he could go on with his lady friend. The man paced up and down the hotel corridor for a period of time, returned, and said, "All things considered, Father, I'd rather go with her." Sheen was never to see this individual again, though he often remarked that his story was one of a man rejecting every grace the Good Lord was offering him. One could only hope that he cooperated with the impulses of grace at some time before his death. Why did that man cave in the way he did? Why were his preferences so much more directed to the flesh than to the spirit? It was a subject Fulton Sheen discussed much in his career, and it can be described under the theme of sin and temptation.

To answer the question why we are tempted, Sheen drew the distinction between temptation and sin. The former was a mere invitation; the latter was the commission of an act, the voluntary doing of something wrong. He traced it to the complexity of human nature, to the fact that human beings are not one entity, but rather a duality of body and soul, matter and spirit. Examples from the cultures of Greece and Rome could be helpful.

> The human personality is like a driver in a chariot, as Plato suggested. Before him are two headstrong steeds: one is the animal urge within us, and the other the spirit. The charioteer or the driver has great difficulty to get both steeds headed in the same direction.... The greatest of Greek dramatists, Sophocles, wrote of the great primeval disharmony that it was "grave with age and infected all men." Ovid, the Latin poet wrote. "I see and approve the better things of life, but the worst things in life I follow."[1]

There is absolutely no one in the world who is not tempted. Temptations vary from one person to another in degree and intensity, and they may even vary with age. Sheen often said that the ancient Chinese philosopher Confucius divided temptations into three life periods: lust preoccupied the young; pride and power the middle aged; and avarice and greed, the elderly. While this can be argued, the fact of the universality of temptation is a given.

Its origins are not to be found exclusively in the individual; nature is also to blame. Nature answers the question of "what," personhood, the question of "who." Something has happened in nature to corrupt it, not completely, but partially. Centuries ago, Sheen maintained, some theologians claimed human nature was completely corrupt; conversely, at other periods of history, other theologians made the claim that it was totally divinized.

Neither is correct. Human nature has inclinations to good (which it is not always able to fully realize), and most certainly has inclinations to evil and corruption. "It is like a man who is down a well of his own stupidity," the Bishop once wrote. "He knows that he ought not to be there, but he cannot get out by himself."[2] This was fine descriptive language for the secular world, but a spiritual answer must be given to complete its meaning, and that spiritual answer was found in the first act of disobedience committed by the first man and woman God placed on this earth, Adam and Eve. Their initial act of defiance has been called Original Sin, and though most believers would consider this the beginning, Sheen recalled an earlier act of disobedience, committed not by humans, but by pure spirits:

> The gifts the angels received were to be confirmed and made permanent only on condition that they would pass the test of love. Their sin was an abuse of freedom. It was a sin of pride. They wanted to be free and likened to God. They could not sin by sex because they had no bodies. They could not sin by avarice because they had no pockets, not even in their wings. They sinned only by an undue exaltation of their intellect, in other words, "I'm going to be independent of God, I'm going to be a god myself." The truth is they wanted to be like the uncreated, though they were the created. The leader of them all, Lucifer, fought his battle cry, *Non Serviam*: "I will not serve." They were guilty because they did not love so they lost all the blessings they received and one third of them fell and became what are known as fallen angels, the devils.[3]

When an angel decides anything, it sees all the consequences of its actions with complete clarity; they saw all the effects of their decisions, and that is why their act of rebellion, their sin, can never be forgiven. With humans, it is quite different; we often do not see all the consequences of our sins, all the ill effects that flow from them; hence, the mercy and pardon of God is forever at our disposal.

Original Sin and humanity is a different story. Satan initiated the temptation by first placing doubt in the minds of Adam and Eve – asking them why God had specifically requested them not to eat the fruit of a certain tree, a question they could not answer. He then removed any fear of consequences if they did eat the fruit of this tree: under no circumstance would they die. He undoubtedly made them feel foolish for believing they would. Then he made the false promise, telling them they would be like unto God, once again, allowing them to believe that the Creator wanted no one on His footing, but that they would be on His footing if they but concurred in the act of defiance. The fallacy, Sheen said, was that they believed the Devil's lies, especially that God did not know the meaning of good and evil nearly as well as they did.

> We have to conclude that God certainly did not create us fallen. There is a voice inside of our moral consciousness telling us our immoral and unmoral acts are abnormal. God made us one way, and we've made ourselves, in virtue of our freedom, another way. He wrote the drama, we changed the plot! We are not just animals who failed to evolve into humans; we are humans who have rebelled against the divine…. We are not depraved criminals, merely weak. We're not just a mass of corruption, for we bear within ourselves the image of God. We are sick; we need healing; we need deliverance; we need liberation. We know we cannot give liberation and freedom to ourselves.[4]

The effects of Original Sin within us leave us victims of concupiscence, the natural attraction to evil. Sin looks good to us. We are naturally inclined to it, and must continually keep avoiding it in our lives. There are many ways of doing this, and, speaking to a secular American audience, Bishop Sheen reminded them that conscience is that inner mechanism that allows us to discern good from evil, that which keeps us on the right path and allows us to avoid those persons, places or things that will cause us to do evil. He described it as an "oughtness" within each of us, something which is not mechanical, or biological, or even instinctive; it is rational. It puts in front of us guiding principles to lead us through life. Each of us has power to regulate things outside us – an example Sheen used was throwing a shoe at a screeching cat at midnight. What many people fail to realize is they have power to regulate things inside of them as well. This is determining our character. "Many things happen to us," the Bishop said, "but what is more important is what we make happen to ourselves. We are self-determining creatures, unlike frogs and stones."[5] Such was the operation of conscience in every human being. What was novel in Sheen's approach was his comparison of this operation to the workings of the national government:

> Conscience is an interior government exercising the same functions as all human government, namely, legislative, executive and judicial. It has its Congress, its President, and its Supreme Court: it makes its laws, it witnesses our actions in relation to the laws, and finally it judges us.... There is in each of us an interior Sinai, from which is promulgated, amid the thunder and lightning of daily life, a law telling us to do good and avoid evil. Without even being consulted, conscience plays its legislative role, pronouncing some actions to be in themselves evil and unjust and others in themselves moral and good.... In like manner, conscience executes laws, in the sense that it witnesses the fidelity of our actions to the law. Finally, conscience... also

judges me accordingly. The breast of every man bears a silent court of justice. Conscience is the judge, sitting in judgment, handing down decisions with such authority as to admit of no appeal, for no one can appeal a judgment which he brings against himself. That is why there gather around the bar of conscience all the feelings and emotions associated with right and wrong – joy and sorrow, peace and remorse, self-approval and fear, praise and blame.[6]

How does one arrive at the source of the legislative, executive and judicial functions of conscience? It is not within myself since no one can be his own law maker; further, if it did come from within myself, I could easily change it. Neither does it derive from society, since its only function is to interpret the law. It must be concluded that a higher power is involved – one capable of legislating, executing, and judging, namely, God, who is all-knowing, all-wise, and supreme. Sheen admitted an objection could be quickly raised that since God knows beforehand that I will be a thief, a murderer, an adulterer, etc., it seems foolish that He would create me. The answer, the Bishop quickly pointed out, is that we make ourselves thieves, murderers, and adulterers; God well knows the final product, but does not interfere with us in the exercise of our free will. "We are self-creating beings," said Sheen. "We have the power within ourselves to choose our actions."[7] This involves self-determination, and the way we exercise it largely determines our final outcome.

At the end of the day the business man will pull out of his cash register all the debits and credits of the day. So at the end of every human life there will be pulled out of our self-conscience or unconscious mind the record of every thought, word and deed. This will be the basis of our judgment.[8]

Solid an approach as this was, the world in which we live and have lived, presented many problems. Human beings most certainly do have consciences, but very often fail to heed their warnings. The voice of conscience may be speaking to them, but they live and act as if the opposite were true. The human condition has become depraved through the continuous violation of our proper inner dictates, and humanity bears the subsequent wounds. Bishop Sheen, trained as he was in Thomism, could not be considered a great admirer of all aspects of modern philosophy – yet, there were some benefits:

> Marx found conflict in society, Kierkegaard in the soul, Heidegger in man's being, and psychologists in the mind. To the credit of all of them, it must be said that they come much closer to an understanding of man than did the Liberals of the last few centuries, who taught that man was naturally good and progressive and on the high road to becoming a god without God. Anyone who would say today that modern man (who has fought two wars in two decades) needs only evolution and education to become a deity would be less observant than the ostrich with its head in the sand.[9]

Something, therefore, is wrong. Saint Augustine was correct when he said that whatever we are, we are not what we were meant to be. And such has been the state of things since our first parents fell. "It was not you or I who sinned in Adam," Bishop Sheen wrote, "but that which we are. Each person is profoundly the way he is, not because of his parents, or grandparents or great grandparents, but because of his first parents."[10]

History is filled with persons who tried to make themselves gods, and Sheen, with his vast knowledge of history and literature, was always prone to give examples. In one of the Greek myths, Prometheus incurred the vengeance of the god Zeus; in the book *Arabian Nights* is told the story of the discovery of a castle set in a mysterious city, one inhabited by a king who tried to accumulate all the gold and material possessions which would make him enormously wealthy – all to little avail, however, when this earthly ruler, attempting to become a god went before the only God. Examples from mythology and literature were plentiful, but those found in real life are even more compelling, and such examples were to be found in Ancient Greece as much as in 20th century America. Men in their forgetfulness of God, never ceased to make themselves minor deities; the story simply played out differently in different times and cultures. Writing in *The Prodigal World*, Bishop Sheen noted:

> Men are no longer objecting to the Church because of the way they think, but because of the way they live. They no longer have difficulty with her Creed, but with her commandments. They remain outside her saving waters, not because they cannot accept the doctrine of Three Persons in One God, but because they cannot accept the moral of two persons in one flesh; not because Infallibility is too complex, but because avoidance of Birth Control is too hard; not because the Eucharist is too sublime, but because Penance is too exacting. Briefly, the heresy of our day is not the heresy of thought – it is the heresy of action.[11]

We are as forgetful of God in the twenty-first century as the Greeks and Romans were in theirs, and we place ourselves in the center of the universe, asking the Creator of the universe to move over, just as earlier civilizations did. The basis of this forgetfulness of God, with its subsequent disordering of our lives, has at its root the sinful human condition we inherited from Adam. Hence, we are tempted, and so often fall into sin.

When a person is tempted to evil, he must not think there is anything abnormal about him. A person is tempted not because he is intrinsically evil, but because he is fallen man. No individual has a monopoly on temptation; everybody is tempted. Saints do not find it easy to be saints, and devils are not happy being devils.... No one can understand human nature, and no one can treat it adequately who thinks that a conflict is exclusively individual, or who thinks that the basic conflict can be healed by human nature itself.[12]

The 20th century's false premise, said Sheen, was the belief that all conflicts can indeed be healed by human nature – that man has it within himself to cure his maladies, simply by explaining them away. The inner conflict resulting from Original Sin was very deep seated, and disciplines like psychology touched only the surface. Man was actually revolting from the moral law, and from his basic unwillingness to accept his place "in the order of being." Because man has been deprived of his original position in the universe, he has become more proud than ever, and pride, by Saint Augustine's definition, was the cause of all sin. But sin is a naughty word for modern man, and the contemporary world places blame elsewhere. Though he was often critical of psychology, Sheen did not hesitate to cite psychologists like Dr. Karen Horney who felt that, because of a disregard for moral values, an analyst may be often "just as blind as the patient." Dr. Fritz Kunkel went further:

> The physical and mental diseases certainly belong to the realm of medicine, and therefore the ethical valuation of these cases must be avoided. But if vices are diseases, they cease to be vices, and theology in sending the drunkard or the gambler to the physician, relinquishes its last connection with reality: the ethical task.[13]

For society, the solution lies in a sound, practical approach to life. For the believer, it was much different. Pride must give way to humility, to a recognition of the creator-creature relationship, a knowledge of our fallen human condition, and a constant realization of the ease with which one can offend God. The loss of a sense of sin must be replaced by the cultivation of a prodigal nature epitomized by the contrite son in Scripture.

> There is no record – there is not even a hint – that he attempted to excuse himself, or to extenuate his prodigality. He offered no theory about sin; he did not say it was a fall in the evolutionary process; he did not blame his environment or his wicked companions; he did not tell his father that he had inherited a queer Freudian complex from him; he did not say that moral decline is only a myth and that sin is just an illusion; [he did not say] men could no longer live according to traditional morality, and must therefore have a new moral code to suit immoral ways of living. He did not excuse himself by saying that a man was justified in sowing his wild oats and then forgetting, living for the present and having no responsibility for the past. There was none of these things in the mouth of the prodigal, and much less was there any such thought in his heart.[14]

This attitude in us as Christians can only come about by a recognition of our own sinfulness and need of God's mercy. In our battle with temptation, one of the finest meditations that can engage our minds, and one to which Bishop Sheen returned frequently in his writings was the temptations of Christ. Though sinless, temptation was put before Him. It was part of His emptying Himself and becoming one of us in all things save that which was contained in the Devil's advances. The temptations were to be seen at the beginning of His public life, and at the hour of His death. They prove that none of us are exempt, and, as the Bishop so often commented, we must die to our lower nature, in order to rise to a higher one.

In his work *The Eternal Galilean*, Bishop Sheen likened the three temptations of Christ to the temptations offered to the modern world against the Church of the 20th century; to make religion social, political and worldly. Such was not the lot of religion, however, nor would it be. On the contrary, its function was to bring the light of Christ to society, His justice to politics, and His forgiveness to all who had become worldly. Because individuals and societies had succumbed to temptation in its many forms, and had sinned profusely, it was in need of reformation, not from without, but from within. This could be said of nearly any society at any time, but its application has rarely become a reality. Sheen wrote *The Eternal Galilean* during the Great Depression. His words ring true in the 21st century:

> It is only by the spirit of Christ and the spirit of prayer that the freedom of man, won by bloodshed and national sacrifice, can be safeguarded and preserved. The shattering of all our material illusions during the World War and during the present economic recession has made the clear-visioned minds of our day see that apostasy from the principles of the Savior, the abandonment of the spiritual life, and the transgression of the commandments of God, have led of necessity to our ruin and confusion worse confounded.... By permitting the Prince of Darkness to tempt Him, even though it was wholly exterior and did not touch His sinless soul, He proved that He is not insensible to our difficulties, our sorrows, and our temptations.[15]

Sheen described Our Lord's three temptations as "shortcuts from the Cross," likewise they were a "negative preparation" for His public life, much as His Baptism had been a positive one. He received a strengthening from His trials, and proved the real meaning of love – something which must be proven by deeds, not mere words. The temptations that come to human beings are easily described in the three categories of pride, avarice and lust. Christ's temptations, on the other hand, were of a very different kind; they involved a laying aside of His Divine mission and His Messiahship. In many ways they were reminiscent of the first temptation of Adam; when Our Lord assumed a human nature, He became the Second Adam, sent to rectify the sinfulness into which our first parents had been led. Hence, Christ came into direct confrontation with Satan.

> The essence of God is existence, and He defines Himself as "I am Who am." The essence of the devil is the lie, and he defines himself as "I am who am not." Satan has very little trouble with those who do not believe in him; they are already on his side.[16]

Our Lord knew well with whom He was dealing. The first temptation to turn stones into bread to feed the multitudes was a sort of temptation for Him to become little more than a social reformer. Sheen drew the interesting comparison with the modern world, and the Communist Commissar who will go into a classroom and ask the children to pray for bread. They soon find out their prayers are not answered, and are told it is because there is no God. The Commissar will then come to the school and give the children bread, and appear to them as the great hero. He is the representative of the state, and the earthly state is all one needs to satisfy his needs, because the satisfying of our earthly cravings is the only important thing; after we die we shall discover there will be nothing else.

> Our Lord was not denying that men must be fed, or that social justice must be preached; but He was asserting that these things are not first. He was, in effect, saying to Satan, "You tempt Me to a religion which would relieve want. You want Me to be a baker instead of a Savior; to be a social reformer instead of a Redeemer.

You are tempting Me away from My Cross, suggesting that I be a cheap leader of people, filling their bellies instead of their souls. You would have Me begin with security instead of ending with it; you would have Me bring outer abundance instead of inner holiness."[17]

Christ was then tempted to pride and egotism when the Devil suggested He throw Himself down to the earth, so that His angels might come and lift Him up. In other words, why take the long and difficult route to win mankind by the shedding of blood and the horrible death of the Cross? A feat of might would just as easily convince people who are always looking for signs, wonders, supernatural manifestations, and the like. The masses were too far below Him to appreciate the Cross, the Devil suggested; Christ should go among them and, with the performance of miraculous feats, He would easily win them over.

The truth that would answer this temptation was that faith in God must never contradict reason. The unreasonable venture never has the assurance of the Divine protection. Satan wanted to make God the Father do something for Our Lord that Our Lord refused to do for Himself; namely, to make Him an object of special care, exempt from obedience to natural laws which were already the laws of God. But Our Blessed Lord, who came to show us the Father, knew that the Father was not just a mechanical, impersonal Providence which would protect anyone, even someone who surrendered a Divinely ordained mission for the sake of winning a mob.[18]

The final temptation was yet another attempt to divert Our Lord from the Cross, this time by entering into a "treaty" with Satan, as he promised Christ all the kingdoms of the world if He would but fall down and worship him. The meaning again was clear; it would be a simple act of homage to him who fell from heaven, and the ignominy of the Cross would be avoided. The Devil promised Our Lord the entire world, provided He did not change it; and all the creatures in the world, provided He promised not to redeem them. Christ let Satan know that He was as much in revolt as His tempter, but in a different way. His revolution would not be carried out with a sword drawn outwardly, but one which was directed inward, to human hearts.

It was a changed, reformed, redeemed, sanctified society that Our Lord had come into the world to establish, and the Devil, with all his trickery, would not divert Him from it. The final temptation of Christ came not from as formidable an adversary as Satan, but from the jeering, laughing, scorning crowds on Calvary. It seemed whenever Fulton Sheen wrote or spoke on this subject, he was at his most eloquent.

> Once on those heights, He offers His hands to His executioners, the hands from which the world's graces flow. The first dull knock of the hammer is heard in silence. Mary and John hold their ears; the sound is unendurable. The echo sounded as another stroke. Then the cross is lifted slowly off the ground. Then with a thud that seemed to shake even hell itself, it sank into the pit prepared for it. Our Lord has mounted His pulpit for the last time.[19]

The crowds immediately began to mock and jeer at Him, saying that He saved others, wondering why He did not save Himself. We know not how many were there, but quite audibly they shouted to Him that if He would but come down from the cross, they would believe. As Bishop Sheen often wrote, they would apparently believe anything; they would believe in His Church, His Pontiff, His Sacraments, etc. Just come down. They wanted no part of a cross, and it was not so much for Christ as it was for themselves. It would be human to come down, the Bishop wrote; it was Divine to hang there.

Rather than imitating Christ in His temptations, the modern world was only too happy to go its own way. The most practical manifestations of this were what Sheen termed the "seven pallbearers of character." They represented the lives of those who fell prey to temptation, and offended the Good Lord by their sinfulness. Egotism was the first manifestation, an "inordinate love of self." This was followed by pride, a "too great admiration of oneself"; avarice, a "perversion of the natural right of every human being to extend his personality by owning the things that minister to his body and soul"; envy, "sadness at another's good"; lust, an "inordinate love of the pleasures of the flesh"; anger, "a violent desire to punish others"; sloth, a "malady of the will which causes neglect of one's duty."[20] These are the areas where most of mankind's temptations are presented, and most of their sins committed. They represent the Devil's major successes in human lives, by his clever approaches into human minds, and his cunning manipulations which can be so convincing. He could be fought, however, and fought effectively. Bishop Sheen often used practical examples from his vast priestly experience, or from hagiography, the study of the saints. One such example was the life of Saint Thérèse of Lisieux, with which he was greatly familiar. In 1973, he journeyed to Ireland to preach a nine day novena in her honor at the Whitefriars church in Dublin. It was the centenary of Thérèse's birth, and Sheen's presence at the famed Carmelite church insured an overflow crowd. One of the conferences dealt with fighting the Devil's advances in our lives, and the famed preacher took an example from the Little Flower's own life. For her final year and a half, she endured the tremendous suffering of tuberculosis, as well as intense spiritual temptations. One night, she had a dream of confronting Satan.

In this dream she saw in the garden of the monastery a big barrel, and two little devils appeared over the top of the barrel. She moved toward the barrel, and the devils went down into the barrel. She got closer and looked down, and they jumped out of the barrel and went into the laundry room. They were at one of the windows, and she went to the window to look at them, and the closer she got to them, the farther they got away. They were fearful of her because she was holy.[21]

Archbishop Sheen also noted Thérèse's response to temptation:

On each fresh occasion of combat, when the devil desires to challenge me, I conduct myself valiantly, knowing that to fight a duel is an unworthy act. I turn my back on the adversary without ever looking him in the face. Then I am ready to run to Jesus and tell Him I am ready to shed every drop of blood in testimony of my belief that there is a heaven.[22]

These were not offered as pious testimonies; the point the preacher was making was that such remedies are available to all at the moment of temptation. We need not fall victim to the allurements of the adversary. There are tremendous resources available to all of us, not the least of which is recourse to great saints like Thérèse.

The reason we have the ability to overcome temptation, and not commit sin is not through any power of our own, not through anything we have accomplished. It is only in the New Covenant wrought by Christ that such is possible. Sheen used the example of a conductor directing a great symphony orchestra, all of whose musicians were in perfect accord in a given composition. Suppose, he said, one musician decided to strike a discordant note, what could be done about it? Initially, nothing. The disharmonious note is floating in time and space, and an element of discord has entered the universe. Man could not stop it because "time is irreversible and man is localized in space." The only way the situation could be remedied would be for someone to write an entirely new symphony, and make that discordant note the first new note of the composition. That is exactly what God did in reestablishing harmony in the universe. It had its beginnings at the Annunciation when the angel Gabriel asked Our Lady if she would give God a human nature, continued in the Incarnation, and was completed in the Paschal Mystery.

This becomes the first note in the new creation, the beginning of the new symphony which will be played again and again by the divine conductor. How are other notes added? We're the other notes if, like Mary, we freely consent to be added to this first note. We become added by the Sacrament of Baptism, by which each person dies to the old Adam and is incorporated into the new Adam, Christ. These notes added to the first note constitute the new body of Christ, or what is known as His Mystical Body, the Church. This is what it means to be a Christian.[23]

Sheen had known many persons in his life who seemed more than willing to be added as notes to the new symphony, people who wanted to put their past behind them and be reconciled to God. One example from the world of journalism was Heywood Broun, a convert of Bishop Sheen decades ago in New York City. Broun had been a friend of Catholic author and convert Fulton Oursler, and the latter suggested he contact the Bishop. The two reasons Broun gave for his interest in Catholicism was his search for the truth, and his fear of dying in his sins, fearing he had little time left on this earth. Sheen instructed him in the faith, and received him into the Church. Broun became the first person Cardinal Spellman confirmed shortly after his appointment as Archbishop of New York, and the famed writer did indeed die shortly thereafter.

Yet another example was a young woman Sheen encountered on one of his many pilgrimages to the famed shrine of Our Lady in Lourdes, France. He had been at the shrine for some days, and went down to the grotto one evening to say good-bye to the Blessed Mother before departing. As he returned to his hotel, he began climbing the several flights of stairs to reach his room. He felt the presence of someone following him, and he turned around to discover a young woman. When he inquired if she were following him, she replied yes, though she could not give a particularly compelling reason. She had simply seen him in procession that afternoon, and decided to follow him. The curious thing was, while at the grotto, Sheen had offered a prayer that Our Lady send him a cross to save a soul. As he listened to the young woman's story, he became more and more convinced she was the cross he had prayed for. He remained in Lourdes several more days trying to teach the young woman how to be good. She had been succumbing to temptation after temptation, leading a sinful life, and wanted to put her past behind her. He succeeded in bringing her back, and upon his final departure for Paris, he encountered the anticipated cross in the tremendous inconveniences he experienced making the long train trip back; delays, invalid tickets, sleepless nights, etc., all of which lengthened a normal one-day trip into a third day. That, he felt, was the price to be paid. An interesting footnote to the story is that this young woman had come down from Holland on a bus trip through the mountains of the Pyrenees, and for a reason explainable only by grace, decided to get off at Lourdes. The bus was later involved in a serious accident, and all its passengers killed.

Such grace was, and is available to everyone at the moment of temptation, a grace that will save us from sin, mortal or venial. Sanctifying grace is the term we give to it, and Bishop Sheen explained it well to a class of potential converts, by using the example of two tadpoles under water. One said to the other that he was going to stick his head up to see if there is anything in this world but water. The other tadpole replied, telling him not to be silly – do you really think there's anything in this world but water? The moral was, there's more in this world than the mere natural; there is the supernatural, and that is to be found in abundant fashion in God's grace.

> Before grace comes, you act in your own way; after you receive grace, you act in His way. That's the difference. Your conscience becomes quickened, and what before was very precious to you, now seems as nothing, and what before seemed as so much dross, now is precious. That's grace. Grace is supernatural power that illumines your mind to see things above reason; it's that supernatural power which strengthens your will to do things which before you could not do. It changes you from a creature into a child of God, and most of all it enables you to call God, Father.[24]

Thus in the war against temptation, in the battle with sin, there were sure remedies which had helped millions of believers through the centuries, and will continue helping till time is no more. If any further proof were necessary, one need only look to the lives of peoples and nations, and a direct correlation could be seen. Bishop Sheen noted that a civil war rages in the hearts of all; the less people do battle with their inner selves, the more they will want to have that battle directed outwardly. The less concerned people are with their own sinfulness, and the evil in their own lives, the more they become concerned with the sin and evil they perceive in others. People who are not at peace on the inside, are that way because they are not sufficiently at war with themselves, and the manifestations of that become discernible to others. Not only did this principle apply to individuals, but it could also extend to nations.

> There are two kinds of swords: one that swings outward, and the other, which is thrust inward. One is to harm the neighbor, such as the sword of Peter that

hacked off the ear of the high priest's servant. It was
this kind of sword the Divine Master bade be put back
into its scabbard. The other kind of sword is the one
that cuts out egotism and selfishness and greed. The
first sword, which nations hold, creates wars against
others; the spiritual sword is a sign of war against
ourselves. The less men wage war against evil in their
own breasts, the more they will wage war against their
neighbors and nations. The more they battle against
their own sins, the less need there is to do battle with
the enemy without. The less we shed our own blood
figuratively, the more we need to shed our neighbor's
blood physically. Self-righteousness in persons and civil
strife against neighbor go hand in hand.[25]

There was, though, another side to the story. Temptations
need not be thought of as always negative; some people are moti-
vated, with God's grace, to move in entirely different directions.
Many persons judge others on the surface, by the way they seem
to act. When they get to know them on a deeper level, they are
often surprised. "Those who seem to have no depth at all," wrote
Sheen, "really contain treasures of surpassing worth."[26] Taken a
step further, the Bishop said what is true of others also applies to
ourselves; atheists are said to be afraid in the dark; Herod did not
believe in the afterlife, but thought Christ to be John the Baptist,
and was very anxious to see him; Communists were people who
professed no belief in organized religion, but spent a great deal of
time talking about it. With the use of such examples, what point
was Bishop Sheen making?

> In [the] subconscious depths of the soul come inspi-
> rations which are too noble to be of our making; the
> mud and slime which sink down to our subconscious
> mind cannot suddenly shoot forth flowers and blos-
> soms. There is some other force from the outside which

completely changes the direction of our lives. Traveling in the pathways of triviality, it takes some alien Power from the outside to divert us into the Highway of the King. The old theologians used to call these motivations to goodness "Actual Graces." A better wording would be temptations to goodness. Why is it we practically always use the word "temptation" to imply an inclination to evil?[27]

Why, indeed? The choice is entirely ours; to give into temptation or not, to sin or not to sin. We can be tempted in two directions. One, if cooperated with, leads to sin. The other, if cooperated with, leads to God. In the story of temptation and sin versus goodness, one thought is overriding:

> The two great dramas of life are the soul in pursuit of God and God in pursuit of the soul. The first has less apparent urgency, for the soul that pursues God can do it leisurely, as Peter followed the Savior from afar. But when God pursues the soul, He proves a Relentless Lover, Who will never leave the soul alone until He has won it or been conclusively denied.[28]

CONVERSION

"Conversion is an experience in no way related to the upsurge of the subconscious into consciousness," Fulton Sheen once wrote. "It is a gift of God, an invasion of a new Power, the inner penetration of our spirit by the Spirit and the turning over of a whole personality to Christ."[1] The Greek word *metanoia* is often used to describe such a transformation, a complete turning around and moving in a different direction from the one which we are taking. Bishop Sheen was once speaking to a group of drug addicts in Harlem, and he used an example from bowling; if he were to role a bowling ball down the center of the aisle of the hall where he was speaking, the ball would go in a straight line unless it was obstructed by some outside force. If our lives are moving in a direction of sinfulness, they will continue unobstructed in that direction unless some superior force, some outside interference stops them. This is a good definition of God's grace, and the power it has to totally change our lives, if we are willing to cooperate with it.

There is no question that many lives were changed because God's grace worked through Archbishop Sheen. Many were converted to the fullness of Catholic truth through his instructions; far more were converted by reading his books or listening to his radio and television programs. Conversion, however, is a far broader topic than merely being received into the Catholic Church;

as the definition suggests, it is a complete turning around of one's life. This may occur in the lives of those already Catholic, or in people's lives in general, whether or not they are blessed with the grace of conversion to Catholicism. It is impossible to estimate how many were thus effected by so powerful a speaker and writer, and, in the end, Sheen would not have cared. He always said it is God who wrought such miracles in persons' lives; he was merely the human instrument.

Nonetheless, the topic of conversion was very important in his writings, and he delved deeply into its roots before offering practical suggestions to be implemented. We are living in days of individualism, he contended; people are concerned only with themselves and their personal fulfillment and happiness, when it is our oneness with others that will give life such tremendous meaning. In a certain cemetery, there was a gravestone of a little girl, with an inscription claiming that her playmates said it was easier to be good when she was with them. Such is how all of us grow rich in the sight of God.

> "No man is an island." This is one of the most quoted
> lines of the poet John Donne. To him every man is part
> of a vast continent. When, therefore, there is a death,
> one should not ask "for whom the bell tolls," whence
> Hemingway derived the title for one of his novels.
> Donne says, "It tolls for thee."[2]

Unfortunately, such solidarity is sadly lacking in many lives – it is the primacy of the ego that surfaces, and there the problem begins. Years ago, Bishop Sheen noted that the personalities of Doctor Jekyll and Mr. Hyde depict the personality of each of us; there is the person we are, and the person others meet – the person others think us to be. The two lives cannot be lived simultaneously; if we attempt such, we will land up in inner dissatisfaction. Our lower natures, our egos must give way to our true selves. "If true freedom is to be found within ourselves," the Bishop wrote, "the ego must yield itself to the birth of our true personality."[3] Every person, in his or her being, is a profound mystery. Decades later, in developing his *Theology of the Body*, John Paul II would refer to each individual as a "being given," one who, in his or her bodiliness, is a presence and a call – a presence to the world of which he or she is a part, and one who is called – to relationality with God and others. As Sheen earlier noted, no amount of public opinion, no particulars of human conditioning, and no individual judgment on the part of others defines who we are. Only the God who created and sustains us is the judge of our innermost personality. Hence there is the "I" we really are, and the "ego" comprised largely of the enemy within.

> The ego is made to the image and likeness of the world in which it lives, as the I is made to the image and likeness of the eternal God. The ego is a conformist; it is "adjusted" to its times; but the Scriptures warn: "Be not conformed to the world." The "I" has attained inner freedom, through transcendence of the worldly. The "ego" is always self-centered; the personality, because it is essentially a mystery, is willing to soar beyond the self if it can return to its source. The "ego" wants the world to serve it; the "I" wants to serve the world.[4]

The "ego" sees liberty as the right to do whatever one pleases; the "I" views it as a response to a call. The real "me" feels that pull toward God, and knows that the totality of life is a response to a gift – my giftedness, the treasure I've been given in the gift of my human life, and in my Baptism into the life of Christ. The "ego," said Sheen, is never aware of other egos. It is so preoccupied with the relentless pursuit of its own pleasure and satisfaction, it never makes time for the needs of others. The "I" on the other hand wants to make the best use of the goods and talents God has given, for His honor and glory. The only way the ego will ever decrease is by putting individualism aside and making communion with others a primordial aim. Love of neighbor, even though the neighbor in himself is not particularly lovable, is very attainable when the other is seen as a child of God, one whose life has also been given, one who possesses the Divine image within him or her. What a contrast this presents to the egotist whose conscience is either dulled, or numbed, or outright killed. The difference between the two was contrasted by Sheen in terms of those who have true peace in their lives, and those whose entire existence consists of a false, or artificial peace.

> Peace is a nice word – but it, too, has a true and a false sense. True peace is a gift of God; false peace is of our own making. True peace flourishes in an increasing friendship with God; false peace is spawned in forget-fulness of God and exaltation of the self. True peace deepens in sorrow; false peace is shattered by reverses. True peace has no wants; false peace is restless and covetous. True peace has a lowly estimate of self; false peace lives in fear of being found inferior. True peace has a firm trust in God despite its own past sins; false peace shrinks from the thought of God because it will not put an end to present sins.[5]

The egotist was further described as being an escapist – one who could not face up to change because he or she was afraid of goodness, or fearful of truth. Sheen used the interesting compari-son of the things which most commonly scare us – the pulling of a tooth, or facing surgery. We must go through pain and suf-fering before the greater good can be achieved. In the same way, spiritual goodness can be feared because it will mean the giving up of oftentimes deeply rooted sinful pleasures and sins before the greater spiritual good can be achieved. Such is reminiscent of Saint Paul's awareness that he did not do the good he intended, and

Saint Augustine's desire to be good, but according to a timetable he would determine. The fact is, both did it, with God's grace, and Sheen's point is very well taken; so can we.

> If Our Lord were liberal about our sins and took them lightly, He would never have been sentenced to the Cross. He had at least four good chances to leave us as we were: He could have courted the Pharisees or wooed the Herodians; He might have disclaimed Divine Authority before Pilate; or spoken to the wicked Herod; or finally come down from the Cross instead of paying the penalty of death for sin. It is no wonder that, in the face of that persistent, resolute Goodness, the bystanders at the Cross pleaded, "Come down and we will believe."[6]

Egotists also feared the truth, Sheen said; another reason for delaying, if not refusing to spiritually better themselves. The truth may be resisted, or hated for several reasons; because of human pride that prevents us from admitting that the position we have taken is incorrect; or a deep seated love of the sin itself that makes us shrink at the thought of having to live without it; or because of its implication that a Divine Mind knows our innermost self far better than we do, and is not for a moment deceived by the public face we put on for the rest of the world. One of the finest examples in all the Scriptures of one who feared the truth was Herod. One day John the Baptist was invited to preach at his court to an audience largely comprised of those whose lives were immoral. John the Baptist immediately told his host it was not right for him to be living with his brother's wife, and for such a remark he was immediately imprisoned. He was martyred by decapitation a few months later, when a drunken Herod, delighted with the dance of Salome, promised to give her anything she wanted, even half his kingdom. When the girl's mother told her to ask for John's head, despite Herod's misgivings, the request was acceded to. "Evil will always kill goodness when it has become a reproach; virtue is a dangerous career."[7]

Despite this, many do change. In fact, man is the only one who has the capacity to change; water, plants and animals have various capacities to assimilate, though each one of them remains, for the most part, fixed in type. Man has the greatest capacity, because "he who is born of the flesh can also be born of the spirit." The conversion of which Bishop Sheen wrote so extensively, the sort understood by Catholic theology, is not a further development in the natural order; rather, it is a transformation to the supernatural order. In his work *Peace of Soul*, he distinguished between the proper types in society; those who use the best grammar, are very well educated, socially prominent, and the like, but "Deity-blind." It is entirely possible for such people to go through the entirety of their lives with no thought about God or their response to Him, "They have eyes, but they are blind." On the other hand, there are those who have experienced a "Deo-version," a turning to God, a putting Christ ahead of their egos. These are people who have experienced the transforming love of God in Christ, and their lives are changed irrevocably. They have undergone a sort of inner civil war; the urge for God conflicting with the results of concupiscence, and have experienced the beauty of the former winning.

> Every conversion starts with a crisis: with a moment or a situation involving some kind of suffering, physical, moral or spiritual; with a dialectic, a tension, a pull, a duality or a conflict. This crisis is accompanied on the one hand, by a profound sense of one's own helplessness and, on the other hand, by an equally certain conviction that God alone can supply what the individual lacks.[8]

This conversion might also be called a great moment of decision in a person's life. In an essay of that title written in the late 1960's, Bishop Sheen used the example of Napoleon, taken no doubt from one of the famous General's biographies. Napoleon believed that the fate of every battle was decided in the space of about five minutes; if the commander had the foresight to take advantage of the situation, the enemy's defeat would be assured, but if he was slow to perceive, he himself would be vanquished. In one battle, Napoleon's forces were stopped in front of a bridge which crossed a deep ravine; if the bridge were not crossed, the battle would be lost, but the smoke from Austrian fire was so dense, the French troops were afraid to cross. Napoleon snatched the French flag from the standard bearer, plowed ahead, renewing the enthusiasm of his soldiers, and within a matter of minutes the battle was won. From this story, Sheen concluded that the life of every person is not so much decided by daily routines, but in the very brief moments when significant decisions are made; reminiscent of Shakespeare speaking of a "tide in the affairs of men, which taken at the flood, leads on to fortune."

> If the opportunity is allowed to slip by unimproved, success turns into failure. There is a name of a place which signifies such a turning point in the affairs of men, and that is Kadesh Barnea, which is situated on the southern border of the Promised Land. There came a point in the pilgrimage when the children of Israel were within striking distance of their inheritance. They sent out spies, twelve of them, to report on the land they were about to take. The majority report, made by representatives of ten of the tribes, was that the land could not be taken because the cities were too fortified and the enemy too numerous. The minority report, brought in by Joshua and Caleb, was turned down despite the fact that God had told the people through Moses that they would possess the land. It was this point in the journey, like the five minutes in the battle, which determined their future. With the fruit of their

tribulations within their grasp, they refused to take it, and thus had to continue wandering in the desert for many years.... There is a Kadesh Barnea in every man's spiritual life. His background may have been filled with unbelief, guilt, dishonesties, adulteries and any of the seven pallbearers of the soul. Then there comes a moment of illumination to the mind, perhaps in a moment of sickness or a startling thought while reading, or the vision of innocence in a child. If this grace is responded to, a person is lifted out of himself, cuts connections with the past and starts out on a new career and new paths, with Heaven shining in his face.[9]

What Sheen describes is a moment when "inner frustration and Divine Mercy meet," a moment experienced in one of Christianity's most famous conversion stories, that of Saint Augustine. The fourth-century convert from paganism who eventually became Bishop of Hippo in North Africa, had heard the story of another convert, one Ponticianus. In hearing that story, Augustine slowly came to realize the Lord was speaking to him. In his *Confessions*, he claimed that he was being shown "how foul I was," though he did not immediately turn from his former life. It was only after a continual Divine prodding that the future Doctor of the Church came to realize his true place. Sheen drew the comparison with Augustine not merely to tell his readers a sublime sort of story, but that they would relate to it, and see in the particulars of Augustine's life, similar situations to their own. "The abyss of powerlessness now cries out to the abyss of salvation," he wrote, stressing the importance of Blaise Pascal's observation that there are only two kinds of reasonable people: "those who love God with all their hearts because they have found Him, and those who search for God with equal intensity because they have not found Him."[10]

The crisis in a person's life that brings about conversion involves a surrender to an all loving Christ, who does with us what no human being could ever do. There is a certain emptiness of soul that our sinful condition has left us with, but ever so gradually one begins to see less of his or her individual sinfulness, and more of the loving mercy of God. Attention is shifted from the self to the Cross. This does not always occur overnight. Bishop Sheen once had a woman come to see him to discuss her life, and especially its many problems. She was a rather well known figure in the world of opera, and came to the meeting with a friend who was a vocal coach. No sooner had the meeting begun, than the woman told the Bishop she would have to leave if he began speaking to her of the Crucifix. She was not a Catholic, had not initially the intention of becoming one, and said he would immediately prejudice her against the Church if he began speaking about it. Sheen responded by telling her if she truly understood the Crucifix she would love it, and instead of avoiding the topic, he intended to begin his discussion with it. She apparently was not put off, for she did, in time, enter the Church, and devoted many years to speaking with actors, actresses, and singers behind the stages of their Broadway productions, placing crucifixes in their hands, and preaching a mini sermonette as she did. Sheen often recounted the story in his books, and was especially fond of relating it during Days of Recollection he gave during the 1970's in various Broadway theatres, sponsored by the Catholic Actors Guild at the famed Saint Malachy's Church on 49th Street in New York City.

Hesitancy of all sorts could be found among the more famous converts to Catholicism. Clare Booth Luce came to him in the aftermath of her daughter's death in an automobile accident; Bella Dodd was an active member of the Communist Party who displayed a noticeable unhappiness her instructor picked up at the outset; Douglas Hyde was editor of the *Communist Daily Worker* in London; Louis Budenz functioned in a similar capacity at the *Worker*'s American edition; Horace Mann played a leading role in fostering anti-Catholicism in Governor Alfred E. Smith's unsuccessful presidential campaign of 1928. All of these individuals had to let go an inner hostility before the Spirit could begin to work. Sheen was the catalyst for most but the "Hound of Heaven" was in continuous pursuit of them all.

In a parish where the future Archbishop worked in the early days of his priesthood, he took a census, visiting all the homes in the geographical bounds of the church, Catholic and non-Catholic alike. He went into one very poor home where the woman told him she had once been a Catholic but had not practiced in years. She seemed a friendly sort, but her son was a very different nature. He was an automobile mechanic, and he came in the back door of the house as Sheen was speaking with his mother. He carried a monkey wrench and, as the Bishop related the story, he let it fly at him. Sheen was able to dodge it, but immediately picked up the hostility in the boy's voice, not to mention his actions. The young priest decided to begin the conversation by asking how much it would cost to put "a new carburetor into a Hudson." This immediately dates the story in the early 1920's, and even then, the man informed the priest Hudsons were no longer being made. Not to be deterred, Sheen kept up the line of questioning, inquiring about prices, installation and service. It took fifteen to twenty minutes, but eventually the man settled down, began answering the questions and provided Sheen the useless information. Finally the priest admitted he did not own a Hudson, nor did he have any interest in the questions he was asking. The young man, either from the point of view of amusement or curiosity, asked why he had been questioned at such length. Sheen explained it was a test to see if he had it in him to be kind. After passing with flying colors, he and his mother went on to be faithful, devout Catholics, and active members of their parish church. But first the inner hostility had to be overcome.

Yet another example of conversion from the same starting point ended in mixed success. A young woman approached Bishop

Sheen in New York describing herself an atheist, and anxious to debate. Sheen replied he would be happy to engage her if she could give three substantial arguments for atheism. Since she could not, she agreed to receive instructions. He received her into the Church at Saint Patrick's Cathedral, and some weeks later called her to see if she were staying faithful. She replied she was attending Mass regularly – daily, in fact, but was not receiving Communion because she was going with a married man whom she shortly intended to marry in a civil ceremony. He was a Jew, and well known in the world of theater. For several years, the girl would come to Saint Patrick's Cathedral on Good Friday to listen to Bishop Sheen preach the Discourses on the Seven Last Words from the Cross. One year he met her and asked if she were happy. Pointing to a crucifix, she said she would be if it were not for Him. She eventually asked Sheen to give her husband instructions. Reluctant at first, he gave the course, and, because he was previously married to a Jewess, would be eligible in the Catholic Church for the Pauline Privilege in his marriage. When this was granted by Rome, the former Jew wired his wife, who was staying at a ranch in Wyoming, to return to New York so they could be married in the Church. She announced she was divorcing him and marrying a cowboy. Heartbroken, he went to Sheen, related the story, and gave him the wedding ring she had given him at their civil ceremony; he had it made into a cross to reflect her gift to him, faith in Christ and His Cross. Sheen reminded him he was still free to marry, and, since this had been his second attempt, and it had ended in failure, the Bishop suggested he select the girl he should marry. His friend did not marry the girl Sheen had in mind, but rather an actress whom he persuaded to enter the Church. Sheen witnessed their marriage in Washington, though in later years the woman became an alcoholic, and her husband was forced to spend the rest of his life alone. In an indirect way, through the failure of two Catholic women, this Jew came to Christ. Interestingly, he and Bishop Sheen became fast friends.

He designed the chapel in Sheen's New York City apartment, and the Bishop officiated at his funeral years later. Conversions take varied routes, with surprising results.

Conversions can also be of a spiritual nature rather than moral. People in this category have usually been leading exemplary lives, but are not yet "possessed of the fullness of Faith and Sacraments." These were situations where Sheen excelled. During the twenty-five years he served as a Professor of Philosophy at the Catholic University of America, he took the train each weekend from Washington to New York City to conduct convert instruction classes, either at Saint Patrick's Cathedral, or at the Paulist Church of Saint Paul the Apostle at 59th Street and Columbus Circle. Because he was on national radio, the numbers seeking such instruction from him were significant. He would give twenty to twenty-five hours of class, and, on average, fifty to one hundred persons from each group would be received into the Church. In his posthumously published memoirs, Sheen recalled that as the course of instruction continued, he could see a decided change in the composition of a group. At first, there would be a scrambling to get the better seats in the auditorium, and the tendency not to give up the good seat once one had acquired it. When the instructor began to preach Christ, however, things changed; the tendency then became one of deference – people would defer to one another in seat placement, and courtesy seemed to reign. Many of these individuals either recognized "they have tremendous potentialities that have not been exercised, or else begin to yearn for a religious life that will make greater demands on them."[11] As such, they were wonderful groups to work with, since the discernible shift in their lives was usually occasioned by the inspiration of devotional reading, the example of a saintly person, or a relentless hunger for God. Sheen felt a convert like G.K. Chesterton could easily be placed in this category. Received into the Church at Beaconsfield, England in 1922, he had written the Foreword to Sheen's earliest book, and had been much impressed by the brilliance of the young graduate priest at the Catholic University of Louvain's Institute of Philosophy. Sheen oft quoted Chesterton's remark that he was the man who "with utmost daring, discovered what was discovered before."[12] Another English convert who interested Sheen was Christopher Hollis, a leading Catholic writer and apologist whose son would become Bishop of the Catholic Diocese of Portsmouth. Hollis is buried in the same cemetery as Monsignor Ronald Knox at Mells in Somerset, just a few graves apart. When one examines his conversion story, it is easy to see how the Bishop could include him among those who yearned for something deeper:

> When I looked at the New Testament, I did not find there any record of Christ talking as a friend talked; I did not find Him saying: "These are a few observations that have occurred to me. I should be very grateful if you would go away and think them over and see if you can find anything in them." I did find Him teaching with authority, hurling dogmas at the heads of His audience, commanding His audience to accept His teaching and holding out to them the appalling threat of eternal damnation if they refused to accept. When I was at school, among my school fellows were a Presbyterian and a Methodist. One term the Presbyterian came back and said that during the holiday his parents had read the New Testament and as a result, they had become Catholics. The Methodist thought this was a very funny story. I did not see at the time why it was so particularly funny and when some years later, I came to read the New Testament myself, I found it was even less funny than I had imagined.[13]

Bishop Sheen was insistent that there were many in the world who earnestly sought, but were hindered from taking any action because of their own fears. "They are thirsty, but they fear to ask Him for a drink lest He pour it from a chalice," he wrote. "They are cold but they fear drawing near His fires, lest those flames cleanse as they illuminate them."[14] Courage is what is lacking, and this courage is nothing less than the desire for God. Unless that desire is stronger than old habits and sins, one will end up in frustration. God never refuses His grace to those who sincerely ask, but many souls cringe at the thought of such grace changing them. They would much prefer to have God take them as they are, and let them retain the same characteristics; "to purge them of the disgust of sin, but not of the pleasure of sin." Sheen compared such types to the onlookers at Calvary who wanted God on their terms rather than His. The sort who would shout, "Come down and we will believe."[15]

Then, too, there were conversions caused by physical events. These usually come through some unexpected catastrophe; the death of a loved one, a significant business failure, a serious illness, or the like; events which prompt one to question the meaning of life, and one's future destination. So long as a person enjoys good health, prosperity, success, and the bounties of life, such questions are rarely in the forefront. When our situation changes, we often realize we cannot stay the same, and this is a marvelous occasion for the working of God's grace. One episode that Bishop Sheen knew well involved Doctor Felix Leseur, a French physician, and his wife Elizabeth. Leseur was a man of science with all of the prejudices such a background could include; his wife, in her younger years, had been a "mediocre" Catholic. Leseur became very interested in atheism, and edited a newspaper in which many fellow thinkers presented their case. Elizabeth Leseur eventually contracted a serious illness, and as the years progressed, her pain began to intensify. She discovered the meaning of suffering, and gladly offered hers in union with Christ, for the intention of her husband's conversion. "Felix," she once said to him, "when I am dead, you will become a Catholic and a Dominican priest." He considered this the wishful thinking of a pious, dying woman, and gave it little credence. At one point he even told her that he had sworn hatred for God, and intended to live and die in that hatred. Following his wife's death, he discovered her Last Will and Testament, containing a notation that, in 1904 "…I asked Almighty God to send me sufficient sufferings to purchase your soul. On the day that I die you will have been bought and paid for. Greater love than this no woman hath." Elizabeth died in 1914, and her husband Felix, who had once written a book against Lourdes, describing it as a hoax and a fraud, suddenly converted to Catholicism. In the early 1920's, a young Father Fulton Sheen made his retreat under Dominican Father Felix Leseur at a Dominican monastery in Belgium, and the retreat master personally recounted the details. Such stories prove that "the desire for God is to the soul what breathing is to the body."

In the late 1940's, the then Monsignor Sheen began to express much skepticism about the future. In his classic study, *Peace of Soul*, he offers an interesting commentary on the times:

> The world may have departed so far from God and the path to its own peace that a tragedy would be the greatest mercy. The worst thing God could do to us would be to let us alone in our present chaos and defilement. Two world wars have not made the world better, but worse. And one wonders if the next catastrophe will be a war in the same sense of the last two or rather some calamity more surely calculated to produce repentance in man.[16]

Much of our concentration to now has been on what Bishop Sheen described as the psychology of conversion. There is a theology to it as well, one which goes beyond adjusting the human mind to the world in which we live, in order to reflect on the Lord's teaching that He has taken us out of the world. "No flat tire can fix itself," the Bishop wrote, "and no frustrated, unhappy person can get well without the introduction into his nature of something that is not already there."[17] This presents an opportunity that is often missed, but it need not be missed – by anyone.

Individuals can live on three levels in the course of their lives. There is first the "subhuman," or animal, in which carnal pleasures are the most important aspect of life. If reason is used at all at this level, it is only to discover new techniques to enhance one's sensate desires. It is also possible to live on a higher, more rational level, following the natural virtues, but without great enthusiasm, those who believe honesty is the best policy, but are unable to provide any underlying rationale for such direction. These people will live a "good pagan life," being tolerant, philanthropic, contributing to community causes, and the like. There is a third level of being, much higher than the first two, in which man, aided only by the grace of God, is able to live as a child of God, elevated as he has been, to a supernatural order.

> The supernatural, the third level on which we may live, is not an outgrowth of the natural, as the oak develops from an acorn. It marks a complete break, a beginning anew. The development is not a gradual progress, in which a person becomes more tolerant, more broad minded, more articulate about social justice, less hateful and less avaricious, until finally he reaches a point where he finds himself a Christian and a citizen of the supernatural order. This is not the way it happens.[18]

As Sheen explained, God must come down to the individual; the Eternal "must invade human history." This is the meaning of the Incarnation, and as a result of this defining moment in the life of every soul, a human response must be made to Divine initiative. Man is the only one capable of making such a response; in the animal species, lower natures are destroyed by surrendering them to man, but because man is a person, his personality is not something capable of being destroyed. What man surrenders is the sinful, ungodlike part of his nature. The Sacrament of Baptism is the specific act by which such sinfulness is surrendered, and its power and efficacy does not simply set us in a new direction, but gives us "an elevation, or better still, a generation." Indeed, the very heart of Christianity is the inspiration for man to aspire to something greater than he is. Sheen noted that "as the soul gives life to the body, so does grace, or participation in the Divine Nature, give life to the soul."[19] Those who have arrived at this level of spiritual life recognize that Christ came among us to restore us to that condition we lost through Original Sin, and to help us each step of the way in our battle with concupiscence, that attraction to sin which the Council of Trent noted has been left in us for the sake of the combat. The Bishop drew the beautiful comparison that what physical birth is to a child of nature, Baptism is in the life of the Spirit, and, just as we resemble our parents in the physical characteristics of the natural order, so Baptism bestows on us a similar resemblance to the Creator in whose image we've been made, and the life of whose Son we sacramentally share.

It is also true that the acceptance of God's grace is a free act on our part, and God will never interfere with the free will He has given us. Many will refuse this gift, fearing they will have to give up too much. They are very much like the rich young man in the Gospel who went away sad because he had many possessions. "Are we willing to surrender the lower to find the ecstasies of the higher?" Sheen asked rhetorically. "Do we want God enough to overcome the obstacles that keep Him away?"[20] The effects of such a surrender, or conversion on our part, can be very significant. For one thing, Christ is no longer someone who is extrinsic to us, as He is to those who view Him merely as an historical figure who lived well over two thousand years ago.

> If Our Divine Savior had remained on earth, they would be right: He would be only an example to be copied, a voice to be heard. But once He ascended into Heaven and sent His Spirit to us, then He ceased to be only a model to be copied and became a Life to be lived.[21]

He described this life of Christ within us as a real possession, a transforming power. The effects of this transformation may be observed on the natural and supernatural levels. Naturally, it translated into altruism, a topic the Bishop discussed at some length in a telecast in the 1950's. Calling it an "evolution of love," he traced the four stages love may take in a person's life: it may be utilitarian, directed at the other for what he or she can do for us; romantic, or sexual love, the sort we bear for another because of the pleasure the other offers; democratic love, where others are respected and their rights recognized because it is important for us to have ours equally recognized; finally, humanitarian love, directed at humanity in general and largely confined to the abstract. Above all of these is Christian love, given by Our Lord as a new commandment, and unique in that it distinguishes between liking, which is an act of the emotions, and loving, which is an act of the will.

> The Commandment is new, not only because it is in the will, but also because the Model of such love is God Himself.... When anyone does us wrong we say, "You lost my love; change, and then I will love you." Our Blessed Lord, on the contrary, says, "Love someone first and then he will change. Let your love be the creation of his betterment." It was the love that He gave Peter the night Peter denied Him that made Peter change. Tradition has it that Peter went out and wept so much that he created furrows in his cheeks, because he had hurt Someone he loved.[22]

Such is conversion, both on the part of one who loves, and on the part of one who has been loved. On the supernatural level, Sheen saw the results of conversion discernible in the unity existing among Christ's members in His Mystical Body, the Church. Just as a human body is one because it has one soul, one visible head and one invisible head, so the Church's soul is the Holy Spirit; its visible head is Peter and his successors, and its invisible Head is Christ in Heaven. The Church is the "Totus Christus," the Whole Christ; it complements the individual Christ. His Spiritual Body is, of course, perfect, but His Mystical Body, consisting of so many cells, is simply growing to perfection. Each cell in that Body is a unique individual, who, upon his or her conversion to Christ has experienced a re-centering of life, a revolution of all its values, a definite change in behavior and conduct, and a degree of certitude.

> Philosophy gives a proof for the existence of God; the science of apologetics gives the motives for believing in Christ, the Son of God; but all the incontrovertible proofs they offer fall short of the certitude that actually comes to a convert through the gift of Faith.[23]

Finally, conversion has a collective, or global effect. Bishop Sheen delivered one particular radio address in 1935, not terribly long after the United States had emerged from the throes of the Depression. He sharply disagreed with critics who held that our world economics had failed us; on the contrary, man had forgotten God, and no economic or political system can help a civilization in that predicament. The solution would come "only by a renovation of the inner man, only by a purging of our hearts and souls." Such was not readily apparent, however, and Sheen was prophetic in comparing the pre-World War II years, before the rise of dictatorships in Western Europe, with the time of Our Lord, when there was intense Nationalism in Israel, and fierce Militarism in Rome.

> What has the birth of God in the form of a Babe to do with the social, political and economic conditions of His day and our own? What possible relation could ex-

ist between a Child in a manger of straw and Caesar on his throne of gold? The answer is: the birth of the Son of God in the flesh was the introduction into the historical world order of a new life; it was a proclamation to the world that social reconstruction has something to do with spiritual regeneration; that nations can be saved only by the men in them being reborn to God as God is now being born to man. Once God entered the created order on the level of humanity He gave man a new strength from above; He gave him a Divine Power along with a human power. In a word, God became man in order that man might become God-like.[24]

Western Civilization in the 1930's, said Sheen, was not simply suffering from a famine of spiritual values, it had given up caring about them. One can only wonder what he would write about the early 21st century! No matter how far, or how low one may sink, Sheen was careful to note that we are always considered exiles from the heavenly homeland for which we were made and are destined. In that sense, it makes no difference which decade or century one lives in; every person who is destined for such a future must prepare for it during his or her earthly sojourn. In 1935, Fulton Sheen saw the remedy in the Church's sacramental life, especially the Holy Eucharist and its frequent reception.

Only by taking the Lord into our hearts and souls would true conversion of the individual be possible, for conversion on a collective level always starts with the person.

The communion rail is for that reason the most democratic institution on the face of the earth; it is even a greater leveler than death, for there the distinction between rich and poor, the learned and the unlearned disappears; there the millionaire must take the paten from the common laborer, the employer must kneel at the same board as the employee, the university professor must eat the same bread as the simple Irishwoman who knows only how to tell her beads. There the dividing wall between nationalities is broken down and rebuilt into that Spiritual Kingdom where all are one, because of One Lord, One Faith, One Baptism.[25]

Chapter Five

CONFESSION

During the Second World War, the National Council of Catholic Men published a small pamphlet written by the then Monsignor Fulton J. Sheen entitled *Friends*. It contained spiritual truths, Catholic teachings, and specific prayers, all of which were designed to lead one into deeper friendship with Jesus Christ. A brief description of each of the seven sacraments is given, and Sheen summarizes the Sacrament of Penance in these practical terms:

> In the natural order it sometimes happens that a part of the body becomes injured, in which case the wound must be bound and healed. In the supernatural order, it may sometimes happen that a soul sins, in which case a member of the Mystical Body becomes wounded, or even dies. The spiritual wound must be healed and the inanimate member revivified – and this is the Sacrament of Penance.[1]

Six and one half decades later, the *Catechism of the Catholic Church* is the normative guide for all of us in our quest to better understand this magnificent sacrament that reconciles us with God and with each other, after the commission of personal sin. The *Catechism* looks at the sacrament from several angles; it is the

Sacrament of Conversion, because it makes sacramentally present the Lord's call to conversion, the necessary first step in any journey home; as the Sacrament of Penance, it makes holy a person's individual return to Christ; as the Sacrament of Confession, it reminds us we must enumerate all our particular sins, their type, gravity, and, to the best of our ability, their frequency; as the Sacrament of Forgiveness, it emphasizes Christ's pardon and peace, bestowed through His priest, from whose fingers, Bishop Sheen often said, the Savior's Precious Blood is, figuratively, dripping when he raises his hands in absolution; finally, as the Sacrament of Reconciliation, it binds up the wounds inflicted on the entire Body of Christ by our individual transgressions.

In his time, Fulton Sheen discussed each of these themes, and helped his readers more deeply love Christ Crucified, through whose merits their sins were forgiven.

During a course of instruction for converts in the 1950's, Sheen emphasized the sacrament's true purpose was the forgiveness of sins committed after Baptism. It showed God's realism in dealing with His creatures; we are given Divine Life in Baptism, but are strongly inclined to turn away from it because of concupiscence within us, that inclination to evil which stems from sin and so often leads us to sin. Sin, properly defined, is an abuse of freedom, and freedom can be maximized or minimized. We maximize freedom when we consider that we are a law of and to ourselves; that we are the final determiners of what is right or wrong. We minimize freedom by denying there is any such thing as guilt, by confusing it with a psychological complex, or by disclaiming any personal wrongdoing.

> You get too fat? You can't help it; you're a compulsive eater! You drink too much? You can't help it; you're a compulsive drinker! You steal? You can't help it; you're a compulsive thief! Behind that word and behind all other escapes there is the assumption, "I am

determined." I am determined by environment; I am
determined by my grandparents; I am determined by
something inside or outside of myself.[2]

Of the two extremes, minimizing freedom is far more
dangerous. Sheen often used the example of Lady Macbeth in
Shakespeare's play; she washed her hands every fifteen minutes in
a bizarre expression of guilt, but it was prompted by real guilt, her
involvement in the murder of the king. Denying sin, explaining
it away, or not mentioning it in polite society are all characteristic
of our age; each makes the forgiveness of sin impossible. And by
separating ourselves from the opportunity of forgiveness, still
graver situations develop.

"Traveling seventy miles per hour in an automobile is already
an excessive speed," the Bishop said. "But if twenty miles per hour
more is added, the danger mounts. Unrepented sins beget new sins
and the dizzying total brings despair."[3]

Authentic teacher of the faith that he was, Bishop Sheen often
used examples from daily life to illustrate supernatural truths. He
once compared mortal sin to receiving a fatal wound, since it kills
the Divine Life in us. Such is far more than a violation of the law
of God; it is more properly a "crucifixion." Venial sin, on the other
hand, does not kill Divine Life, but diminishes it.

> Every sin has a triple effect: it divides a person from
> himself, his neighbor, and God. From himself because
> it makes the soul a kind of battle field; after a sin one
> always feels like a menagerie full of wild beasts. Then
> sin alienates a man from his neighbor. A man who
> cannot live with himself cannot live with his neighbor.
> Cain, after his sin, asked, "Am I my brother's keeper?"
> Finally, it estranges us from God and gives us a sense
> of loneliness. In some way we dam up the mind which
> ought to have communion with God.[4]

There is absolutely no reason why any person in the world be weighed down by the burden of sin and guilt. Our Lord instituted a remedy no human mind could ever have conceived. Tracing the evolution of the sacrament, Sheen noted that a form of confession had existed all through the Old Testament. After Adam had eaten of the fruit of the tree, God asked him if he had committed such an act. The Creator knew that he had indeed done it, but God queried him to elicit a confession. Further on, Cain was asked where his brother was, but in responding with another question, "Am I my brother's keeper?" he was in effect refusing to go to confession. John the Baptist heard the confession of sins from those who wanted to purify themselves for the coming of the Messiah. All of these had been forerunners of the sacrament Our Lord gave us through His Passion and Death and their applied merits.

The power of the sacrament's forgiveness was first conferred on Peter, when Our Lord gave him the power of the keys, and told him whatever he bound on earth would be bound in heaven, and whatever he loosed on earth would be loosed in heaven. He further extended that power to the rest of the Apostles (and their successors) when He breathed on them – a symbol of the giving of the Holy Spirit – and told them to receive that same Spirit, assuring them that the sins they forgave were forgiven, while those they retained were retained. The form of the sacrament is a logical development of Our Lord's words, since no priest would ever know which sins to forgive or retain unless he heard the confession of those seeking Christ's forgiveness.

Why did Christ institute His sacrament in the particular form He did? Why not allow people to simply tell their sins directly to God without any human intermediary? "There is no test of sorrow," Sheen wrote, "if you are the judge. What would happen to justice in our country if all judges and courts, when they had murderers, thieves and dope addicts before them, handed out Kleenex?"[5] In other words, each of us must be held accountable.

Almost anticipating the theology of the body of Pope John Paul II, Sheen wrote decades ago

> Why should a confessor stand between my God and me? For the same reason that the human nature of Christ stands between His divinity and me. If we were angels, there might be a confession of spirit to spirit, but being made up as we are of body and soul, it is fitting that body or a human nature be the means by which we commune with God. When God came down to earth in the Incarnation, He did not come as a flash of lightning, or as an invisible spirit, but He came in the form and habit of man, and through that human nature of His, He forgave sins, lifted up blinking eyes to the light of God's sunshine, and healed hearts wounded with disease and death.... Ascending into heaven, it was only natural that He continue His forgiveness in exactly the same way, namely, through the instrumentality of other human natures, or confessors.[6]

Writing in 1932 in his work *Moods and Truths*, Sheen harkened back to the time of the Communist Revolution in Russia fifteen years before, and the severing of diplomatic relations between the United States and what had become the Union of Soviet Socialist Republics. He noted that if America had had any contact with the Soviets, it was not through direct channels, but through a third party. In the same way, since man had broken off diplomatic relations with God through sin, was it not equally fair that he deal with God through His chosen ambassadors? How, asked Sheen, could one situation be considered just and fair, and not the other? The person confessing his or her sins may be much holier than the priest to whom they are confessing; priests do hear the confessions of many saints. It is also true, that many American citizens may be far more patriotic than the President of the United

States; in both cases, the confessor and the President possess powers that others do not, and, in the case of the sacrament, Our Lord gave the power of forgiveness to His Church; He did not give it to individuals. No human being can forgive the sins of another; when a priest absolves, it is Christ absolving, just as it is Christ acting through His priests in all the sacraments.

Yet another reason for confessing one's sins to a priest is that when one sins it is not a private act; in some way the entire Mystical Body of Christ is affected adversely; hence it is fitting that through a representative of that same Mystical Body an individual be restored to unity with the whole. This argument became particularly compelling during World War II, when Sheen stressed that the sinful world every soul encountered had its impact.

> All the modern explanations given for the existence of evil fail to fit the facts. Biologists have told us that evil was due to a fall in evolution, but if progress is inevitable why have there been two world wars in twenty-one years? Sociologists told us evil was due to systems: Capitalism or Communism or Nazism or Fascism. But how could the world adopt evil systems, if minds were not already fit soil for their growth? Since evil is so universal, must it not be due to a breakdown of a universal moral law? Is not the world in a mess for the same reason I am in a mess, namely, because I have not done what I ought to have done?[7]

One needed penitence, or taking on the role of a penitent. When this decision is made, one must encounter a confessor for the celebration of the sacrament. Every confessor is a judge, a doctor of the soul, and a dispenser of the forgiveness of the Lord. As such, he must resemble the Good Shepherd. Sheen went back to the Old Testament to study the depictions of God in this light, leading His people from slavery into freedom. The Prophet Isaiah depicted God as carrying His sheep in His arms, and Ezekiel saw Him searching out the lost. Zechariah predicted the shepherd would be struck and the sheep dispersed, while Psalm 23 sees the Lord leading His sheep into green pastures. "He was not the Good Shepherd because He provided economic plenty," the Bishop wrote, "but because He would lay down His life for His sheep."[8] In much the same way, modern confessors are called to be the Good Shepherds of today, men who will

> ...look kindly on the denying Peters, speak words of forgiveness to penitent Magdalenes, breathe words of comradeship to betraying Judases, a man who will utter a cry of forgiveness as if from a cross to all those who would malign him or his office; a man with intensity of love for his work and with universality of love for his penitents; a man endowed with a wisdom that comes from training, one in whom the Church has laid the wisdom garnered from twenty centuries' of experience with souls.[9]

And to him comes a soul in search of peace:

> Hard though it is, this narration of sins by a penitent answers a need of the human heart. How often history reveals that a guilty man pressed by conscience alone, and driven on by some mysterious influence, stronger even than the conservation of life, will make him refuse the impunity which silence promises and will force him to proclaim the very sin the avowal of which will bring the punishment he sought to avoid.[10]

If this is true in the natural order, Sheen argued, how much more so in the order of grace. Nor was this simply limited to those with serious sins on their soul. Sheen presented a wonderful argument for frequent confession when he reminded his readers how often human beings are "weighed down with a heart which seems not right with God." There is constant need for an inner renewal, and the daily infusion of God's grace; the special sacramental grace Penance confers provides us a spiritual aid to be gotten nowhere else. The more we avail ourselves of this help, the holier and stronger we become.

We rarely think of the Sacrament of Penance in terms of the social reformation of society, but that theme was developed by Sheen early on. Society cannot be reformed until the individual is reformed. He contended that modern social reform begins and ends with the individual; modern morality speaks of crime, which is a group problem, but the Church in the confessional speaks to the individual criminal; modern society speaks abstractly about the problem of alcoholism, but the Church in her sacrament speaks to the alcoholic, encouraging him or her not to deny the problem, or have it explained away; rather, to seek forgiveness, so that a true healing might begin. Throughout his priestly life, Bishop Sheen saw the lives of many changed by the power of this sacrament, and, as was so often the case, he was the instrument of God in bringing pardon and peace to souls.

On one occasion, he was hearing confession on the eve of a First Friday. A young woman entered the confessional and told him she was not interested in going to confession, she merely wanted to kill time – about ten minutes. Sheen asked her who she was trying to fool, besides God. She responded that her mother was kneeling in the church, thinking the daughter was going to confession. The confessor then asked her if she were afraid to go to confession. When she replied yes, he suggested removing the curtain separating them and turning on the light. He thought that, by seeing her face, he might be able to determine the nature of the problem, and the reason for her fear. She agreed, and Sheen immediately said, "You're a prostitute." She said she was, and he assured her that was her confession, if she were willing to bring it before God. She said she had committed far graver sins and could not talk about them, and with that, she quickly left. All the remaining penitents that evening were asked to say a rosary for the conversion of a sinner, and all agreed, save one. After confessions were over, the priest met her on the steps of the church. He had already tried for twenty minutes in the box to get the girl to tell him the remainder of her problem, and finally she admitted that, after being arrested as a prostitute, she was put in a home run by religious sisters. Hoping to escape, she had made a pact with the devil, telling him she would make nine sacrilegious communions if he would help her. On the ninth day, she escaped. Sheen returned to the church and, by his own recounting, knelt at the communion rail from nine o'clock until twelve thirty praying she might return. At twelve thirty, he heard the door of the church open, and was afraid to turn around, for fear it was the police wondering why the church lights were on till such an hour. When he did turn around, it was the young lady ready to make her peace with God.

Another time, he was working in a parish in what is called the "Hell's Kitchen" section of New York City. One day, two girls came into the rectory telling him that Kitty was sick, and asking him to go to her. The girls were a bit surprised the priest did not immediately know Kitty; she was one who worked the streets, well known to all. Her fifth floor apartment, totally unkempt, was in a tenement building along the Hudson. When Sheen entered the room, he began talking with Kitty, and asked her, at the appropriate time, if she would like to go to confession. She told him she could not because she was the worst girl in the City of New York. Bishop Sheen replied that was impossible, since the worst girl in the city would think herself the best, and give absolutely no thought to sin, let alone sorrow or remorse. Kitty finally went to confession, and later related the story of the terrible life she had with her husband, who would often beat her if she did not bring sufficient monies home from her "employment." He had begun to administer a poisonous substance to her brain which caused her to hallucinate, and tell the other women present with her that she was giving them her arms, eyes, etc., for them to keep as mementoes after her death! Sheen administered the Sacrament of the Sick to her, and she immediately began to revive. Once back in the real world, she did great apostolic work in the parish, being the catalyst for many to enter the confessional, and, before making their peace with God, announce they were there because Kitty had sent them.

Still another story dealt with a family Sheen encountered in his first parish assignment. The pastor of the parish told him he had received a gift of ten thousand dollars to build an altar in honor of the Blessed Mother. The young priest was surprised anyone in the parish would have that much money, and when the pastor named the family and the street they lived on, he was even more surprised. It happened that the brother of the woman who had donated the money had been a bank robber, one who engaged in all sorts of criminal activity. The pastor believed the woman was giving the money in reparation for her brother's soul. Fulton asked the pastor if he had tried to reconcile the brother to the Church, but he replied he had not. When Sheen went to visit, he found the man rather impressive looking, with distinguished features. He asked him if he would like to go to confession, but the man replied no, not because of any particular hatred of God or religion, but in light of his past record; he had spent over thirty years in prison, stolen enormous amounts of money, and violated the law in numerous ways. He felt it too presumptuous at this stage of his life to begin asking God for pardon – almost feeling his actions were unpardonable. Sheen said he would be back the next day, and was bringing the Lord with him; he had the distinct feeling the man would have a change of heart, which indeed he did. He went to confession, and his reception of Holy Communion was actually Viaticum, because he died the following day.

In retrospect, Bishop Sheen had to conclude "he was not the first thief the Lord saved on his last day."[11]

A person's individual reform involves an inner probing of self, or, as the expression has been used in spirituality, an examination of conscience. The concept has ancient roots; the searching of the soul, the attempt to secure an answer to human problems goes back to ancient Greece, with its emphasis on "Know Thyself." Socrates spoke of a therapy of the soul, or the taking care of one's soul, and in the sanctuaries dedicated to the god Aesculapius, mental cures were applied to heal physical ailments; the Stoics recommended a nightly examination of the soul, believing that the deeper one probed, the more peace he would have. Marcus Aurelius wrote a series of meditations in which he communes with his own soul, and tries to determine how well he has lived up to the principles which governed his life. With this sort of background, it was easy to see how Saint Augustine could write that a person should "return into thyself and thou shall transcend thyself."[12] Bishop Sheen spent many years writing about psychoanalysis, its good and bad sides, and particularly how it differed from confession. In the 1950's psychoanalysis had become extremely popular, and as a secular discipline, had convinced the modern world that some sort of confession for peace of mind is necessary in every human life. "This is another instance of how the world, which threw Christian truths into the wastebasket in the 19th century, is pulling them out in isolated, secularized form in the 20th century, meanwhile deluding itself into believing it has made a great discovery."[13] What many people had fallen for through the years, were the false benefits psychoanalysis offered; there was considerable difference between unburdening oneself on a psychoanalytic couch, and doing the same in a confessional.

> There is a twofold difference… the first is in what is told, the second is in the reason for telling it. Psycho-analysis is the communication of mind with mind; the

confessional is the communication of conscience with conscience. In psychoanalysis, there is merely a confession of ideas, and the confession of ideas costs nothing and never craves pardon... but confession is not the communication of ideas; it is the communication of wills.... The reason for telling things in psychoanalysis is to acquire mental ease; but the reason for telling sins in the confessional is to acquire pardon.... Psychoanalysis tells things for the sake of sublimation, but not for the sake of purgation. It is not enough to diagnose a disease, it must also be cured, but there is no cure for a guilty conscience except pardon. The sinner must in some way be brought to Calvary, and made to see the personal equation between himself and the sufferings of Christ, and this is done only in the confessional.[14]

Some decades after he wrote this, Bishop Sheen made the further point that the spirit of confession was not one of fact finding, but of mercy. We human beings are capable of, and often do extend pardon to others who admit their faults and transgressions to us, and Our Lord has done exactly the same thing. He has taken the natural admission of faults, and has elevated it to the dignity of a sacrament. In the Gospels we discover that Christ employs not what we understand as psychoanalysis, but a sort of "Divine Analysis," seeing through people such as the Pharisees, whom He described as "whited sepulchers," clean on the exterior, but interiorly full of foulness. Or the hypocrite who went to the front of the temple to pray as a sort of show of affectation, or again, the way He read the heart of Simon the Pharisee when He visited his home and encountered the sinful woman whom Simon knew, and thought if only the Master knew what sort of woman approached Him – only to have his thoughts read by Our Lord, and told how much would be forgiven those who loved much.

Our Blessed Lord has reminded us that the world will end with a great "psychoanalysis" in which the secret and hidden sins of every person will be revealed and no one will go out until he has paid the last farthing. Because of this basic relationship between the human soul and God, throughout the whole of human history one of the most universal spiritual practices of every saintly soul has been what is known as the nightly examination of conscience.[15]

Bishop Sheen used the example from Matthew's Gospel (9:5) of the paralyzed man let down through the roof of the home to be brought to Christ for forgiveness. There were a number of persons there who took a sarcastic look at the proceedings, questioning who but God alone could forgive sins; individuals described by Sheen as "escapists who laughed at guilt and the moral order [and] scoffed at giving this public importance to sins."[16] Christ became angered at them and asked if it were easier to say the man's sins were forgiven, or to command him to rise and walk. He did immediately walk, but had not been able to recover until his sins were forgiven. It is only in the examination of our faults, failings, and sins, and their confession, that any of us will experience true recovery; hence there is need for a daily, honest examination of who we are and where our lives are headed.

The examination of conscience brings to the surface the hidden faults of the day; it seeks to discover the weeds that are choking the growth of God's grace and destroying peace of soul. It is concerned with thoughts, words, and deeds, with sins of omission and sins of commission. By omission we mean the good that is left undone – a failure to aid a needy neighbor, a refusal to offer a word of consolation to those who are burdened with sorrow. Sins of commission involve malicious remarks, lies, acts of dishonesty, and those seven sins that are the seven pallbearers of the soul; self-love, in-ordinate love of money, illicit sex, hate, overindulgence, jealously and laziness.

In addition to all this, there is the examination for what spiritual writers call our "predominant fault." Every person in the world has one sin that he or she commits more than others. Spiritual directors say that if we blotted out one great sin a year, in a short time we would be perfect.[17]

In addition to defining an examination of conscience, Bishop Sheen offered many positives coming from a person's daily spiritual scrutiny. It is something that prevents us from justifying our actions on the grounds that we are merely following our consciences. We can begin to fit a creed to the way we live rather than the converse – we "sit at the piano of life and insist that every note we strike is right." Also, a daily examination of conscience will free us from the depression that comes from refusing to face our faults. Many people suffer from fears that are nothing less than the effects of sins committed, either in one's far distant past, or as an ongoing habit. The more often we make the examination of conscience, the less we concentrate on our sins, and the more we think of the love and mercy of God, just as one who is wounded focuses more on the power of the physician to heal the wound than on the infliction itself. The examination sees sin as less a breaking of a law than offending one we love. "It develops sorrow not because a code has been violated, but because love has been wounded."[18]

Because the examination is always done in the light of God's love, it begins with a prayer to the Holy Spirit. Such a prayer is made for illumination of mind, that we may place ourselves in God's presence with total honesty. Sheen compared the process to that of bringing our watch to a watch repairman: "We put a watch in his hands because we know he will not force it, and we put our souls in God's hands because we know if God inspects them regularly, they will work as they should."[19]

Finally, by concentrating on God's goodness and love, we are brought to an entirely different level of spiritual appreciation.

> Every soul that examines itself looks at a Crucifix and sees a personal relationship between itself and Our Divine Lord. We admit that the Crown of Thorns would have been a little less piercing if we had been less proud and vain and that if we had been less swift in running down the pathways of sin the Divine Feet would have been less pierced with nails.... This figure upon the Cross is not an MVD [Soviet KGB] agent or a Gestapo inquisitor, but a Divine Physician, Who only asks that we bring our wounds to Him in order that He may heal them. If our sins be as scarlet, they will be washed white as snow, and if they be red as crimson, they shall be made white as wool.[20]

Once a person has examined his or her conscience honestly in the presence of God, the confession of sins follows. One must always tell their number and kind to the best of one's ability, concealing nothing, and bringing to the Lord's loving mercy all doubts, questions, and points which may still remain unclear in one's mind. The sacrament follows with a few words from the confessor, either of a spiritual nature, or correctional, if correction is in order. These are always given by the priest with the knowledge that he acts as an intermediary, speaking and absolving in the name of Christ the High Priest. Hence the element of fear should never enter the penitent's mind; there is no subject matter the confessor has not previously heard, and the priest is himself a sinner, beset with all the temptations and sins that are brought to the confessional by his brothers and sisters in Christ's Mystical Body.

What is very important is the mental disposition the penitent brings with him. Our Lord Himself, shortly before His leave-taking of this world, spoke of the necessity of repentance. Bishop Sheen noted that by Christ's death on the Cross, He "wrote the biography of all whom He redeemed." The fruits of His salvific action now had to be applied to all peoples and nations. Repentance and the remission of sins was to be preached in His name, beginning at Jerusalem: "Of this, you are my witnesses" (Luke 24:47, 48). Both Peter and Paul took up this theme in their first sermons, and repentance was to be the major theme of the New Testament; it was the fulfillment of the Old Testament prophecies, finding its realization on Calvary.

> Repentance implied a turning away from sin and a turning to God. The first four Beatitudes He preached were a description of this inner and radical change of heart, namely, poverty or humility of spirit, sorrow for sin, meekness, hunger and thirst for love of God. In the parable of the Prodigal Son, Our Lord had drawn a picture of the soul penitent who "entered into himself," as if sin had externalized him, and then returned humbly to the father's house. The Angels of Heaven, He said, rejoice more over one sinner doing penance than ninety-nine just ones who need not penance; the publican in the back of the temple mourning over his sins, He said, went back to his house justified. Now in His farewell discourse before the Ascension, He bade the world repent. This preaching of repentance was to begin at Jerusalem, for Salvation was first to the Jews. In that city the one great sacrifice was offered for the sins of the world.[21]

The Church has always distinguished between perfect and imperfect contrition in her teaching, and Fulton Sheen often touched on this in his writings. Imperfect contrition, sufficient for pardon, is the very real fear of hell; the fear of the consequences our sins may bring to us, and the horrifying thoughts of eternal damnation. This mentality brings one to a certain point and no further. It is much like living the letter of the law but missing its spirit. Perfect contrition, always to be aimed at, is the genuine sorrow and contriteness brought about when we know we've offended someone we love very much. When we stop to consider that no human being will ever love us as the Lord loves us, in fact no human being could ever reach such an intensity of love, then the appreciation for perfect contrition follows quite easily. In the late 1940's, the same period in which Bishop Sheen was writing some of his monumental works, a classic study on the Sacrament of Penance was written by Father Alfred Wilson, an English Passionist. In his book *Pardon and Peace*, he develops this idea more fully.

> Christ's infinite merits and satisfactions are enough and yet not enough, because God will not treat us as robots or automatons. There are those who often accuse us of attributing magical effects to the Sacraments. We retort that they are the culprits, who attribute magic to Redemption, whereas we assert that there is magic neither in the Sacraments nor in Redemption. God respects our free will and, without the cooperation of our free will, He will do nothing. His operation is dependent on our cooperation, just as the electric current is dependent on the lamp for the production of light. Confession has the innate power to remove all traces of sin, but, before it can do so, there must be perfect cooperation, i.e., perfect rectification of the will. Free will is the core of the difficulty.... Suppose two men had a quarrel, and one of them got into an uncontrollable rage and struck his companion so hard that he damaged his own hand and wrist. Afterwards the aggressor apologized and his apology was accepted. Would you call that the end of the incident? "No," you would say. "What about the hand?" Acceptance of the apology would not heal the

hand. So it is with *us*. By sin we damage our will; and the damage is not necessarily repaired by God's degree of pardon. Sometimes when we sin we turn to the creature with great intensity. Completely to rectify our will, we must turn back to God with equal intensity; that we frequently fail to do, with the result that our will remains scarred and out-of-the-straight. The will must be rectified before we can be fit for heaven.[22]

Many who have done wrong do not turn to God with such intensity of feeling. Some have the mistaken idea that past is past and should be forgotten about; others, while believing in forgiveness, lose sight of the fact that there is yet more to be done. Such incompleteness can only be overcome by a deepening love of God, and continual awareness of His presence. When we arrive at that plateau, Bishop Sheen wrote, and we discover how we have wounded One we love, our response is apt to be similar to that of Zacchaeus: "I will repay all." Sheen drew a comparison from the natural order: If I have stolen someone's watch, eventually my conscience will start to bother me, and this feeling will intensify until I return it. On returning the watch, I beg forgiveness from the one whom I offended. No doubt the person will forgive me, but will also insist I return the watch! Therefore, we are assigned penances to prove the contriteness of our hearts. They can be of three kinds: prayers, fasting or almsgiving. By praying we beg God's mercy; by works of charity we give back to God some of the gifts He has given us; and by fasting or mortification, we separate ourselves from the many legitimate pleasures of life so that we may better focus on God's loving mercy. Such acts of reparation are not done for ourselves alone, because our sins have wounded the entirety of Christ's Body, and the Body is also in need of healing. The Body of Christ is one because it has one Head, is vivified by one Soul, and professes one faith. "Just as it is possible to graft skin from one part of the body to the other," the Bishop wrote, "so, in the spiritual organism of the Church, it is possible to graft prayer and to transfuse sacrifices."[23] He was describing the mysterious, yet very beautiful Doctrine of the Communion of Saints, and emphasizing the closeness of all its members.

There is a unique experience any sinner may have as a result of a good confession. One description was given by Blessed Angela of Foligno, so beautifully put, that Bishop Sheen felt it worth recounting.

> I resolved to make my confession to him. I confessed my sins in full. I did not feel love, only bitterness, shame and sorrow. Then I looked for the first time at Divine Mercy; I made the acquaintance of that Mercy which had withdrawn me from hell, which gave me grace. An illumination made me see the measure of my sins. Thereupon, I understood that in offending the Creator, I had offended all creatures.... Through the Blessed Virgin Mary and all the saints, I invoked the mercy of God, and on my knees, I begged for life. Suddenly, I believed that I felt the pity of all creatures and of all saints. And then I received a gift; a great fire of love and the power to pray as I had never prayed.... God wrote the Pater Noster in my heart with such an accentuation of His Goodness and of my unworthiness that I lack words to speak of it.[24]

This account proves a point Bishop Sheen wanted to stress; a person must not simply wish to do better, he must will it. There is a vast difference between a desire to be better, and a firm determination for the same. "Pilate wished to save Our Lord," said Sheen, "but he did not will to save Him." Remorse over the past is all well and good, but the determination for the future that must accompany any true repentance involves the hard work necessary to bring about change. It is never easy; it is one of the fundamental challenges of the spiritual life, but God's grace is not merely an occasional aid, it is an ongoing, powerful remedy always at our disposal enabling us to work as if everything depended on us, and to pray as if everything depended on God.

Some souls arrive at a very high degree of repentance in their lives; they feel the obligation to pray for such for all those too blind to see for themselves how necessary it is. They see the face of Christ in the Garden of Gethsemane, taking all the sins of Humanity upon Himself, and they continue His bloody sweat by the quality of their lives and the intensity of their prayers for repentance for the entire Mystical Body of Christ. "The Trappists, Carmelites. Poor Clares, and dozens of other gifted souls renounce the world not because they want to save their own souls, but because they want to save the souls of others." Sheen could identify with much of this; he was a Third Order Carmelite, and had much appreciation for this particular spiritual apostolate. "The cloistered religious are like spiritual blood banks," he wrote, "storing up the red energy of salvation for those anemic souls who sin and do not atone."[25]

The lack of emphasis on Confession and its frequent reception in today's Church would have saddened the heart of Fulton Sheen very much, but with the renewed appreciation for his writings and spirituality, one can only hope that today's readers will be as affected as those decades ago. He often said that the Catholic suffers far more from the commission of sin than those who have not the fullness of faith; those raised in a period when the richness of the sacrament was strongly emphasized can well appreciate his words. To illustrate this, Bishop Sheen paints a picture of the Church in a period of stronger faith, one which aptly concludes our discussion of his writing on Penance.

> If you have ever walked Saturday afternoon or evening to a large city church with rows of confessionals on either side, you have seen feet protruding from the little curtains of the confessionals; big feet, little feet,

male feet, female feet. They belong to people who have finally come to disown their sins by disowning them. The only part of them which is revealed to the world, which sticks out from under the curtain, is the feet, the lowest part, the symbol of the absence of pride. When a Catholic goes to confession, instead of putting his best foot forward, he puts his worst foot forward. Every penitent, who has ever made a confession, as he enters the box has said, "I may fool others but what a fool I am to fool myself, and what a sinful fool I am to think I can fool God."[26]

Chapter Six

THE MYSTERY OF SUFFERING

In his final Good Friday Meditations in 1979 at Saint Agnes Church in New York City, Archbishop Sheen made reference to a thought first expressed by C.S. Lewis regarding pain and suffering. Lewis said that God whispers to us in our pleasures, speaks to us in our conscience, and shouts to us in our pain. "Pain," added Archbishop Sheen, "is God's megaphone; pain is heaven's loudspeaker." His preaching had a particular poignancy that Good Friday afternoon; he surely saw his own physical sufferings reflected in those of Christ. Two years earlier he had undergone open heart surgery in Lenox Hill Hospital, New York City, and his health, though stable, had progressively deteriorated from then on. By Good Friday, 1979, he was within six months of his own death.

More importantly, Archbishop Sheen was continuing a theme he had developed for the sixty years of his priesthood; the mystery and origin of suffering, what to do in light of it, and how to transform suffering into true spiritual liberation. In a radio address in 1932, a much younger Father Sheen said that suffering is of two kinds: pure and impure. Impure sufferings are those which come to us from without, those over which we have no control, such as plagues, famines, earthquakes, natural disasters, and the like. Pure sufferings, on the other hand, are of our own making, and almost always result from our violations of physical and moral laws. Those who eat or drink excessively, smoke, worry beyond measure, etc., run the risk of physical debilitation. Those who violate God's Commandments incur untold sufferings of their own making which may cause tremendous remorse.[1] From whatever source suffering enters a human life, it invites a person, in the words of Franz Werfel, "to heaven or to hell." Suffering makes us concentrate on ourselves; it creates a barrier between an individual and the rest of humanity. "Pain makes us so attentive to the ego as to kill our social instincts," Sheen told a television audience in the 1950's. But on the other hand, it can also "liberate a man from his selfishness and so transform his soul as to reveal the mystery of his being."[2] Such a transformation was clearly illustrated in a story Sheen often related of a Lutheran minister friend of his, who, along with his wife, had spent many years doing missionary work in Russia. After the Communist takeover, they were forced to flee from one village to another, being relentlessly pursued by government officials intent on wiping out religion. The minister's wife's entire family had been killed by Communist soldiers in a particular village they pillaged, though few details of the incident were readily available. Months later, the minister and his wife were living in a small Russian town when he heard a knock one evening on the front door of their home. The minister opened the door, only to be accosted by soldiers; his wife was upstairs and did not hear them enter. Eventually her husband called to her to come down; he informed her that the soldier with whom he was speaking was the one who had killed her entire family. She immediately went up to him, embraced and kissed him, and said, "As God forgives you, I forgive you." Could anything more compelling, one wonders, be found to provide the transforming power of suffering?

The mystery confronts every human being, and has to be dealt with. Sheen contended there were three ways of approaching it:

One is the Stoic solution which is to grit your teeth and bear it. The second is the Buddhist way, which holds that all pain and suffering come from desire. If we could extinguish all our desires, we would eventually reach a point of tranquility where we would be absorbed into the great Nirvana of unconsciousness. The third solution is the Hebraic-Christian philosophy of pain, which believes that pain and suffering can be transcended.[3]

It is that third approach that begins to answer the question why there is suffering at all. Bishop Sheen contended that a clue could be found in the Old Testament Book of Job. The principal character of the story, Job, was an extremely wealthy man, the father of ten children, seven sons and three daughters. He lived in an elaborately large home, owned many acres of land, and huge numbers of oxen, sheep, camels, etc., and each of his children had summer homes. Into what must be considered a well ordered, successfully established life, tragedy struck. One invading tribe stole his oxen, another, his sheep. Lightning struck the home of his eldest son and instantly killed him, and within a brief time, Job himself became covered with sores over his entire body. His faith is readily apparent in his acceptance of trial and his well-known praising of God who both gives and takes away. Job's wife was entirely different; she was not able to understand why God would have sent such adversity to such a good man and his family, and she all too readily cursed her Creator. She would not allow Job entry into his own house, either from fear of a possible contagiousness of his disease, or because of her hardness of heart. Then, some "comforters" assail Job, accuse him of displeasing God, and having to face the consequences by losing many of his possessions. This curious connection between economic prosperity and Godliness would have a modern counterpart in the American Puritan ethic that viewed great wealth as a sure sign of Divine favor, and the opposite, the Creator's displeasure.

Job was not conscious of any transgression, and began to ask himself many questions, none of which he was able to answer. "Suppose the Book of Job stopped there," said Sheen. "What a wonderful opportunity for a Broadway drama." Producers would have God enter the scene, ask Job for his questions, and answer each in turn. "And yet the Divine Dramatist does not operate that way." In fact, God opened a dialogue with Job, out of which emerged Job's appreciation, born of faith, for the Divine presence in his life. "The intelligence of Job was nothing compared with the mind of God," Bishop Sheen reminded his audience. "The mouse in the piano could never understand why anyone should sit down and play the keys of a piano. As the brain of a mouse is below that of a man, so is the brain of man below the mind of God."[4]

In the end, Job regained his possessions sevenfold, because God "never closes a door that He does not open a window." As with all accounts, that of Job only partially penetrates the mystery. It may also elicit such questions as why is there such a thing as sacrifice in the world, and that question is answered only in the life of the Incarnate Son of God. Had the Heavenly Father not sent Him into the world to offer the supreme act of sacrifice, it would never have been possible for men and women through the ages to do what they have done, to transcend themselves, to discover that all happiness is otherness, and to give the mystery of suffering its real definition.

> If, therefore, He who suffered on Calvary, He who was now preaching from the pulpit of the Cross, were not God, but a mere creature or a mere man, then there must be creatures in this world better and nobler than God. Shall man who toils for his fellow man, suffers for him, and if need be dies for him, be capable of doing that which God cannot do? Should this noblest form of love, which is sacrifice, be possible to sinful man, and

yet impossible to a perfectly good God? Shall we say that the martyr sprinkling the sand of the Coliseum with his blood, the soldier dying for his country, the missionary spending himself and being spent for the good of heathens; aye, and more, shall we say that those women, martyrs by pain, who in little hovels and little cottages have sacrificed all the joys of life for the sake of simple duties, and little charities unnoticed and unknown by all save God – shall we say that all those, who from the beginning of the world have shown forth the beauty of sacrifice, have no divine prototype in heaven?[5]

Hence if we are ever able to appreciate the mystery of suffering in its fullness, we must consider Him who suffered; only in light of Christ's sufferings do those of humanity make sense, and only united to Christ's sufferings are those of humanity elevated beyond measure. Some decades ago, Archbishop Sheen was giving a lecture in Florida. He was speaking from a stage, and after the conclusion of the talk, he came down to greet several people in wheelchairs present to hear him. As he was speaking to them, he noticed something in the distance similar to a Grecian statue. Coming closer, he discovered it was a woman in an iron lung. Only her head could be seen, and a small motor was supplying the air needed for her iron lung. She informed the Archbishop she was a convert of his, but he said he had never seen her. She told him her conversion had come from reading his books and listening to his radio and television broadcasts. In answer to his query how long she had been in the lung, she told him twenty-one years; she had been married only one year when she contracted polio. After her husband's initial shock, he decided to leave her, but before he did, he pulled the plug on the machine supplying air to the lung. A family employee saw it, and put the plug back. She told Sheen she was able to move her head, but no other part of her body.

He asked her if she understood suffering; she said not well, and he promised he would write her every day for six months to try to unravel its meaning. She insisted he tell her something then. "Sometimes lovers squeeze too tight," he replied, "and the Lord loved you so much, He squeezed you too tight."[6] He asked her if she ever thought of what her life might have been had her wings not been clipped. Perhaps it was yet a further suffering for her to endure such thoughts for any length of time. In any event, she was continuing the Passion of Christ, and that was the only thing that gave her suffering meaning.

Archbishop Sheen was also fond of relating a story he had once read of three persons killed in the concentration camp at Dachau, two older men and a young boy. Nooses were placed around their necks, and when the chairs were pulled out from under them, the two men died instantly, but the boy lingered for a much longer time. As he swung loosely, an onlooker shouted, "Where is God now?" to which the answer quickly came, "There He is! Hanging on the gallows!"[7]

> Don't you think… that Christ was somehow hidden in the six million victims at Auschwitz and Dachau, all those Jews who went to an incinerated death? Though they did not know it and were loyal to the Law of Moses even as they understood it, they were in some way continuing unwittingly the Passion of Christ and being saved by it.[8]

Such examples compel every believer who wishes to make sense of suffering to meditate on the Divine Sufferer, for in His sufferings we see all of ours. The sufferings of Christ had been predicted in various ways through the Old Testament, and most compellingly by Our Lord Himself during the three years of His public life. Bishop Sheen often emphasized Our Lord was the only one who came into this world to die, and His death was often the subject of His own prediction. Not only that, He made clear He would be hated, really another prediction of the same Passion. Just as one does not find the intensity of love for another as for Christ, so one does not find the intensity of hatred directed against any other person of note on the world scene.

> There are two great passions which entwine themselves around the life of Our Lord, as they do about no other person who ever lived: the passion of love and the passion of hate. He said He would be loved; He said He would be hated. He said He would be adored; He said He would be scorned. He said He would be loved unto folly; He said He would be hated unto fury and that the duel would go on until the end of time. Hate would lift Him up on a cross, but once on it He would lift up all lovers unto His Heart which is love. "If I be lifted up, I shall draw all things unto Myself."[9]

It was a very unusual sort of prophecy for Our Lord to make, that He would be so hated, and makes one easily ask the question what He had done to be so rejected. After all, the Gospel He preached was one of love; His life was offered for the world's redemption; His final act on the Cross was one of pardon and forgiveness for all who had done such to Him; His public life was filled with working miracles, extending Divine Mercy to sinners, and preaching a message which challenged while it consoled. Bishop Sheen rightly observed that there was nothing to hate in such a life, and one must look outside it to find the reason. The Roman Emperor Nero was hated while he lived, for all he had done to prevent the advance of social justice; after his death, few beyond his contemporaries remembered. The same could be said of historical personalities like Tiberius, Domitian, Ivan the Terrible or Nestorius, all of whom provoked intensely passionate reactions from so many, but all of whom "ceased to be objects of hatred, because they have ceased to be obstacles." Such is not the case with Christ; He continues to be an obstacle "to sin, to selfishness, to godlessness, and to the spirit of the world." The reason such hatred continues is because of the one distinguishing characteristic separating Our Lord from all others – His Divinity. "Only the perversion of the sovereign love of God could ever explain such hate," Bishop Sheen wrote. "Only that which continues that divine Life could ever be the object of such hate."[10] In other words, not only is Christ hated through time, but the hatred is extended to His Church, His prolongation in time and space. Just as suffering and hatred was directed to His physical body during the course of His life, so His Mystical Body must expect nothing less.

Bishop Sheen beautifully depicted Our Lord's sufferings in his *Life of Christ*, particularly concentrating on the Piercing of the Side. Such had been prophesied in the Old Testament, and Saint John recorded that when the soldier whom tradition knows as Longinus cast his spear into the side of Christ, blood and water flowed out. Water was present at the beginning of the Public Life when He was baptized by John the Baptist, and the Heavenly Father declared Him to be His Son. Blood was present at the close of His life when He made His supreme oblational offering.

> Though He was spared the brutality that was arbitrary, such as the breaking of His legs, nevertheless, there was some mysterious Divine purpose in the opening of the Sacred Heart of God. John, who leaned on His breast the night of the Last Supper, fittingly recorded the opening of the Heart. At the deluge Noah made a door in the side of the ark, by which the animals entered, that they might escape the flood; now a new door is opened into the heart of God into which men might escape the flood of sin. When Adam slept, Eve was taken from his side and was called the mother of all living. Now the second Adam inclined His head and slept on the

Cross, and under the figure of Blood and water there came from His side His bride, the Church.[11]

Straightaway, Bishop Sheen wrote that "all must look whether they like it or not." The reason was simple: Christ "stands emblazoned at the crossroads of the world." He often noted that the attitudes of sympathy, antipathy and empathy, all found at the Cross on Good Friday, continue in modern man. Once lifted up, Our Lord was jeered and taunted, and these reactions seem to have received more attention than those of Magdalene, or John, or His Mother. His detractors shouted that He easily saved others, but could not save Himself. "Of course not!", reacted Sheen. "This is not weakness, but obedience to the law of sacrifice." Such obedience is always the key to understanding the Crucifixion, and most especially, the mystery of suffering. "What heart can conceive the misery of humankind," the Bishop wrote, "if the Son of God had saved Himself from suffering, and left a fallen world to the wrath of God?"[12]

There was one heart that could have conceived such misery because it was so completely united with the Heart of Christ, His own Mother's. If one is really to comprehend the mystery of suffering, it will be found in the life of Our Lady, in which we have a mutual begetting on the part of Mother and Son. The connection between Bethlehem and Calvary is that Mary gave Christ sonship, and Christ, in turn, gave Mary motherhood. When He gave His Mother to John, who stood in for all believers on that Good Friday, Our Lord addressed His Mother as "Woman." That signified a second Annunciation, while John was the second Nativity. Tradition has always held that Mary was "pierced" seven times with swords of sorrow, or dolors. Bishop Sheen took a different approach, saying there were not seven swords, but seven thrusts of one sword, and the sword that pierced her heart was Christ Himself. He pictured the sword having a double edge; one edge ran into His own Sacred Heart, and the opposite edge into her Immaculate Heart. The sword ran into Our Lord in the sense that He willed all His sufferings from Bethlehem to Calvary. He was the cause of His own death in two ways: directly, because He was such an opposition to the world, His presence could no longer be tolerated; indirectly, because He could have prevented His death in countless ways, had He chosen. Sheen then applied the teaching of Pope Leo XIII that the Heavenly Father had willed that the grace His Son won for the world through His Passion and Death be mediated in no other way than through Mary. If that is so, the Blessed Mother had to "will cooperation in Redemption, as Christ willed it as the Redeemer."[13] In other words, if He willed His death, He also willed her dolors. If He was the "Man of Sorrows," He willed that she be a "Mother of Sorrows." The Bishop reflected that this could hardly have been the case had they not been Mother and Son, two in one flesh, in a spiritual sense.

> This was the first reason why God permitted her Dolors, viz., that she might be the first after the Redeemer Himself to continue His Passion and Death in His Mystical Body.... But she also had to suffer for our sakes as well as His. As Our Lord learned obedience by what He suffered, so Mary had to learn motherhood, not by appointment, but by experience with the burdens of the human heart. The rich cannot console the poor unless they become less rich for the sake of the poor; Mary cannot wipe away human tears unless she herself has been their fountain. The title "Mother of the Afflicted" had to be earned in the school of affliction. She does not expiate for sins; she does not redeem; she is not a savior, but by His will and by her own, she is so much bound up with Him that His Passion would have been entirely different had there not been her Compassion.[14]

The believer can more fully grasp the mystery of suffering by considering the seven individual thrusts of the sword into the heart of Mary. Sheen beautifully developed these in a work entitled *The World's First Love*, published in 1952. The initial thrust was the prophecy of Simeon, when the old man predicted the Sword of Sorrow would pierce her heart. He never predicted a physical attack on her person; that was to befall her Son on the Cross. Rather, hers found a parallel in the Annunciation where she experienced an ecstasy, first in her soul, then in her body. Now, in her compassion, she would experience the "pains of martyrdom" first in her soul, and then in her "sympathetic flesh." Simeon's prophecy was followed by the "summoning of His Mother to share sorrow with all the exiled and displaced persons of the world of whom He Himself was the first born."[15] Herod had ordered the killing of all male children under two years of age, fearful that if the King were indeed in his midst, he would ultimately have to relinquish the earthly authority he possessed. Sheen wrote that "two swords were swinging," that of Herod, and that of the Messiah Himself "Who would have His own Mother see the exodus reversed, as He now goes back to the land from whence He once led His own people out."[16] The Flight into Egypt has many modern counterparts in the lives of people who try to flee the mystery of suffering.

> Now that Mary is crowned in Heaven, as she looks down on the earth, she sees millions of men still banishing the Creator out of their lands, and driving Him out of their hearts. Many men do not spend most of their time making a living; they spend most of it flying from God! He, on His side, will not destroy their freedom, and they on their side, will not choose Him. But as Mary ... was not angry with the wicked, but unhappy for their sakes, so now in Heaven her compassion and love of sinners almost seems to rise with the measure of their sin.[17]

If Mary had her "Dark Night of the Body" in Egypt, she would have her "Dark Night of the Soul" in Jerusalem with the loss of the Divine Child. Until she and Joseph found Christ in the Temple instructing the Doctors of the Law, she suffered not a lack of knowledge as much as a deprivation – something was hidden from her that caused her a spiritual trial. Bishop Sheen compares her loss with Calvary; on the Cross the Lord would take to Himself all the great cries of isolation in His anguished prayer, "My God, My God, why hast Thou forsaken Me?" He was denying His human nature all the joys of His Divinity; prior to that, He had mysteriously denied His Mother all the joys of His Father's household. "Darkness in the saints is not the same as darkness in the sinners," Sheen wrote. "In the former, there is no light, but love; in the latter there is night without love."[18]

Mary's fourth privation was the meeting with her Son on the Via Dolorosa, so beautifully depicted in the fourth of the Stations of the Cross. She now sees fully that the sign of contradiction predicted by Simeon is fulfilled. Words are not capable of describing the emotions of the Mother and Son, though Sheen interestingly drew a contemporary parallel:

> The just Abels slain by the Soviet Cains of Eastern Europe, the Chinese faithful living in mortal dread of execution, the countless multitudes panic-stricken by the injustices of Communists, all these could have raised their eyes to Heaven as so much brass, did not one Man and one Woman feel the bitterness of that terror.[19]

The meeting was followed by the event of the Crucifixion itself, at which no one "looked more closely than the Blessed Mother." Here is the exact moment when Christ thrusts one edge of the sword into Himself, fulfilling His words that no one would take His life from Him, He would lay it down of Himself. "He was upright as a priest," Bishop Sheen noted, "prostrate as a victim." The other side of the sword pierced Mary's heart, since "she had been preparing the priest to be a victim." Curious it was that Our Lord spoke seven times from the Cross, and His Mother is recorded as speaking seven times in Scripture. "As He spoke each word, her heart goes back to each of the words she herself had spoken, making the sorrow more intense as she saw the mystery of the 'sign being contradicted'."[20]

While His death was not the final dolor, it was the culminating one. Even after the fact, Bishop Sheen felt Our Lord continued the thrusts of the sword, making the centurion Longinus the "instrument for opening the treasures of His Sacred Heart." Calvary's deepest significance, seen literally for Christ, and metaphorically for His Mother, was the "piercing of the two hearts with one sword." It is what has always united Christians in adoration of His Heart and veneration of hers. His descent from the Cross, and His Mother's return from Calvary have both been superbly depicted by artists through the centuries. Their masterpieces prove the truth that

> All the fatherless, motherless, sonless, husbandless and wifeless griefs that ever tore at the hearts of human beings, were now bearing down on the soul of Mary. The most any human being ever lost in a bereavement was a creature, but Mary was burying the Son of God. It is hard to lose a son or a daughter, but it is harder to bury Christ. To be motherless is a tragedy, but to be Christless is hell. In real love, two hearts do not meet in sweet slavery to one another; rather there is the melting of two hearts into one. When death comes there is not just a separation of two hearts, but rather the rending of the one heart. This was particularly true of Jesus and Mary.[21]

It is to be remembered that Our Lady lived in a culture where death by crucifixion was common. It was a horrible form of torture, but common nonetheless. She must have witnessed others, at least from the distance, and heard details discussed. One could not envision a form of pain to exceed it, and, in the 21st century, though cultures have drastically changed, the Cross still relates to pain. The vertical bar of life is crossed with the horizontal bar of death. The vertical bar is erect, as all life is upright and erect, and as Saint John tells us Our Lady stood upright at the foot of her Son's Cross. The horizontal bar, on the other hand, represents the prostrate nature of death. The crossing of one bar with another, much like the crossing of joy with sorrow, is a contradiction, if not an absurdity. The pain and suffering associated with the Cross may be of our own making, or fashioned for us according to a Divine plan. In either case, such trials endured in isolation are meaningless and devoid of any real value. What Our Blessed Mother was the first to realize, and what every follower of Christ must realize with her help, is that Mary's Son transformed the meaning of the Cross into something entirely different when He mounted it.

> The difference between the cross and the Crucifix is Christ. Once Our Lord, who is love itself, mounts the cross, He reveals how pain can be transformed through love into a joyful sacrifice, how those who sow in tears may reap in joy, how those who mourn may be comforted, how those who suffer with Him may reign with Him, and how those who take up a cross for a brief Good Friday will possess happiness for an eternal Easter Sunday. Love is, as it were, the point where the horizontal bar of death and the vertical bar of life become reconciled in the doctrine that all life is through death.[22]

It will be interesting some day to discover, once in heaven, how strongly the mediatorial role of Our Lady influenced the two thieves on the right and left of her Son. Bishop Sheen often alluded to them as proof that, at least in one instance, pain can be a true liberator and turn a curse into a blessing. At the outset, the two thieves appear to have been much alike, sentenced for the same crime. Why the heart of one was touched so profoundly we do not know, but he saw the error of his ways, asked for pardon, and was assured by Our Lord he would accompany Him into the Kingdom. Dismas' counterpart experienced no such transformation as far as we know, and may well be an example of those whose pain "unsanctified, can sear, spoil and scorch the soul."[23] The one thief united his sufferings with those of the Lord; the other, it would appear, missed the opportunity. It is in that uniting of one heart with another, the lesson Mary teaches believers so well, that pain is never wasted, and that all suffering has meaning. What we are doing, Bishop Sheen preached and wrote so often, is continuing Calvary.

No more than the Incarnation, Calvary is not an event that occurred at a given moment in history and is completed. It is an ongoing reality, and any image of Our Lord on the Cross makes the event present to us, and vividly reminds us of our redemption. "We can keep a statue of Buddha in a room, tickle his tummy for good luck, but it is never mortifying," the Bishop wrote. "The crucifix somehow or other makes us feel involved."[24]

> Words are so fixed in their meaning that when we hear "crucified," our minds go back to a hill outside Jerusalem, which like the Battle of Waterloo, is gone forever. A doctrine that is only a doctrine has a poor chance indeed to create a glowing enthusiasm or a faith that can move mountains. While theologians and scripture scholars "locate" the Passion in time and space, the mystics and the victims delocalize and universalize it.[25]

Completing the Passion, or giving suffering its true significance, found its best expression in Saint Paul's Letter to the Colossians (1:24), when he wrote of completing in his own flesh the "full tale" of Christ's sufferings for the sake of His Body, the Church. Bishop Sheen saw two ideas hidden in Paul's words; a Christian's sufferings share in those of the Lord, because the two are somehow one; also, there is a specific quota of suffering assigned to the Church. The quota of Christ's personal sufferings have been fulfilled, but those of the Church have not. "What the Church endures until the end of time, and what Israel suffered before Christ in anticipation both enter into Him."[26]

The Passion of Christ continues each time a person consciously unites his or her sufferings to the Cross. Our Lord's death is the condition of our salvation, and whenever trials and difficulties are united to Him, there need be no worry about being on the right course.

> If the Father did not spare His Son, and the Son did not spare His mother, then even the unexplained things of life fit into the Divine Plan. Relief does not always come in harmonious acceptance of Calvary, but peace does. He who does not welcome the Cross does not welcome Christ. God's method in nature is evolution; God's method in man is Calvary.[27]

Bishop Sheen once asked a Christian who spent fourteen years of torture in a Communist prison camp the most impressive thing he had ever seen. He replied it was the way so many souls united their sufferings with those of the Crucified, and received great solace in the midst of overwhelming odds. One cannot escape the thought that the man who told the story was one of those who practiced such transference to the fullest.

Countless souls have united their lives to Christ in this fashion, and the reasons for their doing so are as varied as the individuals themselves. Through his long literary career, Fulton Sheen recounted many such stories, some he knew personally, others through the tale-telling of history. A case in point is that of

Sophie-Charlotte Wittelsbach (1847-1897). At the age of nineteen, she became engaged to the King of Bavaria, a young man already in the early stages of insanity. After a brief courtship, he broke off the engagement, telling her the only love of his life was Wagnerian music. Her mental anguish was somewhat alleviated when she met and married an exiled French Orlean, Ferdinand Phillipe, Duke of Alençon. For him, Sophie was his first and last love; he was a deeply committed Catholic, and told his wife he loved her with a Christian love, the deepest kind of all. It obviously made little impression on the young woman at this point; she had never been religious, and spirituality had little significance for her. Not long after they were married, a deep melancholia began to afflict her. It was an inherited family trait, and manifested itself in fits of "undue sensitiveness, impulsiveness, capriciousness, and morbidity." She became more and more distant to her husband, very hard to reach. He tried to introduce her to the faith, but with little success. A trip to Rome was advised, and when the couple reached the Eternal City, it was providential they happened to visit a certain ruin, very likely one of the Catacombs, where they read an inscription on an ancient tombstone, "Sophronia, may you live." Sophie's husband made that inscription his prayer for his wife, that she be freed from the shackles of mental illness. After he had recited it countless times, he began praying, "Sophie, you shall live!"

Many years followed that visit, and when Sophie had reached the age of thirty-six, she emerged from her final crisis, a renewed and revivified woman, full of energy, enthusiasm, and great strength of character. She, along with her husband, began to devote themselves to charitable causes in the city of Paris; she became a Third Order Dominican, he a Third Order Franciscan. By the age of fifty, she was well known in Parisian Catholic circles, and was asked to head up a mammoth bazaar to aid Catholic Charities. It was held in a large tent, where the primary attraction was a newly invented motion picture machine – quite the rarity in 1897. In the midst of this highly successful bazaar, the machine caught fire. There was a scramble on the part of hundreds of persons to exit by the side doors of the tent. Because Sophie was general chair, many sought to help her out, but she refused, insisting that others be helped first. Her husband, trying to stay as close to her as possible, was crushed in the onslaught, and forced to exit; once outside, he lost consciousness from severe smoke inhalation. Sophie was consoling a young girl, trying to shield her from the sight of so many dying. A Dominican nun standing nearby quietly exclaimed to Sophie what a terrible death they were about to experience. "Yes," Sophie agreed, "but think of it; we shall see God in a few minutes." A few days later, her husband regained consciousness in a hospital and was informed of his wife's death. His thoughts quickly turned back to Rome, to the inscription on the tombstone he had read years earlier, to the prayer he had made his own, and now, in great faith, he prayed not "Sophie, may you live," but simply, "Sophie, you live!"[28]

Another example of one who transformed suffering was Alexandrine d'Alopeus of Saint Petersburg. Raised with no particular faith, she was attracted to the beauty of religious art, especially as found in Rome. On one trip there, she met and ultimately married Albert de la Ferronnays, a young French diplomat, devoutly Catholic, and somewhat instrumental in the famous conversion story of Alphonse Ratisbone, of the internationally famous Jewish banking family. Albert and Alexandrine were married in 1834 and enjoyed an extraordinarily happy married life. Deeply in love as they were, her husband's religious faith had not made a particularly significant impression on his young wife, until she once asked him if the love they shared was not in some measure, a glimpse of the way humans would be allowed to love God in heaven for all eternity.

Her husband eventually fell ill with consumption, but each night, likely at his request, they read together certain excerpts from Thomas à Kempis' *Imitation of Christ*. Even with this, Alexandrine did not receive the gift of faith, and her husband's greatest disappointment was that she was not able to kneel next to him at the altar rail and receive Holy Communion. He began to unite his ever growing sufferings with those of Christ for the intention of his wife's conversion. Not only did this become a reality in 1836, but, following her husband's death, Alexandrine, greatly influenced by a biography of Saint Elizabeth of Hungary, gave herself to incessant works of charity. When many began to warn that she was imposing too many sacrifices on herself, she replied in the same words that Ratisbone had used years earlier, "One cannot give to God less than everything."[29]

Finally, the story of the great French Catholic writer and apologist, Leon Bloy, an inheritor of a Catholic tradition, but one who had never practiced the faith. By 1869, Bloy admitted he had reached the height of an evil life. He, along with his four brothers fought in the Franco-Prussian War, and his mother once wrote to him, fully aware of the foulness of his life, and told him that news of his death would bring her greater consolation than the life he was now leading. Her letter seemed to make him more indifferent, and sensing his attitude, she redoubled her prayers. Bloy recounted his mother's spiritual path:

> One day my mother, while meditating on the sorrowful passion of the Divine Savior, came to see that Our Lord redeemed men by suffering without measure and without consolation, and that we who are His own members can prolong this marvelous redemption through our imperfect sufferings. What Jesus has done absolutely by His perfect oblation of life, Christian hearts could do relatively through their sufferings. She then offered herself to suffer for her children, and to bear their penances. In a counsel of mysterious and ineffable sublimity, she made a pact with God that she would make

the absolute sacrifice of her health, and the complete surrender of all human joy and consolation, if He, in return, would grant the entire and perfect conversion of her children.... She lost suddenly and irreparably her excellent health in a manner as complete as was possible without actually depriving her of life. Her life became a torment twenty-four hours a day, and, in order that this torment be actually complete, her infirmity assumed a character of physical humiliation and abasement that demanded exacting heroism.[30]

Only later in life, firmly entrenched in the Church, and actively defending her, did Bloy come to realize the full import of his mother's sufferings, and their redemptive value in his life.

Although Fulton Sheen was fond of relating such pertinent details, he experienced much the same in his own career in the Church. One could not rise to the heights he did in the sixty years of his priesthood without bearing the Cross in unique ways. In his autobiography, he speaks of the many crosses endured by the Church from the outside, as well as those to be borne interiorly by the members of Christ's Body. Sheen's biographers have presented details that could well be construed as particulars for what he would only speak of in a general way. He felt that "silence about tensions behooves us," and this for several reasons.

Silence is recommended because any discussion of conflicts within the Church diminishes the content of the Christ-love within the Mystical Body – as the hand excessively rubbing the eye diminishes vision. Impatience and blame is a blight to humanity; rebellion against having one's own will crossed is a plague to obedience. If we are right in a conflict the Lord bids us absorb any wrongs like a sponge; if we are wrong, we are to see others as the instrument of working His

Will.… Silence is also imperative in order to avoid the danger of self-justification.… Finally, silence is recommended because if I judge not, I will not be judged. As we hope the Good Lord will throw our sins in the wastebasket, may He not justly expect that we throw our self-righteousness into it also.[31]

One of the finest solutions Fulton Sheen discovered in the relating of human crosses to Calvary came from the writings of Saint Thérèse of Lisieux, whom he considered "far closer to the truth than many of our theologians." Since Christ continues to suffer in His Church, He is much in need of our consolation. A point few but saints think of, but one that is open to anyone. Thérèse wrote often on it, and one of the passages Bishop Sheen was fond of quoting was the young Saint explaining that

> Since our Well-Beloved has trodden the wine press alone, the wine which He gives us to drink in our turn, let us not refuse to wear garments dyed with blood. Let us press out for Jesus a new wine which may slake His thirst [as if our Lord were still thirsty]. And looking around Him, He will no longer be able to say "He is alone." Neglect, forgetfulness, this I believe is what pains Him the most.…[32]

One can almost envision Archbishop Sheen, during the many, many hours he spent in the presence of Our Lord in the Blessed Sacrament, making this practice his own. He learned early on what any of us may learn at any time, that the mystery of suffering may be penetrated, and give us the profoundest joy we have ever experienced.

Chapter Seven

PRAYER

A religious pilgrimage to Catholic Paris, even in the twenty-first century, should include a visit to the Church of Saint Roch. Not only is it interesting from an artistic and historical point of view, but it is one of the few locales where English-speaking Catholics can hear Sunday Mass, in one of its side chapels. Unfortunately, today's pilgrim gets the feeling it is more of a museum than a vibrant house of prayer; decades ago, this was anything but the case. In the 1920's a young Father Fulton J. Sheen arrived in the city, with a two hour wait before his ongoing train to Lourdes. He went to Saint Roch to engage in a daily spiritual practice he had begun several years earlier as a seminarian in the major seminary in Saint Paul, Minnesota; one continuous hour of prayer in the presence of Our Lord in the Blessed Sacrament. In a humorous vein, Sheen often recounted his entering the church and attempting the Holy Hour. There were not three days in the course of a year when he was able to fall asleep in the middle of the afternoon, but this happened to be one. No sooner had he gotten into the pew than he fell fast asleep. He slept for one full hour, and, upon awakening he asked the Lord if he had made his Holy Hour. The Lord replied he had – in fact that was how the Apostles had made their first one! Then a word of caution from above: do not let it happen again!

This story always provoked laughter from his audience, but it was told to underscore the vital part daily prayer must play in our lives. Only in dialogue with God will a human being ever achieve holiness and true self knowledge. This topic of prayer was a central theme of Bishop Sheen's writing, and he approached it, as he did so many topics, from the philosophical view of man's quest for God.

The quest is a simple one: a person need only look into his or her heart to begin, since there is something God-like mirrored there.

> ...whatever is best in the treasured lives of heroic men and the serene unwritten lives of innocent women; whatever is best in the loyalty of human hearts and the unwearying sweetness of a mother's love; whatever is noble in the sacrificing care of a father and the devotion of an unselfish friend, is but the dim reflection, the far-off echo, the faint shadow of that which in God is perfect. We are enjoying but a two billionth part of the light and heat which streams from the sun, and it may equally be that we are receiving even a smaller fraction of the Love and Life and Truth which is in God.[1]

Sheen asked rhetorically, if one's mother appeared to be the most loving person, and one's father, the most kind, what must be the love and kindness of God who created human mothers and fathers? In the same vein, if one's own heart reveled in the size of the planets, and the nature of the spheres, how much more must that human heart be lost in wonder and awe of Him from Whose Hands planets and spheres came to be?

From this, we can gather that God is not hard to find. Thomist that he was, Sheen pointed to Aquinas' teaching that once we have looked upon the order of the universe, our reason immediately concludes some higher power behind it. "As the mind concludes to a watchmaker on seeing a watch," the Bishop wrote, "so, too, it concludes to a Divine Mind on seeing the order of the cosmos."[2] Saint Teresa of Avila, upon hearing that God was present only in His grace, became very disturbed, until a very learned man set her mind at ease with the thought that God was present in His world, and in everyone in it, and that He communed with one and all. It is not only given to Saints to come to this realization, anyone may arrive at it. Sheen was especially fond of quoting the English mystic poet Francis Thompson

> O world invisible, we view thee,
> O world intangible, we touch thee,
> O world unknowable, we know thee,
> Inapprehensible, we clutch thee![3]

Every striving and action of our will is a movement toward God. This is what distinguishes man from the animals; an animal is able to have its desires fulfilled, since it is only interested in the fulfillment of the moment's immediate need. Man, on the other hand, has a never ending desire for something greater, and for someone who will be absolute fulfillment for him. Man enjoys his natural life, which is a gift, and is capable of enjoying, even in this world, the gift of supernatural life. Christianity's entire meaning is to be found in the Incarnation, and every Christian can identify with the Samaritan woman at the well (Jn 4:10) who was asked by Our Lord for a drink. Had she known who was asking, and the gift of God present in His very person, she would have asked Him, and He would have given her living water.

Why, then, do so few people really find God in the course of their earthly pilgrimage? "Most souls are like people living in a dark room during the daytime and complaining that the light is too hard to find," Sheen wrote, "when all they need do to discover it is to raise the blinds."[4] Human pride is to blame in many instances, people too proud to let God enter, thinking they are perfectly capable of working things out themselves. Scripture teaches very clearly that some people prefer darkness to light, and will keep the Lord at arm's length, continually refusing His love. It is not that people do not want to be saved; they do, but not from their sins, not at too great a cost, and in their own particular way. The fact of many not wanting salvation from sin, said Sheen, accounted for the popularity of social Christianity. Many are quite content to focus on the need of churches to concern themselves with problems like slum clearance and "international amity," while not interfering in individual's private lives. Others want an easy salvation – one which will not exact too many demands. They have no fears of God not loving them enough; they do fear His loving them too much. Many have reached a certain knowledge of God, be it academic or practical, but remain outside His "sheepfold," fearing the consequences of entering. In an age of great conversions to the Catholic faith, Sheen surely encountered many whose interest in the Church he personally flamed, but who stopped short, lest too much be asked of them. "As the musician loves the violin and tightens the strings with sacrificial strain that they may give forth a better tone, so God submits us to sacrifice to make us saints."[5] Finally, there were those who wanted salvation in their own way, those who wanted to "remake society without remaking themselves." In a spiritual sense, they are the type who would favor a Christ without a cross, a Savior without a crown of thorns.

There are, however, souls who readily submit to God and allow themselves to be transformed. By submitting to the will of God in all things, they reach a degree of peace and inner tranquility unknown to others. It is not that humanity ceases to have meaning for them, or that the created world is loved any less; now the world is loved in God. These are people who have made a drastic change, taken a significant leap of faith, and made themselves malleable in God's Hands. They immediately begin to have more effect as Christians (and Catholics), because they have put themselves aside, and allowed the Lord to use them as He will. These people found their likeness in the man who had lain at the Pool of Bethesda for thirty-eight years, complaining that every time the waters of the pool were stirred up, there was no one to help him in. When Our Lord met him, He told him to do what he thought impossible – take up his bed. It was his will that had been lacking those many years; he really needed healing, but did not want it badly enough. Many souls in the world are like him, not willing to do what has to be done to be better, while those who have changed have so often done so because of their cooperation with God's grace. The choice is completely up to us.

> Ever since the days of Adam humanity has been hiding from God and saying, "God is hard to find." The truth is, in each heart there is a secret garden that God made uniquely for Himself. The garden is locked like a safety deposit vault. It has two keys. God has one key; hence the soul cannot let in anyone else but God. The human heart has the other key; hence not even God can get in without man's consent. When the two keys of God's Love and human liberty, of divine vocation and human response, meet, then Paradise returns to a human heart. God is always at that garden gate with His key. We pretend to look for our key, to have mislaid it, to have given up the search; but all the while it is in our hand, if we would only see it. The reason we are not as happy as saints is because we do not wish to be saints.[6]

Those who have become saints have done so because they genuinely desired it. This desire is brought about only in silence, only by shutting out the noise of the world. A constant striving for amusement, excitement, thrill, and the like, is an indicator a person is uncomfortable with self. Placing oneself within the noisy atmosphere of the world generally can be taken as a running away from reality. Many souls "do not like to be with themselves because their conscience reproves and carries on an unbearable repartee," Sheen wrote. "They do not like to be quiet because the footsteps of the Hound of Heaven, which can be heard in silence, cannot be heard in the din of excitement."[7] God's voice in the soul was much like a whisper; if you continually live on the city streets with their unending distractions, you will drown out that voice. If, on the other hand, you enter into yourself, God's speaking to you will be unmistakable. An example of this is found in the life of a remarkable Frenchman who experienced a conversion on Christmas Eve, 1886, and never returned to his former way of life.

> Charles de Foucauld, a soldier of France and a man of dissipation, was brought to the very threshold of sanctity by the silence of the Eastern skies, where stars seem so close that one could almost reach up and pluck them out of the heavens. Foucauld died as a priest, perhaps massacred for his faith by the Mohammedans, and yet he came to Christ through the repose and quiet forced upon him by his life in the French Legion.[8]

This silence Bishop Sheen felt so necessary to the human psyche, he also described as quiet time. It takes at least one quarter hour of everyone's day to block out the world's distractions, to get mentally focused, to enter into oneself. One's quiet time should therefore be a minimum of thirty minutes, and perhaps a full hour, circumstances permitting. During that period, a person "begins with a confrontation of self, denudes his pretenses, throws off the mask he wears before others, and looks his faults in the face."[9] Psychology emphasized much the same for generations, but for very different reasons. What interested Sheen was the individual's encounter with Divinity.

There is an old story of a Saracen woman who came to England seeking her lover. She passed through the foreign cities with no word upon her tongue that would be understood by those who heard her except the name of him whom she was seeking. Many today are wandering through the earth as strangers in the midst of it. They cannot translate the cry of their own hearts, but it really means "My soul thirsteth for Thee." There is only One who can respond to these deepest aspirations of the heart.[10]

This "quiet time" is absolutely essential to the development of the human personality. Sheen used the practical examples of the weary traveler who seeks a haven for rest at the end of an exhausting day, or the sailor who has been long at sea, desiring to find shelter. In like manner, our souls are searching for rest, more rest perhaps than the body may need. Interestingly, he makes the point that the restlessness of many souls may account for the numerous physical ills that often beset human beings. It is in this silence, this quiet time, this searching, this restlessness needing to be satisfied, that human beings begin to lift their hearts and minds to God. And this we call prayer.

Bishop Sheen went far beyond the definition of the *Baltimore Catechism*, preferring to describe prayer as a dialogue. "Man breaks silence in two ways," he noted: "a dialogue with his fellow man, and a dialogue with God. My dialogue with others is proof we are both persons. The same is implied in a dialogue with God."[11] One must start with the life of Christ for any true understanding of prayer. Our Lord always prayed before the major events of His life: in the course of His teaching, at the time of His miracles, and on the Cross. Also, He prayed for others: the eleven, the entire Church, His persecutors and, in a particular way, for Peter. Perhaps the most poignant scene of Our Lord in prayer came during His Agony in the Garden, an event that Bishop Sheen often said was more intense than His final hours on the Cross.

> His two natures, the Divine and the human, were both involved in this prayer. He and the Father were One; it was not "Our Father," but "My Father." Unbroken was the consciousness of His Father's love. But on the other hand, His human nature recoiled from death as a penalty for sin. The natural shrinking of the human soul from the punishment which sin deserves was overborne by Divine submission to the Father's will. The "No" to the cup of the Passion was human; the "Yes" to the Divine will was the overcoming of human reluctance to suffering for the sake of Redemption. To take the bitter cup of human suffering which atones for sin and to sweeten it with little drops of "God wills it" is the sign of One Who suffered in man's name, and yet One Whose suffering had infinite value because He was God as well as Man. This scene is shrouded with the halo of mystery which no human mind can adequately penetrate. One can dimly guess the psychological horror of the progressive stages of fear, anxiety and sorrow which prostrated Him before even a single blow had been struck.[12]

Christ always remains our example of and pattern for prayer. In our humanness, we sometimes do not want to enter into such dialogue. Scripture is filled with such stories, such as Adam being fearful when God called him in the Garden, Cain experiencing fear when God questioned him, and Moses being very much afraid before the burning bush. Each of them had a sense of their own inadequacy, and they were very reluctant to speak with God about anything. We are not unlike them. The voice of God in dialogue makes us conscious of our sinfulness, our need to seek His ever loving mercy and forgiveness; it is a constant life-giving invitation. One of the most beautiful examples of this, said Sheen, was the encounter Saint Paul had with the Risen Lord on the road to Damascus. Everything the Apostle would later write to the early Christian communities, all the content of his preaching, was derived from that initial transforming encounter. The assurance that God's grace was sufficient supported him in life, and sustained him at the hour of martyrdom. The point Bishop Sheen wanted to emphasize was that similar transformations are open to us all, if we only give our minds and hearts to God. Keeping this in mind, it is important to

> ...notice we said nothing about the emotions. Prayer does not have very much to do with sensations, emotions or feelings. It's not a feeling in the stomach, just as it is not a pain in the stomach; it is not a capricious feeling, something that makes us purr on the inside. It has nothing to do with the animal part of us. It is not in the glands. Prayer is in the intellect, in the will, and in the heart, as embracing a love of truth with a resolve and determination to grow in love through an act of the will.[13]

The Bishop was clear that very often in life, prayer is neglected because we do not particularly feel like it. In fact, our prayers may be far more efficacious when they require effort. Very likely, while praying, we will not experience a deep sense of the presence of God. Saint Thérèse of Lisieux is a perfect example of this, as is Mother Teresa of Calcutta, whom Bishop Sheen knew well though he did not live to see her beatified. Beyond mere human sensation, prayer was an "interaction between the created spirit and the uncreated Spirit."[14] It might be described as communion, conversation, adoration, penance, happiness, work, rest, asking and submission. Each of these aspects of one's personal prayer provides meditative fodder for a lifetime.

To answer the question why we should pray, Sheen responded

with the further question: "Why breathe?" We must take in new air, new power to be reinvigorated. Much like a battery that has become run down, we continually need our spiritual energies restored. There are three possible ways to do this, three specific forms of dialogue with God: vocal prayer, meditation, and contemplation. "In vocal prayer, we go to God on foot; in meditation, we go to God on horseback; and in contemplation we go to God in a jet."[15]

Practicalities are foremost for those who wish to pray seriously, and the first practical suggestion the Bishop offered was not to do all the talking in prayer. Just as a patient would not go to a doctor, rattle off all his symptoms and then abruptly leave, so one does not invert the words of Scripture to read "Listen Lord, thy servant speaketh." In several of his books, Sheen returned to the theme of "poor, talkative Christianity" seeking in talk a form of escapism.

> If the bodies of most of us were fed as little as the mind, they would soon starve to death. Hyperactivity and love of noise and chatter characterize our age, as a compensation for modern man's profound distrust of himself. Not knowing clearly what he is, the American of today tries to become important by what he does – for the more anxious a person is, the more active he or she becomes.... In the post-Christian era, man is active because of his mind – he works to stop thinking. The external necessity of labor is less exigent and cruel than the inner compulsion to "work off" anxiety. Man keeps in futile motion partly to escape having to ask himself two questions: "Why am I here?" and "Where am I going?"[16]

When we begin to really pray, we are not to make prayers of petition our sole object. We become much like children, constantly wanting. Prayers of petition are indeed valid, but only one part of our relationship with God. Our Lord Himself gave us the Our Father which contains seven petitions. When we ask favors, we are never to think that, because God does not answer our prayers quickly, He is reluctant to do so. There are many people who picture the Heavenly Father reacting in the same way they might react if they purposely crossed the street to avoid a beggar. This is a completely wrong way to picture God; He knows our needs before we do, and answers all our prayers according to His Divine plan.

Liturgical and indulgenced prayers should always be favored. These would include, foremost, the Holy Sacrifice of the Mass, and the many para-liturgical actions and prescribed exercises common to Catholic devotional life. In private, Sheen emphasized our prayers should flow from the sincerity of our hearts. Saint Thérèse of Lisieux once wrote that there were so many beautiful prayers to be found in prayer books, it gave her a headache. Prayer, for Thérèse, was an aspiration of the heart. One almost gets the feeling from reading her autobiography, that prayer from the heart is the most perfect act of personal oblation one may make. In a similar vein, Fulton Sheen encouraged his readers to personalize their dialogue with God. "Your heart has problems like no one else in the world. It has certain worries, hopes, agonies, fears, and weaknesses that constitute the content of your prayer. Your prayer will come out of them; you will be a person who is praying."[17]

He often encouraged people to "cut the deadwood" out of prayer, meaning that when routines and habits of prayer become commonplace, we should not fear changing them, adopting new approaches, methods, etc., that will enhance the quality time we give to the Lord. In his later years of preaching, Sheen admitted that it was very difficult, if not impossible to enter the Lord's presence day after day, and think that total spontaneity will always and everywhere work. He highly recommended a copy of the Scriptures, or a good commentary on Scripture, and even went so far as to endorse William Barclay's *Daily Study Bible* as a very effective means of getting the most out of Scripture. Barclay had been professor of Scripture at the University of Glasgow, Scotland; he was an exegete who knew several languages, and was a believer. He was not a Catholic, and the Bishop admitted there would be points in his works on which Catholics could not agree. That was a small price to pay, however, when contrasted with the author's love of the Lord, and an even smaller price when one considered the many Catholic theologians in the years following the Second Vatican Council whose works so publicly dissented from the Magisterium.

A point one does not always think of, but an important one, nonetheless, is the posture one should assume while praying. Sheen recounted the story of Saint Simplician, successor to Saint Ambrose in the See of Milan. He once asked Saint Augustine why the great King David in the Old Testament did not kneel while in the Lord's presence. Augustine replied that a person should adopt the bodily position most likely to move the soul. Saint Jerome, the great Scripture scholar of the early Church took a similar view; in praying and meditating, he said, the body should take the position most conducive for moving the soul's inner devotion.

Aristotle, by contrast, felt that sitting was the best way to commune with the Divine. Sheen, for all of his love of Aristotelian philosophy, did not agree; he pointed to the period of captivity Israel experienced, and how the prophet Jeremiah sat and wept (Lamentations 1:1). Or again, the prophet Elijah sitting under a juniper tree and praying the Lord take his life from him (1 Kings 19:4). Or again the exiles from Jerusalem pictured by the Psalms as sitting by the streams of Babylon and weeping as they remembered Sion (Psalm 136:1). On the other hand, Scripture records Our Lord kneeling to pray in the Garden; Saint Paul said of himself, "I fall on my knees to the Father of Our Lord Jesus Christ" (Ephesians 3:14); the mother of the sons of Zebedee knelt when asking Christ for privileged positions for her sons in the Kingdom

(Matthew 20:20); the father with the epileptic son knelt to ask for a cure (Matthew 7:14); Peter fell down and caught Our Lord by the knees, begging that He depart from such a sinful man (Luke 5:8), though while warming himself at the fire the night before Calvary, he stood (John 18:18, 25). "The conclusion is obvious. It is best to kneel... for it indicates humility, follows the example of Our Lord in the Garden, makes atonement for our failings, and is a polite gesture before the King of Kings."[18]

Such suggestions are enormously helpful for people sincerely making the effort to pray. There are, however, naysayers who will make the point that praying does no good. Sheen said that in one sense a case could be made for such an argument, not from a theological point of view, but from a psychological one. People who take this position are speaking volumes about themselves. In their own case praying is of little or no value because they are "unwilling to curb their promiscuous habits or to tame their carnality."[19] Their prayers are ineffective not because God refuses to hear them, but because they are unwilling to do their part. They would have God do all the work, take all the responsibility, and through some supernatural means, rid them of all their sinfulness and evil desires.

> To have any effectiveness, a prayer for help must express an honest desire to be changed, and that desire must be without reservation or conditions on our part. If we pray to be delivered from alcoholism, and yet refuse to stop drinking, it is an acknowledgment that we did not really pray. In like manner, the person who prays to be delivered from sexual perversions and excesses – and that very day deliberately exposes himself to such pleasures has destroyed the efficacy of the prayer by a reservation. All prayer implies an act of the will, a desire for growth, a willingness to sacrifice on our own part; for prayer is not passive, but is a very active

collaboration between the soul and God. If the will is inoperative, our prayers are merely a list of the things we would like God to give us, without ever asking us to pay the price they cost in effort and a willingness to change. Prayer is dynamic, but only when we cooperate with God through surrender. The one who decides to pray for release from the slavery of carnal pleasures must be prepared, in every part of his being, to utilize the strength that God will give him to work unreservedly for a complete freedom from the sin. In dealing with others, it is possible to have one's cake and eat it, but with God that is impossible.[20]

What we are really doing, the Bishop said, is asking God to lift the laws of the universe, so that He will give us the reward of having placed our complete trust in Him, while continuing to place at least half of our trust in other things. We're keeping one hand behind our back, and holding on to one or several things that will help us if God should fail us. This sort of approach is unrealistic, and simply will never work.

There is still another type of person who argues that since God's will is going to be done in any event, what use is there in praying? Bishop Sheen compared that to saying that I have a sick friend who will either get better or worse; since that is the case, why bother with a doctor? In the natural world, medical science takes into account the factors within a sick body. In the supernatural order, God's will takes into account our desire to change. God will not answer a prayer that is contrary to His will, but He will answer a prayer He might not have without our prayer. In a philosophical vein, Sheen contended that since we live in a conditional universe, to arrive at an effect we desire, we must proceed along the route of its cause. For example, if a person wishes expertise in a given area, he will pursue the specific course of study necessary to acquire the desired knowledge. Similarly, if we wish to proceed in the spiritual order, we must pursue the course Our Lord has set for us, by asking, seeking and knocking.

Such is the place of prayer in our lives. But there is something deeper than prayer – a means by which we go to God even more quickly, namely meditation, the only way one is able to "personalize a truth."

Meditation is much deeper, more spiritually advanced than the mere saying of prayers. Bishop Sheen compared it to a small child approaching his mother and promising to be perfectly quiet if she would only allow him to sit and watch her work. Or like the elderly man whom the Curé of Ars, Saint John Vianney, used to observe sitting in front of the tabernacle for long periods of time; when the Curé asked him what went on in his mind, the man replied that he merely looked at the Lord, and the Lord looked back. Sheen defined meditation somewhat lengthily, but in classic fashion:

> Meditation allows one to suspend the conscious fight against external diversions by an internal realization of the presence of God. It shuts out the world to let in the spirit. It surrenders our own will to the impetus of the Divine will. It turns the searchlight of Divine truth on the way we think, act, and speak, penetrating beneath the layers of our self-deceit and egotism. It summons us before the Bar of Divine Justice, so that we may see ourselves as we really are, and not as we like to think we are. It silences the ego with its clamorous demands, in order that it may hear the wishes of the Divine Heart. It uses our faculties, not to speculate on matters remote from God, but to stir up the will to conform more perfectly with His will. It cultivates a truly scientific attitude toward God as Truth, freeing us from our prepossessions and our biases so that we may eliminate all wishful thinking from our minds. It

eliminates from our lives the things that would hinder union with God and strengthen our desire that all the good things we do shall be done for His honor and glory. It takes our eyes off the flux and change of life and reminds us of our being, our creatureliness, the dependence of all things on God for their creation, their moment-to-moment existence, and their salvation. Meditation is not a petition, a way of using God, or asking things from Him, but rather a surrender, a plea to God that He use us.[21]

The process of meditation is twofold; first the person must consciously withdraw, then he must begin to concentrate on the nature of God, and especially on His Divine Son. In this process, the memory, intellect and will all come into play; to recall God's goodness, to deepen what we know of Him, and to resolve to love Him more deeply. Saint Luke's beautiful description of the journey to Emmaus on Easter Sunday afternoon was, to Bishop Sheen, the finest biblical description of meditation. The account depicts the disciples walking along, very forlorn, and in pessimistic spirit. They encounter a traveler along the way, and not recognizing who it was, they begin to recount all that had happened. This is the first step in meditation, talking about Christ without realizing His presence. The second step is Our Lord's disclosing His presence to them, as He does eventually to the soul lost in meditation. Finally comes the stage of communion, signified in the Gospel narrative by the breaking of bread, and in our lives by the deepening relationship certain to emerge.

In addition to the many spiritual joys that will accrue in our lives from a daily period of meditation, there are practical results as well; it cures us of the habit of self deception, improves our behavior (if our thoughts are bad, our actions will be bad), and replaces the criticism of others with a self-criticism that will make us far less likely to criticize others.

Nothing ever happens in the world that does not first happen inside a mind. Hygiene is no cure for immorality, but if the wellsprings of thought were kept clean, there would be no need to care for the effects of evil thinking on the body. When one meditates and fills his mind … with thoughts and resolutions bearing on the love of God and neighbor above all things, there is a gradual seepage of love down to the level of what is called the subconscious, and finally these good thoughts emerge, of themselves, in the form of effortless good actions.[22]

To achieve these kinds of results, spiritual and practical, to grow in holiness, to deepen our relationship with the Lord, such colloquy must be done daily, in season and out of season, when we feel like it and when we do not feel like it. It is a practice we must keep up with persistence, not getting away from it for periods of time, with the good intention of returning to it, but making the time daily to spend with Our Lord. Further, it must be uninterrupted time – not a period now, and a period then. Finally, it should, if possible, be spent in the presence of Our Lord in the Blessed Sacrament. For laity, Bishop Sheen recommended at least thirty minutes; for priests and religious, there could be no compromise, one full hour each day.

Why an hour? His reasons were scriptural. The word "Hour" is used seven times in John's Gospel, always in reference to "the wickedness of men and the perversity of Satan."[23] Our Lord used it, first at the Wedding Feast of Cana, when He told His Mother His "Hour" had not yet come (John 2:4). Then follows another reference after Christ's declaration that the heavenly Father had sent Him. His words caused such reaction that the crowd attempted to seize Him, but the evangelist reminds us that His "Hour" had not yet come (John 7:36). Or the time when His detractors used the police of the Temple Treasury Department to arrest Him, but they could not lay hands on Him, because His "Hour" was not yet at hand (John 8:20). "The Hour has come for the Son of Man to be glorified" (John 12:33), Our Lord announced, less than a week before His death. The Beloved Disciple further recorded Christ's words as He anticipated the Cross: "Now My soul is in turmoil, and what am I to say? Father, save Me from this Hour? No, it was for this that I came to this Hour. Father, glorify Thy Name" (John 12:17-29). Finally, Saint John recounts Our Lord's final meeting with His apostles before His Crucifixion in which He prays, "Father the Hour has come…" (John 16:33; 17:1-2).

One hour is therefore not arbitrary. In the last decade of his life, the preaching of priests' retreats became one of Fulton Sheen's primary apostolates. In each retreat, one of the conferences dealt with the daily Holy Hour. What is less known, is that it was Archbishop Sheen's policy to open his retreats to members of the laity as well as religious Sisters. Hence it would have been a rare sight to seen only clerics in attendance. The Archbishop offered practical reasons for the daily hour, encouraged laity to make it if their schedules permitted, but insisted on it for priests and religious. He emphasized this spiritual exercise above all others because, after decades in the priesthood, he claimed to know, or at least have heard of all the devotional practices. The Holy Hour was the only one that worked. Why? Because it was done in the presence of Christ; it helped shake off the "noonday devils" besetting everyone; was a power that overflowed into all the activities of daily life; allowed one to keep a balance between the spiritual and the practical in life; made one practice what he preached; it permitted priests to be "obedient instruments of the Divinity"; helped to make reparation for one's own sins and those of the world; reduced a person's susceptibility to weakness and temptation; was, in essence, personal prayer of a sort that kept one from seeking an external escape from worries; was necessary for the whole Church, and most important of all, was the only thing Our

Lord ever asked of His followers: "Had you no strength, then, to watch with Me even for an hour?" (Matthew 16:40).[24]

Above all, Fulton Sheen truly lived what he preached on this subject. He recounts in his autobiography one particularly difficult Holy Hour which preceded a 4:00 A.M. train trip from Jerusalem to Cairo. Then there was the episode in Chicago when he asked the pastor to open the church for him about seven o'clock in the evening. The good man later locked the church, forgetting Sheen was inside. For close to two hours he sought a way out; finally, he jumped out a small window, landed in a coal bin, scared the house keeper with the noise, and was finally rescued!

Looking back, Sheen often wished he had kept track of letters he received from priests all over the world telling him how their lives had been changed by adopting this practice. In a visit with Malcolm Muggeridge in his apartment in New York City just months before his death, the Archbishop recounted these many missives:

> Got one from England the other day from a priest who said, "I became an alcoholic, I sank into the depths of vice – and – I heard your tape; I started Holy Hours … I'm back."[25]

There were many such, but perhaps the most interesting results were to be found among non-Catholic clergy, Protestant ministers who began praying one hour a day. Sheen spoke to two such groups, of over two hundred each, in Florida and South Carolina, and to a smaller group at Princeton University in New Jersey. He noted that the divisions in Christianity had deprived them of the Eucharist, but strongly encouraged them to make an hour with Scripture. As a result, many came to the Archbishop enquiring about the Eucharist, and asking if they might join him in one hour before the tabernacle.

Once when he was in Los Angeles, he received a phone call

from a minister identifying himself as Jack McAllister. He was quite insistent on seeing the Archbishop. Sheen replied that he was catching a midday flight to New York, but would be happy to see him at the airport. In the course of the visit, McAllister explained he was involved in a work of international evangelization, sending tapes on the Gospel to all parts of the world, and printed sermons and copies of the Scriptures to just as large an area. There seemed to be something missing, and McAllister was at a loss to figure out the problem. Sheen once again recommended one hour with the Lord in Scripture, and one year later he received a pamphlet from the minister titled "Jack McAllister Writes to One Hour Watchers." One particular paragraph shows the Lord working through Archbishop Sheen:

> Please … if you are honestly concerned about making Christ known to literally every creature – give God one hour every day. You are needed in God's prayer-force to prepare for work in the totally unevangelized areas of the world. Do you love them enough to pray? Will you "pay the price" of spiritual battle for one hour daily? "What, could you not watch with me one hour?"[26]

At the end of one year, Rev. McAllister reported to the Archbishop that seven hundred ministers had agreed to pray one hour a day. Within six years of their airport meeting, one hundred thousand "One Hour Watchers" had been trained.

As a student priest at Catholic University of America in Washington, the young Father Sheen would never come to class in Caldwell Hall without taking a moment to walk up the few short stairs to the chapel and make a visit to the Blessed Sacrament. Later, as a graduate student at the University of Louvain in Belgium, he would visit Our Lord in each church he passed on his way to the Institute of Philosophy. The same was also true while studying in Rome, and, in later years as a professor at Catholic

University, he had a chapel installed in his Washington home. In retirement, he did the same in his New York City apartment; on December 9, 1979, he was found, gone to the Lord he had loved so long in prayer, on the floor outside of his chapel.

Archbishop Sheen saw fit to mention these facts in his autobiography, because, to him, they were the most important aspects of his priesthood. He could recommend a daily hour of prayer so forcefully, because he had lived the practice so faithfully. It is a practice that may be started by anyone, any time. All that is needed is faith, desire and perseverance.

> This is the story of the Holy Hour. It seems so long at first, like the seven-mile journey to Emmaus. More than that, there seems to be so little in common between our involvement with the news of the world and the stranger in whose presence we find ourselves. Furthermore, we are sad. The Hour means giving up a golf game or a cocktail party, or a nap. Then, too, we have read pamphlets casting doubts on the Real Presence, and we wonder if Christ knows what is going on and being said about Him... we pick up the Scriptures, find everywhere a confirmation that as in the Old Testament there was the Bread of perpetual presence, so in the New Testament we recognize the presence of Christ. He bids us remain for the Hour, and at the end, we hate to leave for our hearts are still with Him.[27]

Chapter Eight

THE BLESSED VIRGIN MARY

Many times over the years Archbishop Sheen recounted the story of Our Lord walking through the courts of heaven in company with Saint Peter. At a certain point, they came upon some dubious characters, and the Lord wondered how they had gained admittance to the Kingdom, since He had not let them in. Peter responded, "Don't blame me, Lord. Whenever you close a door, your mother always opens a window!"

Stories told in a humorous vein often convey tremendously important truths, and this is no exception. Our Blessed Mother plays a vital role in all our spiritual lives, that of motherly intercession. A Catholic's closeness to the Mother of God was one of the central themes of Fulton Sheen's preaching, and of his own life. He was born on the Illinois prairie, in the small town of El Paso on May 8, 1895. A marker designates the building of his birth, and the original Saint Mary's Church of his baptism was replaced with a newer structure while Sheen was still a young man. On the day of his reception into the Church, his mother, Delia Fulton Sheen, placed him on the altar of the Blessed Virgin, and dedicated her young infant son to her. When he made his First Holy Communion at the age of twelve, he made a conscious dedication of himself to Mary. At his ordination in 1919, he took a resolution to offer Mass in honor of Our Lady every Saturday, for the protection of his priesthood. When he was consecrated a bishop in 1951, he took as his episcopal motto "Da Per Matrem Me Venire," "That I may come to Thee through Thy Mother." Interestingly, when he was still in the first grade, a Sister in school suggested that all the children place the initials JMJ at the top of each page of schoolwork they wrote. At the end of his life, having written thousands of pages, the Archbishop had no recollection of ever omitting this invocation of the Holy Family. His television audiences witnessed the same practice at the blackboard prior to making each new point. As a priest, and later as a bishop, he visited Lourdes over thirty times; one early pilgrimage, at the conclusion of his graduate studies, was especially telling:

> When I finished my university studies, I made another pilgrimage to Lourdes. I was deeply concerned that perhaps I would not be permitted to return to Mary's shrine again, for I knew not to what task the Bishop would assign me. I asked the Blessed Mother some sign that despite the odds of returning to Lourdes, she would do what seemed impossible. The sign I asked for was this: that after I offered the Holy Sacrifice of the Mass and before I would reach the outer gate of the shrine, a little girl aged about twelve dressed in white would give me a white rose. About twenty feet from the gate I could see no one. I remember saying: "You had better hurry, there is not much time left." As I arrived at the gate a little girl aged twelve, dressed in white, gave me the white rose.[1]

It was providential she did. The Archbishop began a career that included much preaching and teaching about the Mother of God, not to mention sixty years of priesthood dedicated to her.

Sheen considered Our Lady from many points of view, beginning with what we learn about her in Scripture. Even before her appearance on the stage of history, and the early Church's meditation on her life, she had been predicted, especially in secular literature. Virgil's *Fourth Eclogue* has always been considered messianic, and a veiled reference to "chaste Lucina, 'tis thy own," has been taken as a prefiguration of the Mother of Christ.

Likewise, the Greek poet Homer, who lived one thousand years before Christ, wrote of the defeated man Ulysses, and his sorrowful wife. While he was away on a voyage, many men pursued her; her response was always the same: as soon as she completed the garment she was weaving, she would consider their request. Each night, however, she would tear out the stitches made that day. "No one understood why this great poet should make history understand a defeated man and a sorrowful woman until a defeated man and a sorrowful woman came."[2]

An oft recurring theme in the writings of Fulton Sheen is God's creation of His own Mother. No creature can create his own mother, but if he could, he would create the most perfect woman he could envision. God, on the other hand, had the Mother of His Divine Son in mind from all eternity. If the Creator took six days to prepare a paradise for man, did it not make perfect sense, Sheen queried, for Him to take an even longer time to prepare a paradise for His Son to enter? Just as no weeds grew in the Garden of Eden, no sin was to be found in the Mother of God's Son, from the first moment of her conception in the womb of her mother, Saint Anne. Just as one would not think of using a barn door as the entrance to a majestic castle, it would have been unthinkable for the Son of God to enter humanity through sinful human portals. Mary is often described as the "paradise of the Incarnation," the "Eden of innocence" for Christ, who not only came into this world through her, but as the Divine Child, subjected Himself to dependence on her.

> He needed lips with which to teach, hands to bless,
> feet to search for wandering sheep, a side whereon John
> might lean; He needed eyes that He might read hearts,

fingers that would mold clay to open blind eyes to the light of God's sunshine, ears to hear the plaintive plea of ragged beggars; He needed a human will by which He might give an example of obedience, hands and feet to nail on a cross for the propitiation for the sins of man; so He made Mary. He Who is joy asked her to give Him tears. He Who is rich asked her to make Him poor, that through His poverty we might be rich. He Who is wisdom asked her to give Him the gift to grow in wisdom by learning through suffering. He Who is the Shepherd bade her make Him a lamb, that He might be the sacrifice for our sins. He Who is Spirit begged her for flesh and blood, that He might give us the Eucharist.[3]

Once accomplished, the Son lived His thirty hidden years in obedience to His Mother and foster father, Saint Joseph. When Mary gave her acceptance to God's plan at the Annunciation, a new society began to be made. A human family had its origins, which was at once an "ideal and an earthly trinity." In earthly families, one has a father, mother and child. In the Holy Family, one has to begin with the Child, who created His parents; next comes the Mother who conceived her Son by the overpowering of the Holy Spirit in her virginal womb; finally, Joseph, that just man called to be the protector of the family, and thereby, "protector of the Church, which is the expansion of that original family."[4]

Because Nazareth was so different, it is since then so imitable. Because it is the light, we can see our way. Once that earthly trinity stood revealed, the family could never again be the result of a lease or a contract alone; it would be a union, a fellowship, as indissoluble as the Trinity of which it was the reflection. Nazareth tells us the kind of love that makes a home, namely, Divine love on a pilgrimage into time from eternity.[5]

There is a deep and impenetrable mystery in the fact that the Mother of this Family conceived by the power of the Holy Spirit. Sheen explained that every child born into the world is the fruit of love, but the love that begot this particular Child was the love of God. "Under the sun one needs no candle," the Bishop reflected. "When conception takes place through Spirit love, there is no need for human love."[6] He was not trying to say Our Blessed Mother conceived without love, merely that she had conceived without passion. Christ was so totally submissive to Mary, that whatever happened to her also happened to Him; thus, when there was no room for her in the inn, there was no room for Him. Likewise, Mary was the only person in the world with whom Christ was safe from contradiction – she understood Him perfectly because she was preserved from the contradiction of sin. Perhaps Sheen's most stirring description of the hidden life reminded his readers that

> As He was formed by her body and given to mankind by her arms, so He was formed by her mind. The world received only three years of His life, but Mary had thirty years of His obedience. Down to Nazareth He went to be subject to her. He, the Divine word, for three long decades responded to a human word. Nazareth was the first university in the history of Christianity, and in it all humanity, in the person of Christ, was trained in obedience under the tutelage of a woman. It was no wonder that, when He was graduated, men marveled at His learning: "No man ever spoke as this man." Nazareth was the school for Golgotha.[7]

We meet Our Blessed Mother in no better place than in Scripture, and her appearances occur both during her Son's hidden and public life. Forty days after His birth, He was presented in the Temple, in accordance with the prescriptions of the Mosaic Law. The prophecy of Simeon about Our Lord, and the sword of sorrow that would pierce the heart of His Mother were intense drama. Simeon, an old man well past the age of singing, opened the "vents of song," when he uttered his *Nunc Dimittis,* his prayer of farewell. It was the "Compline of his life," Bishop Sheen noted, and it has ever since been part of Compline, the night prayer of the Church, required daily of all her priests. God was speaking through the old man, telling Mary she was to guard her Divine Son until the moment of His sacrifice; there was an echo here of the Garden of Eden, where a tree had brought the ruin of the first Adam, and a prediction of another tree on which the second Adam would undo the initial rebellion. The encounter between the old man and the Babe was the meeting of the two covenants, Old and New. "Antiquity had said its last word. History, which had until now recorded its battles and set down the rise and fall of its kingdoms as events before Christ, would henceforth write them down as happening in the year of Our Lord."[8]

The Flight into Egypt was an example of the Blessed Mother's acceptance of trial and sorrow. Most human beings of faith can accept the crosses sent them by God, because a deep inner knowledge sees His providential love and care in the sending, and with that knowledge comes acceptance. Trials inflicted on us from others are a very different sort, and most often present untold difficulties; such were Our Lady's on this occasion, since they came from "the wickedness of men, the injustice of a pagan." Herod's decree was all the more terrible a cross since its end was so uncertain. The loss of the Divine Child at age twelve was an even deeper darkness; Mary had indeed lost God. His discovery on the third day always gives rise to the question of His whereabouts, and Bishop Sheen conjectures if He might not have visited the scenes of His future Passion and Death? In the midst of this dark night, however, Mary is seen as one with sinners, since sin is a separation from God. She therefore knows the horror of loss of Him, whatever the cause, and, as a result of experience, she the inviolate one, is able to lead the fallen back to the fountain of life.

Short of divine Motherhood assigned her from the cross, perhaps the most poignant example of her role of intercession came at the wedding feast of Cana. After she presented her Son the dilemma of the newly married couple running out of wine, Sheen imagined a dialogue that might have transpired.

> Whenever our blessed Lord used the word "hour" it was always in relationship to His Passion and His death.... Our Lord is saying to His Mother, "The hour of My Passion and death has not yet come. What do you want Me to do? Do you want Me to work My first miracle? Do you want Me to prove I am the expected Messiah, the Son of the living God? Do you realize if I work this miracle and announce Myself as the Christ and the Son of God I will be sent to the Cross? Do you want to be a mother who sent her son to the battlefield? My dear Mother, if you want Me to begin My public life now and usher in My death, Passion, and redemption of men, then your relation to Me will change. Up to this point, you have been known as the Mother of Jesus, but the moment I begin My redemptive work, you will not just be My Mother, you will be the Mother of everyone I redeem. Then you will be the Mother of all humanity, the universal Mother of the world."[9]

Sheen described Mary's last recorded words in Scripture as a most beautiful valedictory: "Do whatever He tells you." In other words, she speaks not simply to the waiters at Cana, but to all who would follow her Son through the ages; in these words are to be found her directive to all who seek her motherly intercession.

She would meet her Son again on the Via Dolorosa, that narrow street through Jerusalem leading to Calvary, filled with merchants' stores on either side, through which many convicted criminals carried their crosses to death, while the business of the world continued uninterrupted. Good Friday would be like all others from this point of view, but when Mother met Son, Bishop Sheen felt her mind went back to the Old Testament account of young Isaac carrying the wood for burning, and asking his father, "Where is the lamb?" This, Mary knew, was the true Isaac, about to offer the true sacrifice. "Every nail in that carpenter shop suggested a crucifixion, every thorn in their humble garden a crown, every tree a cross, and every red rose His crimsoned Self."[10]

Our Lord spoke seven words from the Cross, and for his entire priesthood, Fulton Sheen would spend three hours every Good Friday afternoon meditating on them with thousands of people gathered to listen, either in New York City, or wherever God placed him. Christ's third word from the Cross was that in which He entrusted His Mother to the care of John, the beloved disciple, and John to her. At that moment, she became the universal Mother of all humanity, since John, to whom she was given, stood in for all believers. Hence, we were all spiritually begotten from Mary on that fateful afternoon. It is not a figure of speech, nor pious rhetoric, when the Christian claims two mothers, one biological and the other spiritual, and both just as validly mothers to their offspring. Sheen captured the moment as few spiritual writers have.

> The mystery came to an end on Calvary. There she became our mother the moment she lost her Divine Son. What seemed an alienation of affection was in reality a deepening of affection. No love ever mounts to a higher level without death to a lower one. Mary died to the love of Jesus at Cana, and recovered Jesus again at Calvary with His Mystical Body which He redeemed. It was, for the moment, a poor exchange, giving up her Divine Son to win mankind, but in reality, she did not win mankind apart from Him.... The Fiat she pronounced when she became the Mother of God now became another Fiat, like unto creation in the immensity of what she brought forth. It was also a

Fiat which so enlarged her affections as to increase her pains. The bitterness of Eve's curse – that woman would bring forth children in sorrow – was now fulfilled, and not by the opening of a womb, but by the piercing of a heart, as Simeon had foretold. It was the greatest of all honors to be the mother of Christ; but it was also a great honor to be the mother of Christians. There was no room in the inn for that first birth; but Mary had the whole world for her second.[11]

The Lord's Mother was present as He was taken down from the Cross, and buried in a nearby tomb. In fact, the return from Calvary, traditionally depicted in Christian art, has moved countless souls through the centuries. The Son and the Mother are inseparable, which prompted Bishop Sheen to ask, how one could love Christ without loving His Mother. In human terms, how could one have a friend, go to visit him, and each time he visited, ignore the friend's mother? From that, he took it that Christ could never be pleased with those who disregard His Mother and any closeness with Him must come through her. A fear among non-Catholics, originating at the Reformation, and continuing until the present, is that Catholics adore Mary, and place her on an equal footing with God.

> To show her veneration is not to adore her. Only God may be adored. Mary is an abstraction of love from Love.... Love for Mary no more derogates from Christ's divinity than the setting robs the jewel, or the hearth the flame, or the horizon the sun. She exists but to magnify the Lord, and that was the song of her life. Knowing her as the Tower of Ivory, He climbs up the stairs of her encircling virtues, to "kiss upon her lips a mystic rose." Acknowledging her as the Gate of Heaven, through her portals He comes to us. He who slams the gate in the face of the Queen bars the entrance of the

King. As His Mother, she must be ours for, as our Lord said: "I will not leave you orphans."[12]

The Church has given four major dogmatic affirmations about Our Blessed Mother; she is the "Theotokos," or Mother of God, forever a Virgin, Immaculately Conceived, and Assumed body and soul into Heaven. Of the four, Sheen concentrated more on Mary's Immaculate Conception and Assumption, though not in a strictly apologetic sense. His concern was explaining the Church's teaching, especially to inquirers. The Immaculate Conception was solemnly defined by Pope Pius IX in 1854, and the Assumption nearly a century later, by Pope Pius XII, in 1950. In one sense, they were part of the modern age, and in his classic work on Our Lady, *The World's First Love*, Sheen tried to relate the significance of each to present times. He noted that within five years of the definition of the Immaculate Conception, and within six months of Our Lady's revelation of herself to Bernadette in the Grotto at Lourdes, Charles Darwin wrote his *Origin of the Species*, Karl Marx produced *Introduction to the Critique of the Philosophy of Hegel*, and John Stuart Mill, his *Essay on Liberty*. Darwin took man's mind off his Divine origin, and tried to paint a future in which the creature would take on qualities of godliness; Marx was so impressed with Darwin's ideas on progress, he desired to dedicate one of his future books to him. The founder of Communism did not advance an intellectual atheism denying God, so much as a world in which God played no part. Mill's contribution was to define liberty as the right to do whatever one chose, charting the way for a "chaos of conflicting egotisms."

The dogma of the Immaculate Conception wilted and killed the false optimism of the inevitable and necessary progress of man without God. Humbled in his Darwinian Marxian-Millian pride, modern man saw his doctrine of progress evaporate. The interval between the Napoleonic and Franco-Prussian Wars was fifty-seven years; the interval between the Franco-Prussian War and World War I was forty-three years; the interval between World Wars I and II, twenty-one years. Fifty-five, forty-three, twenty-one, and a Korean War five years after World War II is hardly progress. Man finally saw that he was not naturally good. Once having boasted that he came from the beast, he now found himself to be acting as a beast.[13]

There was yet another reaction in society; modern man, the eternal optimist who felt himself "immaculately conceived," that is, incapable of doing wrong or being a sinner, was now replaced by man who was filled with uncontrolled sexual or "libidinous" drives, over which he had no control. The influence of philosophers and political writers, said Sheen, was now replaced with the psychology of Freud. In the Immaculate Conception, the Church had to remind the world that perfection is "not biologically inevitable," so in her doctrine of the Assumption, it had to "give hope to the creature of despair." The Bishop saw in the life of Our Lady a "triple transition." At the moment of her Annunciation, she moved from the holiness of the Old Covenant to the holiness of Christ. At Pentecost, the beginning of the Church, she moved from the holiness of the Historical Christ to that of His Mystical Body, the Church. And at her bodily Assumption, she "becomes the first human person to realize the historical destiny of the faithful as members of Christ's Mystical Body, beyond time, beyond death, and beyond judgment."[14] As such, Mary remains, for all ages, a beacon of hope in the midst of despair, confusion, and all the passing fancies of humanity at variance with her Son, His teaching, and His Church.

How does Mary, the woman of faith for all generations, affect modernity? Bishop Sheen's life spanned nearly eight decades of the 20th century; he could easily separate its early decades from those that followed, to outline Our Lady's influence in each generation. During one broadcast of his Emmy-award winning television series, *Life Is Worth Living* in the 1950's, he dealt with the beginning of the modern world, which he specifically dated October 13, 1917. On that day, three extraordinary events occurred, in Moscow, in Rome, and in the Portuguese village of Fatima. In Moscow, a young woman named Maria Alexandrovich was teaching religion to a class of nearly two hundred children in the church of the Iberian Virgin. Suddenly, a group of soldiers entered through the main door, went down the middle aisle, began destroying the church's icons, religious images, furnishings, etc., then turned on the children, killing several of them. The young Russian noblewoman rushed out of the church screaming. She seemed to know there was an imminent revolution brewing and went immediately to the offices of a local government official to report what had happened. He not only was aware of it, he told her he had ordered it. Such was the beginning of the Russian Revolution which brought the Communist Party to power, and began the Soviet Union.

On the same day in the city of Rome, a very different event was taking place, amid rejoicing and the ringing of church bells. A new bishop was being consecrated, Eugenio Pacelli, a name not well known, but destined to be. His first assignment was in the Vatican Diplomatic Service in the city of Munich where, in April of 1919 Communist forces under the leadership of one Rudolph Egelhofer, and two Bolshevik Commissars, were attempting to establish a Soviet Republic. Calling themselves Spartacists, they assembled a considerable army, which roamed the streets of Munich, killing nearly three hundred twenty-five people in one day, April 25, 1919. One man, Bishop Pacelli, had become a threat to Communist operations in the short time he had been in the city. A plot was hatched to assassinate him, and Communist soldiers forced their way into his residence on April 29, literally threatening him with drawn pistols. One of the soldiers threw out his pistol hand with such force, it hit the pectoral cross the Bishop was wearing; Pacelli grasped it for safety, and told them to go ahead and kill him, though they would gain nothing – he was only trying to save Germany from the onslaught of a godless regime. Within minutes, the soldiers left the Bishop's residence; they could offer no explanation either on the spot, or later when they returned to their commanding officer, why they had not killed the Bishop. He was no match for their force; he was soft spoken; it simply appeared that his penetrating glance was too much for their emotions. Pacelli, of course, would become Pius XII in future years, and gave the pectoral cross he was wearing that day to his great friend in New York, Francis Cardinal Spellman. On the night Bishop Sheen gave the telecast in which he related the story, the Cardinal loaned it to the Bishop, knowing the powerful effect it would make on so large a television audience.

Finally, on October 13, 1917, the three children of Fatima – Lucia, Jacinta and Francesco – received one of a series of private revelations from the Blessed Virgin Mary, but one which was particularly significant. In the course of her messages, Mary had told them the approximate time the First World War would end; she predicted an era of peace if humanity would stop offending God. If that were not the case, a future, more terrifying conflict would overtake the world. She also foretold the rise of Russia, the spread of its errors, and the consequent crosses the Holy Father would have to bear. Finally, the children related that a special sign would be given on October 13, 1917.

Seventy thousand people gathered at Fatima on that rainy day with the children, awaiting a sign. Most of them were unbelievers. Portugal in those days was an anarchistic, Communistic, anticlerical, and atheistic nation. Most of the people came out of curiosity, not out of faith. They doubted that anything would happen, but the children assured them that the Heavenly Lady would show a great sign as a proof that she had actually appeared. The proof was what has since been called the "Miracle of the Sun." The testimony of these seventy thousand people, as well as the records of the atheistic, anarchistic newspapers of the time that I have read, attested the fact of what happened. One anarchistic paper stated that there was a miracle of the sun, but it hoped that nobody would interpret it in a Divine way.[15]

From that time on, said Bishop Sheen, Fatima became the gathering place for all who believe that peace is made in places other than the tables around which politicians gather. Thirty-four years after the "Miracle of the Sun," on October 13, 1951, the Bishop found himself at the shrine of Fatima; it was one of about ten pilgrimages he had made there in his lifetime, and this particular year, over one million people gathered to pray for peace. They had begun to arrive the evening before, an especially rainy night, common during the Fall in Portuguese mountainous regions. People either knelt or stood throughout the night. The next day's ceremonies were particularly noteworthy:

> ...as the statue of Our Lady of Fatima was carried through the throng, these million people waved white handkerchiefs as white flags of purity, in tribute to the Lady of Peace. One's mind suddenly left that white Square of Fatima and went to the Red Square of Moscow, where there were flags, dyed red in the blood of the victims. Somehow one felt that the white Square was giving the only answer there is to the Red Square. A great change seemed to come over the Communist hammer and the sickle. The hammer that had beaten down so many homes, and profaned so many sanctuaries, will one day, in virtue of such prayer and penance,

be held aloft by millions of men and begin to look like a cross; the sickle which the communists used to cut human life like unripe wheat will also change its symbolism and begin to look like "the moon under the Lady's feet."[16]

While Archbishop Sheen happily lived to see the election of John Paul II to the Papacy in 1979, he did not live to see the correctness of his prophecy, wrought through the influence of this man who so totally captured the world's imagination.

Although the political freedom, so long prayed for, became a reality, another misdirected freedom had a life of its own, and continued to grow stronger as the 20th century progressed. The concept of "freedom from" came to be far more accepted than "freedom for." "Freedom from" was equated with liberation, sexual license, moral perversity, equal rights, the women's liberation movement, and the like. In the later decades of the 20th century, Fulton Sheen would write of Our Blessed Mother's influence and intercession in much different terms.

In an era of women's liberation, he found it strange that there be so little emphasis on the woman who brought about true liberation. Liberation, Sheen wrote, was of two sorts; political and moral, and the former depended on the latter. Women's liberation really originated at the beginning of time when God made it clear to the serpent that He would "put enmity between you and the woman" (Genesis 3:15). The type of liberation Our Lady would bring about would not be from evil – that was for her Son to accomplish. Rather, it would be from guilt. Just as little children understand Divine truth better than the "self-wise," so, the Bishop noted, woman, who is considered the weaker sex, becomes powerful because she has been chosen by God for a very specific purpose, one which is discovered in her very feminine makeup; women have greater capacities for love and surrender and victimhood than men; a woman's whole personality is involved in love, hence she is slower to love because when she does, she gives the totality of herself. Further, women use intelligence or intuition rather than reason, much as Pilate's wife intuited the real nature of Our Lord. Because of this, a woman is more "amphibious" than man; she can move from the human to the Divine in a second. Her nature is more adaptable to the spiritual; she has a greater measure of eternity than a man, who lives primarily in time. From all this, it was clear why one woman's liberation helped save the world. In a word, women stand up far better in crises than men; one need only look at the Cross.

> When we come to this great drama of Calvary, there is one fact that stands out very clearly: men failed. Judas, who had eaten at His table, lifted up his heel against Him, sold Him for thirty pieces of silver, and then blistered His lips with a kiss, suggesting that all betrayals of Divinity are so terrible that they must be prefaced by some mark of esteem and affection. Pilate, the typical time-serving politician, afraid of incurring the hatred of his government if he released a man whom he already admitted was innocent, sentenced Him to death. Annas and Caiphas resorted to illegal night trials and false witnesses and rent their garments as if scandalized at His Divinity. The three chosen apostles who had witnessed the Transfiguration and, therefore, were thought strong enough to endure the scandal of seeing the Shepherd struck, slept in a moment of greatest need, because they were unworried and untroubled. On the way to Calvary, a stranger, interested only in the drama of a man going to execution, was forced and compelled to offer Him a helping hand. On Calvary itself, there is only one of the twelve apostles present, John, and one wonders if even he would have been there had it not been for the presence of the Mother of Jesus.[17]

Contrasted to this were the figures of Pilate's wife, Veronica, Mary of Magdala, Mary of Clophas (the mother of James and John), and Our Blessed Mother. The last three were specifically at the foot of the Cross, the three types of personalities, said Sheen, who will always be found there, "penitence, motherhood and virginity." There must be a harkening back to the feminine. All times of difficulty in world history have proven this true; after the Fall, it was to a woman and her seed that the Creator promised relief; at a period of time when so many had forgotten Old Testament revelation and prophecies, it was to a woman God sent an angel at the Annunciation, and whenever the world has been in danger of collapse in whatever form, there has been renewed emphasis on devotion to "the woman who is not salvation but who renders it by bringing her children back again to Christ."[18]

> This would seem to be the reason for the frequent revelations of the Blessed Mother in modern times at La Sallette, Lourdes and Fatima. The very emergence of woman into the political, economic and social life of the world suggests that the world needs a continuity that she alone can supply; for while man is more closely related to things, she is the protector and defender of life.... Her very body commits her to the drama of existence and links her in some way with the rhythm of the cosmos. In her arms, life takes its first breath, and to her arms life wants to die. The word most often used by soldiers on the battlefields is "Mother." The woman with her children is "at home," and man is "at home" with her.[19]

Bishop Sheen saw a triple role for the eternal feminine: restoring constancy in love, respect for personality, and the infusing of the virtue of charity into souls. A deepening of the world's appreciation for these would restore what was lost in the late 20th century, and indeed at any time. By returning to the feminine, we are letting Mary form Christ in us, so that we will be totally His, and reflect His life, especially to those we meet. Such may sound simplistic, but transformation of any culture at any time begins with transformation of the individual. In one of his books, Sheen has Christ speaking to the individual soul, and informing it that "no one can be an adopted son of My Heavenly Father without being My brother; but no one can be My brother who does not depend on our Mother."[20] There was no vocation exempt from this but, in a very special way, the priest Fulton Sheen sought to impress it on the hearts of his brother priests.

> The priest first gives up the earthly love of a woman, as Mary gave up the earthly love of a man. In the Incarnation God established a beachhead in humanity through the free choice of a woman; now Our Lord finds an extension of His priesthood in the free act of a priest … His surrender is like Mary's. She willed her Son and she conceived. So the priest willed to be God's, and he can identify the day and the hour.… If there is to be a generation of souls and he is to be a "father" begetting others in Christ, there must be love. That love is the same as Mary's; the fire and passion of the Holy Spirit overshadow him. As in her were united virginity and motherhood, so in the priest there is to be a unity of virginity and fatherhood.… The priest has a deep love for Mary not only in his better moments, but even in his failings. He trusts in her intercession to combat his weakness.[21]

Whether one's vocation is to be a priest, a religious, or a member of the laity, devotion to Mary is an essential ingredient in wholistic Christian development. But, how be devoted to her? There is no question that spontaneity in prayer, spiritual reading, and prescribed devotional practices and prayers to Mary are tremendously important. Of all, however, Fulton Sheen believed the recitation of her Rosary to be the most effective. Nor did he accept the argument that the Rosary was repetitious. He was once instructing a convert class in Washington, D.C. At the end of an hour's explanation on the Rosary, a young couple approached him, of whom the young woman was the spokesperson. She claimed that after such a detailed explanation, she would never become a Catholic, because she did not believe anyone who kept repeating the same thing over and over could be sincere about it. Sheen inquired who the young man with her was, and she proceeded to introduce her fiancé. "Does he love you?" Sheen asked. "Yes, certainly he loves me," was her reply. When he pressed her how she could be certain of the young man's love, the girl said he told her continually of his love. At that, Sheen said, "I wouldn't believe him. I don't think he's sincere!"

> The beautiful truth is that there is no repetition in "I love you." Because there is a new moment of time, another point in space, the words do not mean the same as they did at another time or space. A mother says to her son, "You are a good boy." She may have said it ten thousand times before, but each time it means something different; the whole personality goes out to it anew, as a new historical circumstance summons forth a new outburst of affection. Love is never monotonous in the uniformity of its expression. The mind is infinitely variable in its language, but the heart is not. The heart of a man, in the face of the woman he loves, is too poor to translate the infinity of his affection into a different word. So the heart takes one expression, "I love you," and in saying it over and over again, it never repeats. It is the only real news in the universe.[22]

The Rosary is the most perfect prayer because it combines each of the elements one seeks in prayer: mental, vocal and physical. It is mental because each of its mysteries asks us to meditate on some aspect in the life of Our Lord or His Mother. As we personalize each mystery, we vocalize our faith in Christ and His Mother with the recitation of the prescribed prayers. Finally, it is physical; the movement of one's fingers over the beads. There is something very soothing, if not therapeutic, in such action; at the end of the First World War, one of the therapies given to shell-shocked soldiers upon their return home was to teach them knitting. Nervous energy is somehow released through the fingers, and the exercise of knitting had a calming effect; just so, the Rosary bestows a spiritual calmness, a peace of soul. Those devoted to this wonderful prayer to Our Lady are sure to remain close to her Son, and out of such devotional practice, all sorts of results may accrue.

> I know of a Jew who, in World War I, was in a shell hole on the Western Front with four Austrian soldiers. Shells had been bursting on all sides. Suddenly, one shell killed his four companions. He took a rosary from the hands of one of them and began to say it. He knew it by heart, for he had heard others say it so often. At the end of the first decade, he felt an inner warning to leave that shell hole. He crawled through much mud and muck, and threw himself into another. At that moment a shell hit the first hole, where he had been lying. Four more times, exactly the same experience; four more warnings, and four times his life was saved! He promised then to give his life to Our Lord and to His Blessed Mother if he should be saved. After the war more sufferings came to him; his family was burned by Hitler, but his promise lingered on. Recently, I baptized him – and the grateful soldier is now preparing to study for the priesthood.[23]

Bishop Sheen was not content merely to relate such inspira-

tional stories; as National Director of the Society for the Propagation of the Faith, he designed what became known as the World
Mission Rosary, with each of the five decades a different color,
symbolic of the five continents of the world. These were distrib-
uted in the hundreds of thousands, and one cannot measure their
spiritual effect. Speaking on radio, on the Catholic Hour in 1951,
he put Our Lady and her Rosary in global perspective:

> Then too, as the servant of 97,758 missionaries to
> Moslems, Indians, Chinese, Africans, Japanese, and the
> millions of others who have not yet come to Christ, we
> think of Mary and beg her to hasten the day when the
> fullness of their time will come! Already their native
> art is picturing her as if she were their own, and rightly
> so. As she rose French out of the stone of Chartres
> and Lourdes, and Portuguese from the white lime of
> Fatima, so she comes with the merciful face of night
> to Africa, and with the glow of the morning sun to the
> Japanese, changing her unchanging beauty with every
> nation as a lady changes her dress but not her loveliness.
> May I urge you for the sake of the peace of the world
> to pray for all the five continents on our World Mission
> Rosary. Each continent has its specific color; when you
> finish all five you have circumnavigated the globe.[24]

Finally, we consider the influence of Our Lady in Fulton
Sheen's own life. It was immense. Every priest, Sheen noted, feels
the tension of celibacy. We live in an erotic civilization that pulls
us in many directions, and tries its utmost to sell a convincing
message. The celibate is bound to feel lonely in that atmosphere,
but it is a different sort of loneliness than that plaguing modern
man. The celibate is lonely because he seeks the Infinite; modern
man is often lonely because he seeks the Infinite in the finite. The
Mother of Christ, who nurtures her Son's life in all believers, works
particularly hard in the priest dedicated to her.

Another dimension of Our Blessed Mother's influence in the life of Fulton Sheen was the measure in which she allowed him to share her Son's suffering. He had always believed he received fewer blows than he deserved; at the same time, if Christ desired His Mother's participation in the Passion, why should any Christian be exempt from the same?

> When I had my open heart surgery, only gradually did it dawn on me during my first four months in the hospital, that the Blessed Mother not only gives sweets, but she also gives bitter medicine. Too striking to be missed was that on three feast days of Our Lady I was brought to the door of death, and endured great suffering. The first was the feast of Our Lady of Mount Carmel, July 16, when the doctors stayed with me all day and night trying to preserve the small flickering spark of life. Then came another operation on the Feast of her Assumption, August 15, and the implanting of a pacemaker. By this time I was beginning to feel a kind of holy dread of what might happen on September 8, when the Church celebrates her birthday. Sure enough, a kidney infection developed which, over a period of several weeks, made me feel some new tortures. As I reflected on this concomitance of the Church festivals of Mary and my enforced solidarity with the Cross, I took it as a sign of the special predilection of Mary. If the Lord called her who "deserved" no pain to stand at the foot of the Cross, why should He not call me? If I had expressed a love for her as the Mother of the Priesthood, why should she not, in maternal love, make me more like her Son by forcing me to become a victim?[25]

One could find few priestly examples in our age who more closely resembled Mary's Son, and it was surely through the intercession of that Mother of Priests that Fulton Sheen reflected the life of Christ in the measure he did. Those who listened to him on radio or television, those who heard him preach in person or who read his books, remember his frequent recitation of Mary Dixon Thayer's poem "Lovely Lady Dressed in Blue."

The cadences of his voice were not merely theatrical; they were expressive of the Mother to whom he had such deep recourse. He once told the story of George Bernard Shaw, the Irish playwright, known for his inability to believe in the Divinity of Christ. He once confided to a Mother Superior in Dublin his belief that Christ's Mother will "see me through."

> Shaw put his finger on the sublime truth that those who are not yet ready to accept Christ as the Mediator between God and man, will come to that truth through Mary who will act as the mediatrix between widowed souls and Christ. As Our Lady of Equity she gives hope to man who would otherwise be hopeless.[26]

During his years as a member of the American hierarchy, Fulton Sheen and his brother bishops produced a pastoral letter on Our Lady for Catholics in the United States, titled "To Him She Leads." Could any title be more expressive of all Archbishop Sheen had written on her?

Chapter Nine

MARRIAGE

Archbishop Sheen wrote a great deal on the topics of marriage and courtship, love and sexuality. It is regrettable he was unable to see the full ramifications of the sexual revolution in the 21st century for his insights would have been tremendous. The breakdown of family life, cohabitation, abortion, and all the many effects wrought on the Church traceable to 1968's dissent of Pope Paul VI's magnificent defense of human life, *Humanae Vitae*, were all in embryonic stages when the Archbishop died in 1979. The insights he offered in many of these areas in earlier decades are, however, very beneficial to understanding how today's problems emerged, as well as shedding light on the past.

As early as 1931, Sheen was critical of those who took "advanced" views on morality; those who felt humanity had progressed so far that a more "modern" approach was in keeping with contemporary man.

> When one has read one book on morals by any "new" thinker of our day, he has read them all. Two dominant ideas run through each of them: the first is the decay of old traditions through the advance of modern culture; the second is a plea for a new morality suitable to the way men live today. The first argument is generally

couched in some such language as this: "We do not live in a patriarchal society. We do not live in a world that disposes us to believe in a theocratic government. And therefore insofar as moral wisdom is entangled with the promises of a theocracy, it is unreal to me. It is the unconscious assumption that we are related to God as creatures to a creator, as vassals to a king, as children to a father that the acids of modernity have eaten away." Men no longer believe seriously that they are governed from Heaven, and anarchy will result from all this confusion unless by conscious effort they find ways of governing themselves. The second part of these books is generally consecrated to the elevation of Humanism to a system of morals. Starting from the premise that the history of every man is a history of his progress from infantilism to maturity, they conclude that a goal for moral effort can be found in the notion of maturity. "To replace the conception of man as the subject of a heavenly king, which dominates the ancestral order of life, humanism takes as its dominant pattern the progress of the individual from helpless infancy to self-governing maturity." Maturity, then, is the goal of morals, and a successful passage from childhood to maturity means a breaking up and reconstruction of those habits which were appropriate only to our earliest experience.[1]

This is one of many observations about society that prove it was receptive to "advances" in thinking, especially on sexual morality. Sheen gave much concentration to the effects of Sigmund Freud, though he did not assign Freud blame for making the culture the way it was. There was an openness in the 19th century that would not have been present in the 13th, for example, or at other times in history. There had to be a "materialist preparation for sexism"; Freud was simply the expression of what was already present in society. "Far from being the founder of an age," the

Bishop wrote, "he was its postscript."[2] The question then followed, how did society come to enshrine sex?

> The principal reason for sex deification is loss of belief in God. Once people lose God, they lose the purpose of life; and when the purpose of living is forgotten, the universe becomes meaningless. Man then tries to forget his emptiness in the intensity of a momentary experience. This effort sometimes goes so far that he makes someone else's flesh a god; there are idolatry and adoration, which eventually end in disillusionment when the so called "angel" is discovered to be only a fallen angel and one of no great attraction.[3]

Several other reasons accounted for society's sexual preoccupation. Many people live with such fantasies to escape the real burdens of life, as well as fleeing the guilt of an uneasy conscience. Once God has become irrelevant to them, anything becomes permissible, and their consciences, once guilty, become deadened. If this is true at the level of persons, families are next, and with family breakdown, the very real possibility for social anarchy exists.

Another reason accounting for the primacy of sex is the denial of immortality. The eternity for which all human beings were made becomes unimportant or non-existent, and the present moment, with all its pleasures, becomes the only important thing in life. The vocation of the family is once again denied as a hindrance to individual pleasure, though even in the pursuit of that pleasure, the person lives in continuous fear of death, and what it might imply. On the other hand, the person who lives with a view to the unending reality for which all were created, and who subscribes to the moral law during earthly life, has the advantage of being happy in this life while he prepares for the best which is yet to come.

Yet another reason for sex's dominance is the denial of a

rational soul. This is somewhat related to a denial of immortality, since the soul, the life-giving principle in man, is our first entry into everlasting life, where our flesh will ultimately be reunited. Once the soul is denied, human instinct takes over as the determining factor in moral behavior. Bishop Sheen noted the tragedy of modernity "is not that human beings give way more often in their passions now than in previous ages, but that, in leaving the right road, they deny that there is a right road."[4] All of this is the result of Original Sin, something rarely if ever thought of. Man is not inherently corrupt, but his will has been weakened; he is often prone to be governed by emotions rather than by reason. There is a basic restlessness in him, which, though he often does not know it, is a desire for God. This manifests itself in a restlessness continually seeking perfection; through knowledge, through generation or through economic security. There is a validity in all of these; when any one of them begins to dominate, disorder will result.

The sex instinct, therefore, good in itself, can become perverted. Bishop Sheen often used the example of the ancient Romans at a banquet, who would eat excessive amounts of food, excuse themselves from table, tickle their throats, disgorge the food, and return to the banquet to continue feasting. This was a contradiction of reason that tells us one eats to live, not the opposite; when the pleasure is separated from its function, it ceases to be a pleasure in the right sense. "When the fires of life are aroused deliberately," Sheen wrote, "not to light new torches of life, but to scorch the flesh, there is the sin of lust."[5]

The interesting fact is, whenever the Church calls this to the attention of modern man, it is accused of being opposed to sex. Sheen found this difficult to understand, since the Church never minimized the human body; it dignified it. Church teaching clearly points to this: in the teaching of Clement of Alexandria who wrote that man should never be ashamed to mention what God was not ashamed to create; or Saint Thomas Aquinas who taught there was more pleasure in marriage before the fall because there was more peace and harmony in man's soul; or Saint Augustine who often wrote about the goodness of the flesh, noting that "the flesh is good, but to leave the creator and to live according to this created good is mischief."[6]

There is nothing new, therefore, in the Church being ridiculed for her teaching on the correct use of the gift of sexuality. Such criticism takes a variety of forms, such as the expression "sex is nothing to be ashamed of." That is correct; it is a gift of God to be used according to His purposes. If carnal license is being described in this phrase, the statement is very wrong. Another popular slogan is that we must be "self-expressive." If we are striving to perfect our personalities, it's true; if we're giving free rein to every sexual instinct our fantasy can think up, once again popular sentiment is wrong. Finally there is the belief that God would not have given us this gift, would not have made us the way He did, if He did not intend us to use the gift of our sexuality. True, to be sure, provided the gift is channeled in the divinely planned fashion. Bishop Sheen did admit some agreement with the complaints of those who say that Church teaching on sexuality tended to be negative; a list of don'ts. It is regrettable he did not live to study the *Theology of the Body* given the world by Pope John Paul II, in which Church teaching is presented to modern men and women just as clearly, though from a different, and very convincing perspective.

Sheen may have been a trend setter in the positive manner in which he approached the virtue of purity, describing it as "reverence paid to the mystery of sex." He stressed that sex is both known and unknown; it is known in the sense that we are all male or female; it is unknown in its creativeness, its sharing in some mysterious way in the creative power of God. God gave married couples the tremendous privilege of being co-creators, of sharing in the mystery of creation through their human instrumentality. He noted that most bodily functions are involuntary and unconscious – they go on independent of our will. The act of creation, though, is very free, and corresponds to the Creator's command to increase and multiply. Pagan peoples believed in this great gift humans had to create, and they felt it should be surrounded by some type of religious sanction. In the Christian understanding, said Sheen, men and women supply the flesh, and God supplies the mystery. For this reason, something so profound may not be trivialized by being used outside of marriage

> ...certain powers are to be used only in certain relation-ships. What is lawful in one relationship is not lawful in another. A man may kill another soldier in a just war, but not in his private capacity as a citizen. A policeman can arrest someone as a duly appointed guardian of the law fortified with a warrant. The creativeness of man and woman is lawful under a relationship sanctioned by God called marriage. Purity will never separate the two. The things which God has joined together will not be separated.[7]

Purity is far from the virginal intactness of bride and groom on the day of their wedding. It is the steadfast act of the will on the part of man and woman to wait until their vocation as husband and wife is actualized. Purity is something which begins in the will, and is carried out with determination, and especially with God's help. Such help we know as sanctifying grace, and to all who sincerely pray for it, the Lord is never outdone in generos-ity. Bishop Sheen further described purity as the "sacristan and guardian of love," and said that life only becomes impure when our wills are impure. Just as one would not want to see the Ameri-can flag trampled on, because the external appearance of the flag symbolizes the much deeper meaning of our country's greatness, so when purity is trampled on, the reverent is made irreverent, it is a "turning of the inner mystery into a jest."

Suppose a director of an orchestra becomes very conscious of his hands, focusing on how he is going to
hold the baton. Do you think it is going to have an
effect upon the music? Suppose he concentrates on the
music, the orchestra, and the production of harmony.
Everything fits into place. He is unconscious of the
hand. When sex becomes a part of love and the purpose of life, it is a dedication and fits into the whole.
Sex is not something isolated from life. Self-control is
subordination of a part to the whole to serve a higher
enthusiasm. Purity properly understood matches love
and the sex instinct.[8]

As Bishop Sheen expressed it, sex is integrated into the totality of the love experience. It is a visible manifestation of love, but
love itself is something much broader and deeper. To be understood properly, love must be seen from two perspectives: the one
who loves and the one who is loved. There is a reciprocity to love;
I love and I am loved. Between these two there is a bond, hence
men and women can speak of our love, "a bond that enchains
and an embrace wherein two hearts leap with but a single joy."[9]
Sheen often said it takes three to make love, because what binds
lover and beloved is an outside force; it is impossible to understand
love without God.

There is much more of the Divine in love than those
in love know. First of all, they always speak of "our"
love. "Our" love is more than the sum of the love of
each. It is a reference to something outside themselves
of which they say: "This thing is stronger than we are."
What is this love that is outside of them which pulls
them together, except a reflection of that mysterious
cycle of love in the very Heart of God. So long as the
Divine is kept in marriage, there will never be cynicism.
Every man will know that every woman promises him

something that only the Divine can bestow. True love is really Divine Love on pilgrimage.[10]

The failure to see God in any love relationship dooms it from the start. Love of the self without love of God is selfishness; love of neighbor without love of God is merely loving those we choose, those who are pleasing to us. "One cannot tie two sticks together without something outside the sticks," the Bishop said. "One cannot bind the nations of the world together except by the recognition of a Law and a Person outside the nations themselves."[11] Duality in love Sheen described as "extinction through the exhaustion of self-giving." Love must be Triune, it must be God contained, and God centered, or it dies.

> It requires three virtues, faith, hope, and charity, which intertwine, purify, and regenerate each other. To believe in God is to throw ourselves into His arms; to hope in Him is to rest in His heart in patience amidst trials and tribulations; to love Him is to be with Him through a participation of His Divine nature through grace. If love did not have faith and trust, it would die; if love did not have hope, its sufferings would be torture, and love might seem loveless. Love of self, love of neighbor, and love of God go together and when separated fall apart.[12]

This love finds its fullest expression between a man and woman in the Sacrament of Matrimony. Sheen told a class of future Catholics the Church understood this sacrament as an "unbreakable bond until death," and two decades after he gave this series of instructions in the faith, he would be describing life as filled with "unfinished symphonies": chalices left behind in sacristies, and marriages not lived out until death do them part. In the years following the Second Vatican Council, with theological tensions brewing, and a cultural revolution with a life of its own, society had greatly minimized the idea of permanent commitment. In the 1950's, Sheen said there was "one divorce for every 2.3 marriages, and remarriages after such divorces,"[13] in the United States. Such figures are extraordinarily mild contrasted with the early years of the twenty-first century.

The Bishop was clear that divorce was not something prohibited to Catholics, but to everyone "whether he is Tibetan, Muslim, Hottentot, or Christian." This was so, because marriage is a union, not a contract. A judge may grant a civil decree of divorce attesting that a couple is no longer married in the eyes of the State, but God looks upon such couples as "fragments of a joint personality, like a babe cut in two."[14] Love, said Sheen, had only two words in its vocabulary, you and always: you, because it is unique, and always, because it is enduring. A man never said to a woman that he would love her for two and one half years, after which his love would cease.

Likewise, all love songs have an idea of permanence about them; they portray love as eternal, made in heaven, lasting forever. In one sense, they mirror the Divine.

> When the Son of God came to this earth and took upon Himself a human nature, which flowered into His Mystical Body, the Church, He did not take it for three years, but for all eternity! A husband takes a wife as Christ took the Church until death does him part. To symbolize the enduring union of espousals between Christ and His Church, they are to love one another until separated by death.[15]

Whenever two baptized persons marry, they are symbolizing another marriage, between God and His people. This idea is traceable to the Old Testament, where God spoke to His people in a covenant relationship, through His prophets, who describe God's closeness in terms of the closeness of married love. God was the Bridegroom, the husband of Israel, one who was always true, and who loved His people deeply, no matter how unfaithful they might be. In the course of time, the Incarnate Son of God came into the world, and would describe Himself in similar terms. He was once asked why His disciples did not fast in the same way as those of John the Baptist, and He replied that people do not fast while the bridegroom is with them, but only when he has been taken away.

> I think that there is beautiful mystery hidden in the marriage feast of Cana. Our Lord began His public life by assisting at the marriage feast, showing His relationship with His Church could be exactly like the relationship unfolded in the Old Testament. The old *qahal* of Israel became the new Church, or the new Israel. Through redemption and Pentecost, we had continuation of this symbolism. Eve was the continuation of man, bone of his bone, flesh of his flesh. The continuation of the new Adam is Christ. A human marriage is like the union of our Lord and the Church. When the bridegroom and bride stand at the altar, we read the marriage ceremony informing them: "You, the bridegroom stand for Christ, and you, the bride, stand for the Church."[16]

Bishop Sheen also took from this symbolism the fact that there was only one Church; it is impossible to think of Our Lord having several brides; that would be "spiritual adultery." Christ has only one spouse, and it is a union that continues forever, and just as there is fidelity in that relationship, so too with husband and wife. Describing fidelity as an "eternal engagement with the future," one could not escape the fact that as Christ's love is never withdrawn from His Church, so with spousal love. Beautiful a symbol as this may be, its daily living presents a challenge.

There is a natural order and a supernatural order. We live in the order of the human and the divine. In addition to physical life, there is supernatural life which is grace. Our intellects are illumined with faith and our wills are strengthened with power in the divine nature. Our blessed Lord makes marriage a sacrament. To those who are united in His Church, He gives grace, strength, and power to live out their mutual existence. Every sacrament has two elements. The visible is the exchange of consent signified by the joining of hands and witnessed by a priest. Invisible grace is communicated for their married state.[17]

Much cooperation with God's grace is needed to live out the vocation to marriage, as it is in every calling. Couples often encounter situations after marriage which were totally unseen during the courtship. Some even discover another person from the one they married. Great maturity is needed, and exceedingly careful preparation should accompany growing in love. In an era before cohabitation became the norm, many young couples simply married too young. At least their objective situation before God was infinitely better than those who simply decide they will live together, possibly getting married, possibly not. Even in the case of early marriage, however, Sheen saw difficulties. He felt that going steady and marrying in the teenage years was very much like buying a home with only the foundation laid; one does not know how many stories there will be, nor the size of each room, nor the arrangement of the floors, "In marrying young, one does not make a choice of another partner; one just falls into a habit."[18]

It was not only those who married young who often made a mistake; there was what the Bishop described as an "aloneness together" in couples married for years. In such cases, husband and wife seem to get no closer than "two ships colliding in a harbor." The reason was that the other person was made an idol;

the man was considered a god, while the woman was looked on as a goddess, able to provide an unending ecstasy of love. This is a mistaken notion, failing to see that no finite creature can ever satisfy infinitely. "He who forgets the body is a vestment of the immortal soul is destined to boredom."[19]

This is also related to possession. Many will marry looking for happiness, believing it will be found in the possession of another. Sheen likened this to buying a new car; one is pleased with it at first, but after six months, the particulars of the body of the car, so important at the outset, are hardly noticed. To marry someone with the idea of possessing him or her is to deprive the loved one of liberty. "If that other person is mine like a cocktail, then he or she can never make a present of himself or herself."[20]

A maturity has to be present that distinguishes between knowing and loving, both objects of the will. We are all like animals in that we have sensations and passions, but knowing and loving are uniquely human. Sheen spoke of our intellects and wills operating in very different ways; when the intellect knows something, it will bring itself down to the level of the object known; on the other hand, the will always goes beyond itself to meet the object loved. For example, if a person loves music, he or she will become accommodated to its scales and harmonies. Or, if you love a foreign language, you will adapt yourself to its laws of grammar and syntax. In much the same way, if a person is truly loved by another, each will go out of him or herself to meet the other. There were, said the Bishop, significant differences between men and women in terms of knowing and loving; men are concerned principally with things, women with persons. A man will always give reasons for loving, but a woman, because she loves totally, needs no particulars – she gives the totality of herself, and hence is slower to love than a man. Finally, defects often get in the way of a man's loving, but a woman, because the totality of her being is involved, allows for no roadblocks whatever.

These differences, instead of being opposites, are actually in a marriage correlated. Man is like the roots of a plant; woman is more like the blossom that bears the fruit. One is in communion with the earth and business; the other with the sky and life. One is related to time, the other to eternity. The fusion of both is the prolongation into the home of the Incarnation where eternity became time and the word became flesh, and the divine became human in the person of Christ. Differences are not irreconcilable; rather, they are complementary qualities.[21]

Television audiences in the 1950's listened to Sheen speak of the "three tensions of love": unity and separateness, the personal versus the social, and human longing contrasted with satiety. In the first case, each human being is composed of matter and spirit; one person is not able to be united completely with another because "matter is the basis of impenetrability or division; spirit is the basis of unity."[22] We come close to unity because of our spirit, but the ideal unity sought by "body-love" is never an abiding or permanent part of life. On the personal-social aspect: personal is the deliberate will toward mutual love; social is "automatic, and of a reflex nature, which, to some extent, is outside personal control."[23] Finally, human beings feel an interior tug of war – between being loved too little and being loved too much. They want human affection, and they do not want it. This tension might be likened to a young boy asking his mother for a third dish of ice cream; on finding the little fellow could not finish it she exclaimed "See! Too much ice cream!" to which the youngster replied, "No, not enough boy."[24]

Problems will arise and must be dealt with. What is to be done when the husband becomes an alcoholic, or unfaithful, or the wife a spendthrift? The answer was very simple: "Stick it out! Remain faithful!" Very different advice than one finds in the twenty-first century. But Sheen had a definite rationale; suppose that same husband, instead of being an alcoholic, had pneumonia. Is it not likely the same wife would nurse him and care for him? Giving in to the sin of alcoholism is a form of "moral pneumonia," and must be treated accordingly.

> A young German girl, at the close of the last World War, who was very learned and had read Homer at seventeen, was courted by one of our American GIs in Berlin. She married him, and they came to this country where she discovered that he wanted only to read Western stories while frequenting saloons and refused to work. While supporting both of them, she wrote to me saying, "I was thinking of divorce, but I know that if I divorce him, I am contributing to the ruin of civilization. It does not mean very much if I pull my own individual finger out of that dam; just a little water will come through. But if every woman in the world in a similar position does the same, then the floodtides will sweep over the world. So I am going to stick it out; but I cannot do so without faith, and you must help me to get it." We gave her instructions, and God gave her the gift of faith. The husband is now an officer in the army, a different kind of man, and both are raising a fine family.[25]

Sheen did not deny for a moment that a marriage could be living hell, but he said the person who is faithful and remains has the great peace of knowing he or she has not been deprived of honor or fidelity. Why, the Bishop queried, should we expect our American soldiers to be faithful to their country on the battle-fields, in the midst of one war after another, and think it perfectly alright for a husband or wife to up and leave as soon as the going gets tough in marriage? Further, it isn't so much the trials and sufferings that come to men and women in married life that make the union unbearable. It is how they react to those trials and sufferings. If they are seen as depriving a spouse of pleasure and the cultivation of the ego, etc., then the marriage is headed to ruin. If, however, such are viewed as sent from God for the accomplishment of some higher good, they are a cause for inner joy in the knowledge a person is sanctifying him or herself.

> If you object and say, "God never intended that anyone should live under such difficulties." The answer is flatly, "Oh yes He does!" Our blessed Lord said, "If any man has a mind to come my way let him renounce himself, take up his cross and follow Me. The man who tries to save his life shall lose it. It is the man who loses his life for my sake who will secure it." We would all like to have tailor made crosses. We are very willing to take on the mortification and self-denial which we choose, but when God chooses it, then we say, "Oh no, I cannot take that cross!"[26]

To many in today's contemporary society, this sort of approach would sound rather foreign. We are not living in times of sacrifice, or in times that place great stress on permanent commitments. There is no question that very real problems arise in married life, and in many instances the Church must take a pastoral approach. On the other hand, one cannot escape the thought a certain Bishop expressed some years ago, when he commented how interesting it will be getting to heaven and seeing how many annulments were granted invalidly! In other words, much needs to be done to impress on our Catholic faithful the permanence of the marriage bond and the seriousness with which that must be taken by both parties. When Archbishop Sheen used the seemingly incredible example of no one ever saying, "I will love you for two years and six months," little did he think society was moving in precisely that direction. He would be greatly dismayed with today's cultural idea of man and woman, and many in today's society would do well to meditate on his words which were challenging, to be sure; but he would also take heart at some of the wonderful movements like Married and Engaged Encounter that have been gaining popularity in recent years. He understood well the basic natures.

> There can never be a giver without a gift. Man is generally the giver, woman the gift. The man has, the woman is. Man has a sentiment; woman is sentiment. Man is afraid of dying; woman is afraid of not living. She is unhappy unless she makes the double gift: first of herself to man, and then of herself to posterity, in the form of children. This quality of immolation, because it involves the wholeness of self, makes a woman seem less heroic than a man. The man concentrates his passions of love into great focal points.... The woman, however, identifies love with existence, and scatters her self-oblation through life.... It may well be that the woman is capable of greater sacrifice than man, not only because she is gift, which is the same as surrender, but also because she sees ends rather than means, and destinies rather than the present, she sees the pearl of great price for which lesser fields may be sacrificed.[27]

Few Popes of the 20th century will be better remembered for their defense of human life than Paul VI. When his encyclical *Humanae Vitae* was issued in July, 1968, he seemed to be a lone crier. Much like Saint Athanasius, centuries earlier, Paul was *"contra mundum."* The Holy Father had commissioned a preparatory theological commission some years earlier to study the question and submit their report to him. This committee looked into the problems modern Catholics supposedly had in living up to Church teaching, as well as the "threat" of overpopulation that certain protagonists advanced, a concern one rarely hears in the 21st century. As a result of these influences, the Pope was advised that some modification in Church teaching was called for, so that modern men and women would not be lost to the Church. It appears, also, that for some time prior to the issuance of the encyclical, many individual Catholics were making up their own minds on the question, and practicing contraception. Worse yet, some confessors were giving advice in the confessional that the use of contraception, given the particular circumstance of the couple, was legitimate. This misdirected pastoral sensitivity is a study in itself, and it was something that would continue in the Church for decades.

When the Holy Father, under the inspiration of the Holy Spirit, made his decision and issued his letter, the outcry surprised many with its highly vocal and bitter character. Individual hierarchies of Bishops, that is national Bishops' Conferences, refused to give wholehearted support, and some even expressed disagreement. Seminaries became infested with professors and spiritual mentors whose advice to seminarians studying for the priesthood was anything but supportive of Church teaching. Sermons were rarely, if ever preached in defense of the Church's well reasoned and divinely guided position, and subsequent generations of young people were to grow up in a world that told them contraception was the correct way to live, and in a period of Church history where they never heard it was wrong. Catholic families became much smaller, and the influence of Church teaching practically non-existent.

This was a far cry from the years in which Fulton Sheen did much of his writing and teaching in moral areas. As a young priest, he would have well remembered a decision made by the Bishops of the Anglican Church at their Lambeth Conference in the 1930's, in which they permitted the limited use of contraception in certain cases. This is always seen as Christianity's capitulation to modernity, since every Protestant denomination quickly followed suit, letting individual conscience be the determining factor. The early 20th century years in which Fulton Sheen was growing up in

Illinois were still a period when the entire Christian consciousness looked askance at birth control.

Thus, America's most popular Catholic preacher addressed contraception according to the background of his time, focusing, among other things, on those who stress the "primacy of the economic," saying that having too many children was simply too costly, strained family resources, and deprived couples of needed priorities. Applying the principle, Sheen asked: "Suppose a husband says that he can no longer support his wife. Should he be entitled to shoot her?"

> To the extent we put ourselves outside the environment and area of God's love we exclude Divine assistance that would otherwise come to us. Those who put the primacy on the economic are really not interested in saving or earning; they are interested in spending which dictates the frustration of life.[28]

Whenever Fulton Sheen gave convert instruction classes, he was interacting with many whose backgrounds would undoubtedly be tolerant of contraception. On one occasion, he stressed that real love in marriage creates the deepest kind of unity, and such depth of love tends, by its very nature, to an incarnation. Turning to Scripture, he showed significant passages where the verb "to know" indicates love. The Book of Genesis states that Adam had "knowledge" of Eve, and Saint Paul encouraged all men to possess their wives "in knowledge." Marriage is spoken of as knowledge because one of the closest forms of unity to be found in the natural order comes from knowledge. The sort of unity between the knower and the thing known is like that of husband and wife. Their love is a sort of knowledge, and the fruit of that knowledge is always directed to generation. At the same time the knowledge produces unity, it also demands fidelity. As one must be faithful to a specific academic discipline in order to master it, so the knowledge love of marriage is not one that can be walked away from.

> The power of generation is a gift from above. The motive power of begetting children is in the Trinity and in the Incarnation because all love ends in an incarnation, even God's. God so loved man, He became enfleshed in the human nature. What is our blessed Lord but God's love incarnate, God's love walking this earth in the form and habit of man. You see how beautiful love is? If one could give a definition of love in the light of the Trinity and the Incarnation it might be that love is mutual self-giving which ends in self-recovery.[29]

There was another way of looking at the question, and Bishop Sheen did so on television in the 1950's. He devoted a program to considering whether children were burdens or joys. It is no surprise that his solution was the latter, but for very interesting reasons. Children rescue love from boredom. When only two are loving, there is a danger that their relationship can degenerate into an "exchange of egotisms, like two shipwrecked sailors on an island supporting themselves by taking in each other's laundry."[30] Children are really the bond of love holding father and mother together. They prevent love from hitting bottom; they rescue it from barrenness. Also, they are a sort of "resurrection of beauty and strength." The approach was somewhat novel; the point was, many men and women felt their distinguishing characteristics, beauty and strength, will last forever. The physical makeup which initially attracted marriage partners wears away with age; children are their progeny, the strength and beauty of a once young husband and wife endures in their children, and for that matter, in their grandchildren. Sheen did not mean to suggest one should become conceited with his or her appearance; rather, the positive, beautiful qualities of both partners will perdure.

Finally, children reveal the mystery of fatherhood and motherhood. The child makes the husband a father, and fatherhood is a mirroring of the Divine paternity from which all blessings flow. Children also make the wife a mother, and here, Sheen was especially profound.

> Man more commonly cooperates with nature, but a woman cooperates with God; she is the bearer of the gift of God to man. The word of woman is "Fiat," submission, surrender, cooperation with life. A woman's unhappiest moment is when she is unable to give; there is hell within when she refuses to give. Bearer of the cosmic plentitude, she fulfills her mission when she brings a child into the world. Looking down at the babe, a new paradox is revealed: it is the only time self can be loved without selfishness. A mother now loves a non-self in herself as her body becomes the ciborium of the new life, and her arms become its bearer as she passes on culture to ages yet unborn.[31]

The question of abortion burst on the national scene in the United States following the rendering of the Supreme Court's decision in Roe vs. Wade in January, 1973. It is an interesting fact of American culture that giving something legality seems to bestow approval in the public mind. In years prior to 1973, Americans opposed abortion in overwhelming numbers. Not too many years before Roe, the word "abortion" could not be mentioned on television; a hint might be given in the script of a program, but was never vocalized. Archbishop Sheen spent most of his priesthood in a vastly different culture, though he lived six years after America's fateful turnaround, and had opportunity to preach against the horrible destruction of human life that had begun.

At a Right to Life Mass in the National Shrine of the Immaculate Conception in Washington, D.C. in the mid-1970's,

Sheen said that abortion was based on two false philosophies: a misunderstanding of freedom, and a misunderstanding of love. Freedom is not a right to do as one pleases, but as one ought. A selfish ego will deny all limits, and when the ego becomes supreme, abortion naturally follows. Secondly, love is misunderstood, because it is equated solely with sex, and if this is so, it makes little difference who the other person is, or what the relationship results in. True love, on the contrary, is reciprocal; it involves persons, and demands responsibility. America in the 1970's, said Sheen, was divided into two classes: lovers of life, or biophilics; and lovers of death, or necrophilics. In Victorian England, sex was taboo; in 20th century America, death is taboo; hence, women are described as carrying a fetus, or terminating a pregnancy. If one wears a rose on his lapel, eyebrows are raised in polite society.

The Archbishop noted that on any given day (in the 1970's), there was a killing by abortion every twenty seconds in the United States, and in any given year (of that decade), five out of every ten children born in New York City were murdered in wombs. These dismal statistics were balanced, however, by stories of heroism the Archbishop was fond of telling, of mothers who did not "terminate pregnancies" at various periods of history. Beethoven's mother was one; how much the world would be deprived, had his birth never occurred.

Such, then, were some of Fulton Sheen's contributions to the question of marriage. He seemed to see married life as a reflection of the love of Mary and Joseph, and family life as a reflection of the Holy Family. These thoughts are not simply applicable to the great period of Catholic faith Archbishop Sheen knew so well, but are valid for every age. Every couple is to see in Our Lady and Saint Joseph the model of what a marriage can and must be. While none are called to live the unique circumstances of Christ's Mother and foster father, all are called to model their self-surrender on the example that they set.

How much more beautiful Mary and Joseph become when we see in their lives what might be called the first Divine Romance! No human heart is moved by the love of the old for the young, but who is not moved by the love of the young for the young, when their bond is the Ancient of Days, Who is God? In both Mary and Joseph there was youth, beauty, and promise. God loves cascading cataracts and bellowing waterfalls, but He loves them better, not when they overflow and drown His flowers, but when they are harnessed and bridled to light a city and to slake the thirst of a child. In Joseph and Mary we do not find one controlled waterfall and one dried up lake, but rather two youths who, before they knew the beauty of the one and the handsome strength of the other, willed to surrender these things for Jesus.[32]

Chapter Ten

EUCHARIST AND PRIESTHOOD

Our Lord's most precious gift of Himself, the Holy Eucharist, is inseparably linked with His institution of the Sacrament of Holy Orders; without the priesthood, Christ's Body, Blood, Soul and Divinity, His real presence in our midst would cease. It is appropriate, then, that our final consideration of Archbishop Fulton Sheen's spiritual legacy, develop these two topics. The Archbishop wrote extensively on them, was deeply devoted to a daily holy hour in Our Lord's Eucharistic presence, and lived six decades of the most exemplary priesthood.

His teaching on the Eucharist is best begun by his comparing this sacrament with the others.

> The Eucharist is the greatest of all the sacraments because it contains in a substantial way the person of Christ, the Author of life. It is the one sacrament to which all of the other sacraments look. Imagine six arrows in a circle all pointing to a center. The center is the Eucharist; the six arrows are the other sacraments. The Eucharist is the sun around which the other sacraments revolve as planets. All other sacraments share in its power and they perfect themselves in the celebration of the Eucharist. It is a sublime sacrament that human

reason could never guess. Divine love is far deeper than we know.[1]

Our Lord's formal institution of the Eucharist at the Last Supper was foreshadowed by the Heavenly Father's gift of Manna for His chosen people as they traversed through the desert to the Promised Land; it was predicted often in the pages of the New Testament, especially in the account of the multiplication of the loaves and fishes. Christ saw thousands traveling in a Passover caravan to the city of Jerusalem, making their way in small groups, many exhausted by the long journey. He took pity on them, and, as Scripture relates, took five barley loaves and two fishes, and fed the huge multitude. While many were grateful, and followed after Him, others were expecting a bread king, that is, a savior who would not only satisfy their natural cravings, but also politically liberate them from the yoke of the Roman Empire. To such, Our Lord was a disappointment, including one future priest, who, according to Bishop Sheen, had already begun to weaken.

> This flight from political kingship might have disillusioned Judas. Do you know the first record we have of the fall of Judas takes place when Our Blessed Lord announces and promises the Eucharist? The fall of Judas comes when Our Blessed Lord gives the Eucharist at the Last Supper. It was the Eucharist that disillusioned Judas. Judas knew Our Lord was not going to be an economic king.[2]

The next day, at Capernaum, Our Lord begins to discourse on working not for food that perishes, but for that which lasts for eternity, the sort of food the Son of Man would give them. They were very skeptical, wondered if Christ were setting Himself up as greater than Moses; after all, Our Lord had fed the multitude only once, while Moses had supplied the Manna from heaven for many years. In replying that He was the Bread of Life…

He makes the shadow of the Cross appear. Bread must be broken. He who came from God must die on the Cross as a result of the sins of the world. These are His words: "And now, what is this bread which I am to give? It is my flesh given for the life of the world." ... Notice He is picturing Himself as one who gives Himself in death. The flesh and blood He will give them is not just that flesh and blood they see; it will be the flesh and blood that will be ascended into heaven at the right hand of the Father. He said He would give it for the world.[3]

Writing in his masterful *Life of Christ*, Sheen gives more explicit detail:

He was setting two kinds of bread before them: the bread that could perish, and the bread that could endure unto life everlasting. He cautioned them against following Him as a donkey following the master who holds a carrot. To lift their carnal minds to eternal Food, He suggested that they seek the heavenly bread the Father authorized or sealed. Oriental bread was often sealed with the official mark or name of the baker. In fact, the Talmudic word for "baker" is related to the word "seal." As hosts used in the Mass have a seal upon them (such as a lamb, or a cross), so Our Lord was implying that the Bread they should seek was the Bread affirmed by His Father, therefore Himself.[4]

Our Lord not only pictured Himself as the One who had come down from heaven, but also as the One who had come into this world specifically to die. It would only be through His death on the Cross that His followers would be able to see the significance of the Bread that would give them eternal life. When He spoke of the Bread which He was to give, His choice of a verb was not coincidental. Giving referred to the sacrificial action of Calvary, and His Flesh and Blood, separated on the Cross, would be the source of eternal life for all who followed Him. When He referred to giving His Flesh for the life of the world, He referred to the human flesh He had assumed from His Mother at the Incarnation; it was only because that human flesh was hypostatically linked to a Divine nature, that His Body and Blood could be spiritually life-giving. Sheen sums up this very beautiful scene of John's Gospel poignantly:

> How carnal was the eating of the manna, and how spiritual was the eating of the flesh of Christ! It was a far more intimate living by Him than a baby's living by the nourishment supplied by the mother. Every mother to every child at her breast can say, "Eat, this is my body; this is my blood." But actually the comparison ends there; for in the mother-child relationship, both are on the same level. In the Christ-human relationship, the difference is that of God and man, heaven and earth. Further, no mother ever has to die and take on a more glorious existence in her human nature before she can be the nourishment of her offspring. But Our Lord said that He would have to "give" His life, before He would be the Bread of life to believers.[5]

Since Our Lord was the only one in human history who came into the world to die, it was fitting there be a memorial commemorating that death. What is most significant, is that this particular death would not be left, as Sheen often put it, "to the chance recollection of men." Christ at the Last Supper instituted a New Covenant, one which brought the Old Covenant to fruition. A covenant is an agreement, or compact, and in Old Testament times, it was made by God with His chosen people. God promised His many blessings if Israel remained faithful, but much of her history is a record of human unfaithfulness. Abraham was the first to receive the Covenant, and to him God guaranteed the gift of progeny; to David, the promise of kingship; and to Moses, deliverance from bondage in Egypt and the promise that Israel would be, for Him, a kingdom of priests. When the Jews were in Egyptian captivity, Moses received instructions for a new ritual. God struck the Egyptians by smiting the firstborn of every household; the Jews were to save themselves by offering a lamb, and sprinkling the blood of the lamb over their doorposts. When the avenging angel "passed over" the land, those doorposts so designated would be spared, and those spared would make the journey to the Promised Land. The Book of Exodus speaks of the sacrifice of the Paschal lamb, after which God initiated the covenant with Moses making Israel a nation. Such agreement was ratified by numerous sacrifices on the part of the people, especially by Moses erecting an altar with twelve pillars. He took the blood of sacrifice, applied half of it to the altar, and the other half to the people, with a specific prayer. By doing so, Moses was symbolically stating that both God and His chosen people were brought into a special sacramental union. The prophets would later testify that the exile of the Israelite people was the result of their infidelity, but the God who loved them, and was always faithful, brought them back again to His loving embrace. It is against this background that Our Lord instituted the New Dispensation. We have no reason to believe that the twelve Apostles, entering the Upper Room with Our Lord on that Holy Thursday evening, thought they were doing anything more than celebrating the Passover supper with the Rabbi.

> The Last Supper and the Crucifixion took place during the Passover, when the Eternal Son of the Father mediated a New Testament or Covenant, as the Old Testament or Covenant was mediated through Moses. As Moses ratified the Old Testament with the blood of animals, so Christ now ratified the New Testament with His own Blood. He now instituted for His

Apostles and posterity a Memorial Action of His Redemption, which He promised when He said that He was the Bread of Life.[6]

Summarizing Christ's words of institution of the Eucharist, and emphasizing that He said, "This IS My Body" – not this represents or symbolizes My Body, Bishop Sheen continues:

His coming death on the following afternoon was set before them in a symbolic or unbloody manner. On the Cross, He would die by the separation of His Blood from His Body. Hence He did not consecrate the bread and wine together, but separately, to show forth the manner of His death by the separation of His Body and His Blood. In this act, Our Lord was what He would be on the Cross the next day: both Priest and Victim. In the Old Testament and among pagans, the victim, such as a goat or a sheep, was apart from the priest who offered it. In this Eucharistic action and on the Cross, He, the Priest, offered Himself; therefore He was also the Victim.[7]

One question Bishop Sheen treated in several of his writings on the Eucharist, was why the Lord had used the accidents of bread and wine in the Eucharistic Sacrifice. The first reason was that no two expressions of nature better symbolize unity; bread is made from a multiplicity of grains of wheat, and wine from a similar multiplicity of grapes. Both substances represent the oneness of the many who believe in Christ. Second, there is a certain suffering which must be undergone by both substances before they emerge in their final shape; bread must undergo "the rigors of winter, be ground beneath the Calvary of a mill, and then subjected to purging fire"; at the same time, grapes must be subjected to "the Gethsemane of a wine press and have their life crushed from them."[8] They both symbolize the sufferings and death of Christ, and remind us that we must all die to our lower natures in order to rise to a higher one. Finally, there are no two substances that have more traditionally nourished man's physical life; when we eat bread and drink wine in the natural order, they become assimilated into our organism; when Christ took their accidents and changed them into His substance, however, He insured our assimilation into Him.

"Only a Divine Wisdom could have conceived such a memorial," Sheen wrote, because if man had devised it, the recollection of Our Lord's death would be relegated to some sort of historical event one would read about in a textbook. Men would have regarded it as "a drama presented once in history like the assassination of Lincoln," in which case it would have been "only an incident, not a Redemption." Or, Sheen feared, it would have been an incident played out only once, and to be forever meditated on merely by reading and rereading the accounts left of it by the writers Matthew, Mark, Luke and John. The Bishop noted Plato recorded the death of Socrates, a life for all to dwell on with appreciation; left to mere mortals, the death of Christ would have been no different. Instead, Christ wanted "the great drama of Calvary to be played not once, but for every age of His own choosing."[9]

A very important consideration, for Catholic apologetics, and for the searching non-Catholic mind, was the answer to the question how Calvary and the Mass are the same.

> What happened there on the Cross that day is happening now in the Mass. On the Cross the Savior was alone; in the Mass He is with us. Our Lord is now in heaven at the right hand of the Father, making intercession for us. He therefore can never suffer again in His human nature. How then can the Mass be the reenactment of Calvary? How can Christ renew the Cross? He cannot suffer again in His own human nature which is in heaven enjoying beatitude, but He

can suffer again in our human natures. He cannot renew Calvary in His physical body, but he can renew it in His Mystical Body – the Church. The sacrifice of the Cross can be reenacted provided we give Him our body and our blood, and give it to Him so completely that as His own, He can offer Himself anew to His heavenly Father for the redemption of His Mystical Body, the Church.[10]

It really is Christ going out into the world and gathering to Himself the human natures of all who will give them; those natures consist of sufferings, trials, difficulties, anxieties, sorrows, fears, as well as all that is positive in life – our joys, happiness, successes, spiritual conquests, and the like. Nothing of a person's human nature is isolated, nothing can be held back. All of them are united, massed together, one could almost say harvested, and joined with the ongoing sacrifice of Christ on the Cross. Sheen accented the idea that when we assist at Mass, we are not doing so as isolated individuals, but as "living parts of a great spiritual order," into which the Infinitude of God penetrates our finiteness. The particular beauty of this is that the mystery perdures – it takes place somewhere in the world at every moment in time. We are capable of uniting ourselves with this mystery at any hour of day or night, wherever Mass is being offered. In an era before people watched Bishop Sheen on television, they listened to him on radio; for the people of that time, he offered this thought:

An imperfect illustration may be drawn from the radio. The air is filled with symphonies and speech. We do not put the words or music there; but, if we choose, we may establish contact with them by tuning in our radio. And so it is with the Mass. It is a singular, unique divine act with which we come in contact each time it is represented and re-enacted.[11]

Even more concrete was his next example:

> When the die of a medal or coin is struck, the medal
> is the material, visible representation of a spiritual idea
> existing in the mind of the artist. Countless reproduc-
> tions may be made from that original as each new piece
> of metal is brought in contact with it, and impressed by
> it. Despite the multiplicity of coins made, the pattern
> is always the same. In like manner in the Mass, the
> Pattern – Christ's sacrifice on Calvary – is renewed on
> our altars as each human being is brought in contact
> with it at the moment of consecration; but the sacrifice
> is one and the same despite the multiplicity of Masses.
> The Mass then is the communication of the Sacrifice
> of Calvary under the species of bread and wine.[12]

The reason we may make contact with this Divine Mystery
at any time and in any place, is because Christ saw to its continu-
ance through the ages, until the end of time, through the human
instrumentality of His ordained priests. "A great American patriot
once said he regretted he had only one life to give for his country,"
Sheen once stated in a lecture. "He meant his love was greater
than his sacrifice, his life could be given only once in time and
could not be repeated."[13] Once the Bishop had fully developed
how the giving of the life of Christ could be, and was repeated,
he sought to develop this sacrifice as a "drama in three acts." It
is significant that years after the Second Vatican Council's Con-
stitution on the Liturgy, *Sacrosanctum Concilium*, rethought the
Church's understanding of the Mass for the contemporary world,
especially in terms of the Liturgy of the Word and the Liturgy of
the Eucharist, Bishop Sheen continued to present his theme of the
three act drama, the Offertory, Consecration and Communion.
So much did these three actions signify our redemption, the good
Bishop did not want them forgotten.

At the Offertory, Our Lord is figuratively looking out from heaven on all who are uniting themselves with His sacrifice, and He is telling them that He can no longer offer Himself in the physical manner He did on Calvary. He can, however, die in them, and they in Him, and He asks them to make this offering of themselves. "We are standing on the paten that the priest is offering," Sheen wrote. "We are in the chalice, participants; we are co-offerers to Christ, through Him to the heavenly Father."[14] What happens to us as a result of that self-offering is explained in the Consecration, the moment when the accidents of bread and wine are transubstantiated into Christ's Body and Blood. The primary meaning of the words of Consecration are very clear; "mystically divided by the separate consecration of the bread and wine, Our Lord renews the sacrifice of Calvary."[15] It is the secondary meaning of those words that Bishop Sheen greatly stressed: we are saying to Christ, "This is my body, this is my blood". In other words, we are sacrificing ourselves, giving the totality of our being to Him, and asking Him to do with us whatever He may will. The Bishop often included in his writings a prayer that anyone could personalize at this pinnacle of the Mass.

> I care not if the species remain, or that, like the bread and wine I seem to all earthly eyes the same as before. My station in life, my routine duties, my work, my family – all these are but the species of my life which may remain unchanged; but the substance of my life, my soul, my mind, my will, my heart – transubstantiate them, transform them wholly into Thy service, so that through me all may know how sweet is the love of Christ. Amen.[16]

Finally, Communion. Bishop Sheen compared all who participated in the Mass to lambs being led on to Jerusalem at the Offertory, and offered in sacrifice at the Consecration. In Holy

Communion, our reception of the Lord's Body and Blood, we experience a recuperation, a discovery that we did not lose a thing, but have gained enormously. By dying to our lower natures in the Consecration, we "get back our souls ennobled and enriched." We find that our death was no more permanent in the Consecration than the death of Christ was permanent at Calvary. We surrender our humanity, only to receive a share in His Divine life; we give up the seemingly important aspects of time, and exchange them for His eternity; we turn away from sin and are given a measure of His grace; we surrender our self will so that we might look at life through His eyes and with His mind. Sheen could not have described the exchange more beautifully, and in doing so, he reminded his readers that there is a triple incorporation that takes place whenever we receive Holy Communion: we are incorporated into Christ's life, His death, and His Mystical Body. While the incorporation into His life is more obvious, that of His death is less thought of. Saint Paul reminded the early Christians of Corinth that whenever they received the Lord in the Eucharist, they proclaimed His death until His return; he meant in order to share the Christ life, we who are victims of concupiscence, must continually put to death that which is sinful in us. It is a lifelong process, the condition for inheriting life. Communion into Christ's Mystical Body was even less understood by many, and Sheen sought to explain it:

> When we receive Communion we are being united with every member of the Church throughout the world. Your body is made up of millions and millions of cells. These cells are nourished by blood plasma, or lymph. It courses through all the gates and alleys of your body to nourish and repair. It knocks at the door of each individual cell. What blood plasma does to your human body is a faint echo of what Our Lord does for His Mystical Body. The Mystical Body is made up

of persons, not cells. Instead of human nourishment, there is the Divine life of the Eucharist, as the divine lymph, or all of the cells or persons of the Mystical Body of Christ.... The Communion rail is the most democratic institution in the face of all history. We are communing at the rail not only with every member of the Church, but with the joys of the Church wherever they are in any part of the world and with the sorrows of the Church.[17]

The Offertory, Consecration and Communion, then, were the three great acts of Redemption. They may be viewed together as a sacrament and a sacrifice. Bishop Sheen used the analogy of a human meal; in order for one to partake of certain foods (which could be likened to a sacrament), there had to be a sacrifice. Animals must be killed, vegetables plucked from their roots, cooked, and the like. "Running through all nature," wrote the Bishop, "is the law that we live by what we slay." In this vein, he rhetorically asked who of us can claim innocence of the Crucifixion? When we gaze upon Christ on the Cross we realize we live by what we have slain. He who died as the "great captain of our salvation"

...was both Priest and Victim. He differed from every other sacrifice in the world since He offered Himself; He gave His own life, He was the offerer and the offered. This was still a vicarious sacrifice. He took our place as if the sins were His own. What is the Mass? It is the commemoration of the death and application of that sacrifice of the Cross to us.[18]

Sheen reminded his vast audiences through the years that the Mass was not some sort of souvenir; rather it was an action, one that is played out in time and eternity. It is in time because humans see it taking place before their eyes; it is in eternity because its merits contain all the particulars of the Lord's life, and are continually applied to our redemption. Not only is the mystery enacted in time, but it is savored in time through the abiding presence of Jesus Christ in the Most Blessed Sacrament. "Think of what our churches would be if we did not have a red tabernacle light telling us Our Blessed Lord was there?" Sheen wrote. "They would just be meeting houses or prayer halls. We would almost feel we were standing alongside of the empty tomb on Easter morn and an angel was saying 'He is not here'."[19] It is because of that presence we can look up to heaven and heaven down upon us, and that presence remains because of the ordained priesthood Christ established. "When I offer the holy Mass," the Bishop noted, "I am merely the instrument of Christ. He offers the Mass. He's the offered."[20] Such describes the priest's ontological and sacramental configuration to Christ the High Priest, inextricably interwoven with the Eucharist.

As he wrote much on the Eucharist, so Fulton Sheen concentrated a great deal on the priesthood, especially for the last decade of his life, when much of his work consisted of going from diocese to diocese in the United States to preach priests' retreats. In addition, this work brought him to several foreign countries. He believed he had received an inspiration to perform this work in the years following his resignation as Bishop of Rochester, New York. A spirit of worldliness, want of prayer, overemphasis on the social order were all elements that affected the priesthood of the late 1960's and 1970's, and Sheen resolved, through his preaching, to try to give priests a renewed and deeper appreciation of the great vocation to which they had been called. Decades earlier, in a convert instruction class in Washington, D.C., he had expressed very well the nature of that vocation:

> In the Divine, supernatural order, in the Mystical Body of Christ, there must be government, and the sacrament of government of the Mystical Body is Holy Orders. In this government there are degrees, order, hierarchy. The

division of these orders is principally three: diaconate, priesthood, and episcopacy... We are dispensers of the great mysteries of God. Why did He not choose angels? Because sympathy, compassion, and suffering together with One who has already suffered would be lacking to an angel. Is not this the whole principle of the Incarnation? Did not Our Lord come down, take upon Himself our human nature, become a kind of a slave?[21]

Every priest is a mediator between God and man, bringing God to man and man to God, "continuing the priesthood of Our Blessed Lord." The Bishop described all priests as "sons of Adam, sons of sinners of a fallen nature," underscoring the humanity of each weak individual called by God. Every priest was a sort of Simon/Peter; Simon, in the sense of a sinful nature, one which is always capable of denying the Lord; Peter, in that one's poor human body, mind and will are used by Christ to forgive sins, to renew the sacrifice of Calvary, and to achieve the Divine purpose of salvation.

When reading the Mass, we take Our Blessed Lord upon the Cross out of that locale to Paris, Cairo, Tokyo, and the world's poorest mission. Our work is to extend Christ's forgiveness of our sins and to give His blessing with our poor hands. We mount the altar wearing our chasuble. Hanging on that chasuble are the millions of souls in the world who know not Christ Himself. When we take a host into our hand, we have to see our fingers heralded from slavery in the salt mine of Siberia. We have to see our feet as bleeding feet of refugees tramping westward toward barbed wire beyond which lies freedom. When looking at the candles, we think of the glow of the blast furnaces tended by gaunt men who have had their lives devastated by those who deny economic justice.[22]

Modernity had brought countless changes from the time Sheen penned those thoughts until his senior years as an Archbishop. By then, many were claiming they wanted to be priests to work in the inner city, or to assist in gaining political rights for the deprived. On the contrary, Sheen observed, a priestly vocation never begins with the thought of what the individual wants to do. If my thoughts are purely sociological, why enter a theological seminary? If all one wants is identification with the world, he likely forgets the admonition of Him who reminded all His followers He had taken them out of the world. A true vocation, as Bishop Sheen saw it, had three steps; first, a sense of the unworldly, the holy, the transcendent. Then follows one's own unworthiness, in which "the heart is shocked at the simultaneous vision of the clay and the treasure".[23] This second step is essential, since God can do nothing with one who thinks he is worthy. Finally comes the response, the genuine desire, after ordination, to be sent, to be totally at the disposal of Christ and His Church. Bishop Sheen never ceased to compare the vocation and life of the priest as one configured to Christ who was both Priest and Victim. No priest should expect anything less than to be an offerer and the offered.

> The dialectic between the sublimity of the vocation on the one hand, and the frailty of the human clay on the other, is a kind of crucifixion. Each priest is crucified on the vertical beam of the God-given vocation and on the horizontal beam of the simple longing of the flesh and a world that so often beckons to conformity with it. The best vintage of wine is sometimes served in tin cups. To be a priest is to be called to be the happiest of men, and yet to be daily committed to the greatest of all wars – the one waged within.[24]

There were several types of priest-victims to be emulated and applied to one's life, but Sheen especially stressed three. First, the models found in the lives of Abel, the just son, Abraham, our father in faith, and Melchizedek the high priest. Abel had offered a blood sacrifice, upon which God looked with favor. He serves as a model of all priests who were martyred for the faith, and for those who have suffered under anti-God persecutions throughout the world at all periods of history. Then, Abraham, and the sacrifice God asked of him in the person of his young son Isaac, representative of "those who endure all the stages of martyrdom under tyranny yet are denied the formal crown of the shedding of their blood." This would include all who are brainwashed, tortured, spend their lives in concentration or labor camps, and the like. Finally, there was the sacramental offering of Melchizedek, the archetype for all those priests who live by the mystery they enact sacramentally in the Mass, uniting themselves to the Lord's passion in all its aspects.

Secondly, there was victimhood symbolized by the breaking of the bread, that portion of the Mass prior to the *Agnus Dei,* when the priest takes a fraction from the large, consecrated host, breaks it, and commingles it with the Precious Blood in the chalice. As Christ's Body was broken on the Cross, so the priest is forcefully reminded that, only if he is "broken," can he effectively bring the light of Christ to a world overcome with the darkness of Satan. Finally, how apply the concept of victimhood to vocations? Sheen remarked that many seminarians announce they are studying for the priesthood, but does the thought ever occur to them they are really preparing to be priest-victims?

> Could it be that one reason for the lack of vocations is our failure to stress sacrifice? The young have a sense of victimhood that we underestimate. They want a mission, a challenge! When we follow the type of advertising appeal used by Madison Avenue to sell toothpaste, when we use commercial techniques in our vocational literature, do not the hearts of the

young spurn our distance from the Cross? Do we not recruit fruits of propaganda rather than fruits worthy of penance? Could it not also be that our failure to be victims discourages those who enter the seminary from persevering and becoming priests?[25]

To prove his point, Bishop Sheen cited a survey taken in the 1970's among three hundred young men, asking what sort of priest inspired them the most. The first category was foreign missionaries, then those who worked with the poor, and finally those who were involved with workers. A heroic, sacrificial priest seemed to be the mold, and while that could be highly admirable, one must never be so taken up with this world that he forgets the world to come. So much depended on the holiness of the individual priest to keep him focused, to keep his priorities in order, to keep him renewed in the priestly commitment he made on his ordination day. With this in mind, the priest's individual spiritual life became a central focus of Sheen's retreats.

The holier a priest is, the holier the people will be. This is applicable not only in the parish, but the diocese, the nation, the world. The holiness of the priest will affect the faithful in such a way that their growth in spirituality will, in turn, have a similar effect on the priest. In Our Lord's Priestly Prayer, He left all priests a model by first consecrating Himself, so they may be consecrated, and in the individual petitions of that Prayer (John 17:11-24), the Son's supplications to His Father are meant to give His priests perseverance, joy, deliverance from evil, holiness through sacrifices, unity, the constant companionship of the Lord, and the enjoyment of His glory in heaven.[26] Such must be taken seriously by every priest, for,

> What we are, the Church is; the world is. The world and all it contains is a highway on which the bride, the Church, goes to meet the Bridegroom for the heavenly

nuptials. Politics do not ultimately determine war and peace. What is decisive is the spiritual state of the Church living in and leavening the world. To read the Old Testament is to recognize that history is the hand of the Lord, Who blesses and punishes nations according to their deserts. What we do to sanctify ourselves sanctifies the world. When the shepherd is lazy, the sheep are hungry; when he sleeps, they are lost; when he is corrupt, they grow sick; when he is unfaithful, they lose their judgment. If the shepherd is not willing to be a victim for his sheep, the wolves come and devour them.[27]

For this reason, it is absolutely essential the priest be a holy man. There were two principal ways to insure this: personal prayer, and the Eucharistic sacrifice. By personal prayer, as we have seen, Sheen meant one daily, continuous Holy Hour in the presence of the Blessed Sacrament. It must be daily, and continuous – the only interruption would be the Mass, and if that were the case, one could make thirty minutes before Mass, and thirty minutes after. The priest was largely on his own as to the structure of the hour; he could read his breviary, say his rosary, meditate on the eternal truths in the most effective way for him. One thing was certain, however: no priest could keep coming into the Lord's Eucharistic presence day after day without a copy of the Scriptures, or some good commentary on Scripture. This was, in the end, superior to the many devotional practices with which Sheen confessed great familiarity.

The second vital lifeline for priestly spirituality was the Mass itself, and the spirit with which the celebrant entered into it. Much was riding on this, for his own salvation, and for those he was sent to serve.

The Sacrifice of the Mass that we offer is performed without any satisfaction to the senses. But when does it become sensible, tangible, lived out, concrete? When the morning sacrifice is made visible in the living sacrifice of the priest's body. Any excesses that dull the spirit and make it unfit to serve Him, any absorbing care about outward things that checks the growth of Christ in us – such things erect a barrier against the power of the priest to sanctify others *ex opere operantis*. There is no such thing as a "six o'clock Mass." The Mass is continuous, a "living sacrifice." What is mystically presented in the morning Mass must be bodily presented throughout the day. Having died with Christ on the altar, we continue the death in instructing converts, in burying the dead, in consoling the sick, in almsgiving for the Propagation of the Faith.[28]

One of the most significant effects of priestly spirituality is the practice of mental and physical transference so necessary to the life of the priest. Christ both physically and mentally transferred our sins to Himself in His agony and crucifixion, and the priest's configuration to Him demands nothing less. A practical example of mental transference is a priest's willingness to visit the mentally ill, rather than excusing himself on the grounds that the patient would not recognize him. "The inability to be loved back," wrote Sheen, "is never a reason for not loving." Physical transference, so epitomized by the painting which depicts a young boy carrying on his shoulders a younger boy, with the caption, "He's not heavy, he's my brother," was one aspect of the priesthood Bishop Sheen learned amid difficulty. As National Director of the Society for the Propagation of the Faith, he once visited a leper colony in Africa where he brought with him.

Five hundred silver crucifixes, each about two inches in height. I intended to give one to each victim of leprosy. The first one had his left arm eaten away to the elbow by the disease. Around the stump of the arm he carried a rosary. He reached out his right hand for the crucifix – the hand was the most foul, loathsome sight. I held the crucifix above it, and dropped it into that volcano of leprosy. Immediately it was swallowed up, as if by hands voracious for devouring. All of a sudden, there were five hundred and one lepers. And I was the five hundred and first, for I had taken the symbol of Christ's identification with man, and refused to identify myself with one who was a thousand times better on the inside, where it counts, than I was. Then realizing what a traitor I was to Christ's identification with lepers, I dug my fingers into his hand, pulled out the crucifix, pressed it again to his hand, and so on for the other five hundred lepers.[29]

The point Sheen was trying to make is that all priests, of any time in history, but especially the late 20th century, had to experience a conversion first to Christ, then to the Church, and finally to the world. That was the only order that would work, and any reversal of these would land in disaster. From this, the Bishop continued to five "missions" of the apostle in the world, words of advice, as it were, to all priests. Social action must always be apologetic, meaning that good works must always be done with the intention of leading others to God; the mere physical presence of a priest or religious in the secular order is not necessarily a "witnessing," such must be accompanied by a solid spirituality; the priest-victim plays the role of prophet, not public critic of the political or social order; the priest-victim's role in the world is to be seen as "agonistic," that is, he is in combat, and his battlefield, the world, is the "theatre of redemption"; finally, the priest-victim actively engaged in the world acts as a leaven for society, but also views the Church holistically, not critical of others engaged in other pursuits, because the Church is a Body, in which all work together for the good of the entire organism.[30]

Lastly, what of Fulton Sheen's own priesthood? He remarked often that never in his life did he remember a time when he did not wish to become a priest. His maternal grandparents had come from Croghan, a small village near the town of Boyle, in County Roscommon, Ireland; his paternal grandfather had likewise been born in Ireland, and his paternal grandmother in Indiana. These pioneers had all eventually settled the Illinois prairie. Sheen's parents, who gave him the gift of life, in El Paso, Illinois in 1895, eventually moved to Peoria where young Fulton served as an altar boy at Saint Mary's Cathedral, attended Catholic schools, and eventually entered the seminary. The memory of his ordination on September 20, 1919 in the very Cathedral where he had once served Mass, evoked this thought:

> The stirrings which the Holy Spirit put in my soul in the early days were now fulfilled or were they? I was now a priest. Yes. But is not that just half the story? I never asked myself that question the day I was ordained. In due time, and not in an easy way, I was to learn that a priest is also a victim.[31]

He knew the sufferings common to all priests, and, as he admitted, the more popular and well known the priest is, the greater the trials, temptations, and crosses he encounters. The one biblical story that epitomized the life of every priest was that of Jacob and his vision of the ladder. As a young man, he had the vision of glory and divine protection; but as the years progressed much changed. He began to wrestle with someone, not knowing who, but eventually he discovered it was God, the "Heavenly Wrestler," and in the end Jacob ceased fighting and begged supplication. So with every priest, he begins in "peace and pleasantness," and ultimately, hard, cold reality sets in, either by way of the cross given him from above, or through his own failures here below.

Celibacy, too, as related to every priestly life can be a great burden or a tremendous joy. It is not something a priest gives to the Church in the gift of his being; rather it is a gift he receives from his configuration to Christ, and with the gift, the sufficient grace to keep it. Celibacy is hardest when we fall out of love with Christ; once a priest begins to put celibacy "in the context of the Church and discuss its history, its sociology, its psychology and the like there is a groaning under the burden." Related to Christ, it becomes a matter of love. It is a redirecting of one's passions; if they burn for creatures, the priest will eventually move in that direction; if for Christ, the celibate life is not only bearable, but a sheer joy.

On the occasion of his first apostolic visit to the United States in October of 1979, Pope John Paul II greeted Archbishop Sheen in the sanctuary of Saint Patrick's Cathedral in New York City, just two months before the Archbishop would be buried beneath the same sanctuary. The Holy Father told him he had written and spoken well of the Lord Jesus, and was a loyal son of the Church. Despite such praise from the Vicar of Christ, Sheen's one regret, stated as sincerely as it is given us to be sincere, was that he had not loved the Lord sufficiently. It is difficult to be objective summing up one's own life. This was Sheen's attempt:

> Looking back on about sixty years of my priest-victimhood, how would I answer this question before God: "Do you think you have lived the life of a good priest?" When I compare myself with missionaries who have become dry martyrs by leaving their own country and family to teach other peoples, when I think of the sufferings of my brother priests in Eastern Europe, when I look at the saintly faces of some of my brother priests in monasteries and in the missions, and the beautiful resignation of priests in hospitals who suffer from cancer, and when I just even look at my many brothers in Christ whom I admire so much, I say: "No, I have not

been the kind of priest I should have been or would liked to have been." But I know there is more to the answer of this question. When you put a painting in candlelight to examine it, the imperfections do not appear; when you put it under the full glare of the sun, then you see how badly chosen are the colors and ill defined the lines. So it is when we measure ourselves by God, we fall infinitely short; and when we compare ourselves with many who have given us inspiration, we feel a deep sense of unworthiness. But behind it all, and despite all of this, there is the tremendous consciousness of the mercy of God. He did not call angels to be priests; He called men.[32]

In His infinite wisdom, God called Fulton J. Sheen to be His priest, and for the spiritual legacy of this priest, the Church can never thank its Lord sufficiently enough.

BIBLIOGRAPHY

Leahy, Maurice (ed.) *Conversions.* New York: Benziger Brothers, 1933.

Reeves, Thomas C. *America's Bishop: The Life and Times of Fulton J. Sheen.* San Francisco, CA: Encounter Books, 2001.

Riley, Kathleen L., Ph.D. *Fulton J. Sheen: An American Catholic Response to the Twentieth Century.* New York: ST PAULS/ Alba House, 2004.

Sheen, Fulton J. *Armor of God, The.* New York: P.J. Kenedy and Sons, 1943.

_____. *Characters of the Passion.* Liguori, MO: Liguori/Triumph, 1998.

_____. *Choice, The: The Sacred and the Profane Life.* New York: Dell Publishing Co., 1963.

_____. *Christmas Inspirations.* New York: Maco Publishing, Inc., 1966.

_____. *Church, Communism and Democracy, The.* New York: Dell Publishing Co., 1964.

_____. *Coalition in Support of Ecclesia Dei.* Glenview, IL, 1996.

_____. *Communism and the Conscience of the West.* Indianapolis and New York: Bobbs-Merrill Co., 1948.

_____. *Communism Answers Questions of a Communist.* New York: The Paulist Press, 1937.

_____. *Crisis in History.* St. Paul, MN: The Catechetical Guild and Educational Society, 1952.

_____. *Cross and the Beatitudes, The.* (Originally published in New York by P.J. Kenedy and Sons, 1937.) Liguori, MO: Liguori Publishers, 2000.

_____. *Cross and the Crisis, The.* (Originally published in Milwaukee, WI by The Bruce Publishing Co., 1938.) Manchester, NH: Ayer Company Pubs. Inc., 1977.

_____. *Declaration of Dependence, A*. Milwaukee, WI: The Bruce Publishing Co., 1941.

_____. *Divine Romance, The*. (Originally published in 1930, this book was re-issued in New York by Garden City Books in 1950.) New York: ST PAULS/Alba House, 1982 and 1997.

_____. *Divine Verdict, The*. New York: P.J. Kenedy and Sons, 1943.

_____. *Enrollment of the World, The*. New York: The Paulist Press, 1928.

_____. *Eternal Galilean, The*. (Originally published in New York by Garden City Books in 1934 and re-issued in 1950.) New York: ST PAULS/Alba House, 1997.

_____. *Footprints In A Darkened Forest*. New York: Meredith Press, 1967.

_____. *For God and Country*. New York: P.J. Kenedy and Sons, 1941.

_____. *Freedom Under God*. Milwaukee, WI: The Bruce Publishing Co., 1940.

_____. *Friends*. Washington: The National Council of Catholic Men, 1944.

_____. *Go to Heaven*. (Originally published in 1949.) New York: The Dell Publishing Co., 1960.

_____. *God and Intelligence in Modern Philosophy*. (Originally published in London and New York by Longmans, Green and Co. in 1925.) Garden City, NY: Doubleday and Co., 1958.

_____. *God and War*. New York: P.J. Kenedy and Sons, 1942.

_____. *God Love You*. Garden City, NY: Doubleday and Co., 1955.

_____. *Guide to Contentment*. (Originally published in New York by Maco Publishing Company, 1967). New York: ST PAULS/Alba House, 1997.

_____. *Ideological Fallacies of Communism*. Washington, DC: U.S. Government Pamphlet 197608, published with Dr. S. Andhil Fineberg and Dr. Daniel A. Poling for the House Committee on Un-American Activities, 1957.

_____. *Lenten and Easter Inspirations.* New York: Maco Publishing Company, Inc., 1967.

_____. *Liberty, Equality and Fraternity.* New York: The Macmillan Co., 1938.

_____. *Life Is Worth Living.* San Francisco, CA: Ignatius Press, 1999.

_____. *Life Is Worth Living – First Series.* New York: McGraw-Hill Book Co., 1953.

_____. *Life Is Worth Living – Second Series.* New York: McGraw-Hill Book Co., 1954.

_____. *Life Is Worth Living – Third Series.* (See *Thinking Life Through.*)

_____. *Life Is Worth Living – Fourth Series.* New York: McGraw-Hill Book Co., 1956.

_____. *Life Is Worth Living – Fifth Series.* New York: McGraw-Hill Book Co., 1957.

_____. *Life of All Living, The.* (Originally published in 1929.) New York: Garden City Books, 1951.

_____. *Life of Christ.* New York: Popular Library, 1960. An abridged edition was published in New York by Doubleday/Image books in 1977.

_____. *Lift Up Your Heart.* (Originally published in 1950. Garden City Books of New York then published an edition in 1952.) Liguori, MO: Liguori/Triumph, 1997.

_____. *Love One Another.* (Originally published in 1944.) New York: Garden City Books, 1953.

_____. *Malcolm Muggeridge: A Conversation.* New York: The National Committee of Catholic Laymen, Inc., Undated.

_____. *Misery of Soul and the Mother of Mercy.* Washington: National Council of Catholic Men, 1951.

_____. *Missions and the World Crisis.* Milwaukee, WI: The Bruce Publishing Co., 1963.

_____. *Moods and Truths.* New York: Appleton-Century Company, 1932.

_____. *Moral Universe, The: A Preface to Christian Living.* (Originally published in Milwaukee, WI by The Bruce

Publishing Co. in 1936.) Manchester, NH: Ayer Co., Pubs., Inc. 1977.

_____. *Mystical Body of Christ, The.* New York: Sheed and Ward, 1935.

_____. *Old Errors and New Labels.* (Originally published in New York by The Century Co., 1931.) New York: ST PAULS/Alba House, 2007.

_____. *Peace of Soul.* (Originally published in New York in 1949 and in Garden City, NY by Doubleday and Co. in 1954). Liguori, MO: Liguori/Triumph, 1996.

_____. *Philosophies at War.* New York: Charles Scribner's Sons, 1944.

_____. *Philosophy of Religion.* New York: Appleton-Century-Crofts, Inc., 1948.

_____. *Philosophy of Science.* Milwaukee, WI: The Bruce Publishing Co., 1934.

_____. *Power of Love, The.* New York: Maco Magazine Corporation, 1964.

_____. *Preface to Religion.* New York: P.J. Kenedy and Sons, 1946.

_____. *Priest Is Not His Own, The.* (Originally published in London, England by The Catholic Book Club in 1963.) San Francisco, CA: Ignatius Press, 2005.

_____. *Prodigal World, The.* (Originally published by the National Council of Catholic Men in collaboration with Our Sunday Visitor, 1935-36.) New York: ST PAULS/Alba House, 2003.

_____. *Rainbow of Sorrow, The.* New York: P.J. Kenedy and Sons, 1938.

_____. *Religion without God.* (Originally published in 1928.) New York: Garden City Books, 1954.

_____. *Rock Plunged into Eternity, The.* (Originally published by the National Council of Catholic Men in collaboration with Our Sunday Visitor, 1950.) New York: ST PAULS/Alba House, 2003.

_____. *Saint Thérèse: A Treasured Love Story.* Irving, TX: Basilica Press, 2007.

_____. *Science Psychiatry and Religion*. New York: Dell Publishing Co., 1962.

_____. *Seven Capital Sins*. (Originally published by the National Council of Catholic Men in collaboration with Our Sunday Visitor, 1939.) New York: ST PAULS/Alba House, 2001.

_____. *Seven Last Words, The*. (Originally published by the National Council of Catholic Men in collaboration with Our Sunday Visitor, 1940. It was later published in New York by Garden City Books in 1952.) New York: ST PAULS/Alba House, 1982 and 1986.

_____. *Seven Pillars of Peace*. New York: Charles Scribner's Sons, 1944.

_____. *Seven Virtues, The*. New York: P.J. Kenedy and Sons, 1940.

_____. *That Tremendous Love*. New York: Harper and Row, 1967.

_____. *These Are the Sacraments* (Photographed by Yousuf Karsh and described by Sheen.) New York: Hawthorn Books, Inc. 1962.

_____. *Thinking Life Through*. (Third in the series of *Life Is Worth Living* published in New York by McGraw-Hill Book Co. in 1955). It has been re-issued under the title *Simple Truths: Thinking Life Through with Fulton J. Sheen*. Liguori, MO: Liguori/Triumph, 1998.

_____. *This is Rome* (A pilgrimage conducted by Sheen, photographed by Yousuf Karsh and described by H.V. Morton.) New York: Hawthorn Books, Inc. 1960.

_____. *This is the Holy Land*. (A pilgrimage conducted by Sheen, photographed by Yousuf Karsh.) New York: Hawthorn Books, Inc., 1961.

_____. *This is the Mass*. (Celebrated by Sheen, described by Henri Daniel-Rops and photographed by Yousuf Karsh.) New York: Hawthorn Books, Inc., 1959.

_____. *Those Mysterious Priests*. (Originally published in Garden City, NY by Doubleday and Company, Inc., 1974.) New York: ST PAULS/Alba House, 2005.

_____. *Thoughts for Daily Living*. (Originally published in New York by Garden City Books, 1956.) New York: ST PAULS/Alba House, 2008.

_____. *Three to Get Married*. (Originally published in New York by Appleton-Century-Crofts, Inc., 1951.) Princeton, NJ: Scepter Pubs., 1997.

_____. *Treasure in Clay: The Autobiography of Fulton J. Sheen*. (Originally published in New York by Garden City Books, 1980.) San Francisco, CA: Ignatius Press, 1993.

_____. *Victory Over Vice*. New York: P.J. Kenedy and Sons, 1939.

_____. *Walk with God*. (Originally published in New York by Maco Magazine Corporation, 1965.) New York: ST PAULS/Alba House, 2008.

_____. *Way to Happiness*. (Originally published in New York by Garden City Books in 1954.) New York: ST PAULS/Alba House, 1997.

_____. *Way to Inner Peace*. (Originally published in New York by Garden City Books in 1955.) New York: ST PAULS/Alba House, 1994.

_____. *Way of the Cross, The*. New York: Appleton-Century-Crofts, Inc., 1932.

_____. *Whence Comes War?* New York: Sheed and Ward, 1940.

_____. *The World's First Love*. (Originally published in New York by McGraw-Hill Book Co. in 1952 and later in Garden City, NY by Doubleday and Company, Inc., 1956.) San Francisco, CA: Ignatius Press, 1996.

_____. *You*. (Originally published by the National Council of Catholic Men in collaboration with Our Sunday Visitor, 1944-45.) New York: ST PAULS/Alba House, 2003.

_____. *Your Life Is Worth Living*. Schnecksville, PA: Saint Andrew's Press, 2001.

Wilson, Alfred, C.P. *Pardon and Peace*. London: Sheed and Ward, 1947.

FOOTNOTES

Chapter 1: The Life of All Living

[1] Fulton J. Sheen (ed.). *That Tremendous Love* (New York: Harper and Row, 1967), 16.

[2] *Your Life Is Worth Living: The Christian Philosophy of Life* (Schnecksville, PA: St. Andrews Press, 2001), 13.

[3] *The Life of All Living* (New York: The Century Company, 1929), 7.

[4] Ibid.

[5] Ibid., 13-14.

[6] Ibid., 26.

[7] Ibid., 28.

[8] Ibid., 29-30.

[9] Ibid., 33-34.

[10] Ibid., 34.

[11] Ibid., 40.

[12] Ibid., 79-80.

[13] Ibid., 107.

[14] *Old Errors and New Labels* (New York: The Century Company, 1931; New York: ST PAULS/Alba House, 2007), 21.

[15] Ibid., 24-25.

[16] *Your Life Is Worth Living*, op. cit., 14.

[17] *Footprints in a Darkened Forest* (New York: Meredith Press, 1967), 217-218.

[18] Ibid., 238.

[19] *Way to Inner Peace* (New York: Garden City Books, 1955; New York: ST PAULS/Alba House, 1995), 204-205.

[20] *Lift Up Your Heart* (New York: Garden City Books, 1950, 1952; Liguori, MO: Liguori/Triumph, 1997), 62-63.

[21] *Guide to Contentment* (New York: Maco Publishing Company, 1967), 126.

[22] *The Life of All Living*, op. cit., 122.

[23] Ibid., 132.

[24] Ibid., 133.

Chapter 2: The Incarnate Son of God

[1] *Life Is Worth Living* (San Francisco: Ignatius Press, 1999), 33.

[2] Ibid., 48.

[3] Ibid.

[4] *Your Life Is Worth Living: A Christian Philosophy of Life* (Schnecksville, PA: St. Andrews Press, 2001), 31.

[5] *Life of Christ* (New York: Popular Library, 1960; originally published in 1958. An abridged edition was later published in New York by Doubleday/Image Books, 1977), 13.

[6] *Christmas Inspirations* (New York: Maco Publishing, Inc., 1966), 14.

[7] *Your Life Is Worth Living*, op. cit., 42.

[8] Ibid., 44.

[9] *Lenten and Easter Inspirations* (New York: Maco Publishing, Inc., 1967), 47.

[10] *Your Life Is Worth Living*, op. cit., 69.

[11] Ibid., 68.

[12] *Malcolm Muggeridge: A Conversation* (New York: The National Committee of Catholic Laymen, Inc., undated), 21.

[13] *Your Life Is Worth Living*, op. cit., 105.

[14] Ibid., 106.

[15] Ibid., 108.

[16] Ibid., 115.

[17] Ibid., 118.

[18] *Life of Christ*, op. cit.,525.

[19] Ibid., 526.

[20] *Malcolm Muggeridge, A Conversation*, op. cit., 28.

Chapter 3: Temptation and Sin

[1] *Walk With God* (Originally published in New York by Maco Magazine Corporation, 1965; New York: ST PAULS/Alba House, 2008), 42.

[2] Ibid., 43.

[3] *Your Life Is Worth Living: A Christian Philosophy of Life* (Schnecksville, PA: St. Andrews Press, 2001), 154.

[4] Ibid., 165-166.

[5] *Life Is Worth Living* (San Francisco: Ignatius Press, 1999), 68

[6] Ibid., 69-70.

[7] Ibid., 71.

[8] Ibid.

[9] *Peace of Soul* (Originally published in 1949. Garden City, NY: Doubleday and Co., 1954; Liguori, MO: Liguori/Triumph, 1996), 33.

[10] Ibid., 42.

[11] *The Prodigal World* (Originally published by the National Council of Catholic Men in collaboration with Our Sunday Visitor, 1935-36; New York: ST PAULS/Alba House, 2003), 63.

[12] *Peace of Soul*, op. cit., 46.

13 Cited in ibid., 45.

14 *The Prodigal World*, op. cit., 61-62.

15 *The Eternal Galilean* (Originally published in New York by D. Appleton-Century Company, Inc., 1934; Garden City Books of New York re-issued it in 1950; New York: ST PAULS/Alba House, 1997), 172.

16 *Life of Christ* (Originally published in 1958; New York: Popular Library, 1960; an abridged edition was published in New York by Doubleday/Image Books, 1977), 55.

17 Ibid., 58.

18 Ibid., 60.

19 *Your Life Is Worth Living*, op. cit., 102.

20 *Lift Up Your Heart* (Liguori, Missouri: Liguori/Triumph, 1997), 83-93.

21 *St. Thérèse: A Treasured Love Story* (Irving, Texas: Basilica Press, 2007), 120.

22 Ibid.

23 *Your Life Is Worth Living*, op. cit., 168.

24 Ibid., 174.

25 *Guide to Contentment* (New York: Maco Publishing Co., 1967; New York: ST PAULS/Alba House, 1997), 64

26 *Walk With God*, op. cit., 56.

27 Ibid., 57.

28 *Lift Up Your Heart*, op. cit., 260.

Chapter 4: Conversion

1   *Treasure in Clay: The Autobiography of Fulton J. Sheen* (Garden City: Doubleday & Company, Inc., 1980; San Francisco, CA: Ignatius Press, 1993), 252-253.

2   *Walk With God* (Originally published in New York by Maco Magazine Corporation, 1965; New York: ST PAULS/Alba House, 2008), 71.

3   *Lift Up Your Heart* (New York: Garden City Books, 1950, 1952; Liguori, MO: Liguori/Triumph, 1997), 3.

4   Ibid., 7-8.

5   Ibid., 14.

6   Ibid., 28-29.

7   Ibid., 33.

8   *Peace of Soul* (Originally published in 1949. Garden City, NY: Doubleday and Co., 1954; Liguori, MO: Liguori/Triumph, 1996), 224.

9   *Guide to Contentment* (New York: Simon and Schuster, 1967; New York: ST PAULS/Alba House, 1997), 43 -44.

10 *Peace of Soul*, op. cit., 234.

11 Ibid., 230-231.

12 Ibid., 233.

13 Maurice Leahy (ed.), *Conversions* (New York: Benziger Bros., 1933), 68-69.

[14] *Peace of Soul*, op. cit., 234.

[15] Ibid., 241.

[16] Ibid., 236.

[17] Ibid., 246.

[18] Ibid., 249.

[19] Ibid., 253.

[20] Ibid., 256.

[21] Ibid., 260.

[22] *Life Is Worth Living* (San Francisco: Ignatius Press, 1999), 216.

[23] *Peace of Soul*, op. cit., 268.

[24] *The Prodigal World* (New York: Alba House, 2003), 4.

[25] Ibid., 48.

Chapter 5: Confession

[1] *Friends* (Washington, DC: The National Council of Catholic Men, 1944), 36.

[2] *Your Life Is Worth Living: A Christian Philosophy of Life* (Schnecksville, PA: St. Andrews Press, 2001), 217.

[3] Ibid., 218.

[4] Ibid., 221.

[5] Ibid., 224.

[6] *Moods and Truths* (New York: The Century Company, 1932), 323.

[7] *Friends*, op. cit., 27.

[8] *Life of Christ* (New York: Popular Library, 1960), 213.

[9] *Moods and Truths*, op. cit., 323.

[10] Ibid., 327.

[11] *Treasure in Clay* (New York: Doubleday & Company, Inc., 1980), 277.

[12] Ibid.

[13] Ibid., 118.

[14] *Moods and Truths*, op. cit., 330-331.

[15] *Peace of Soul*, op. cit., 88.

[16] Ibid., 101.

[17] Ibid., 104.

[18] Ibid., 109.

[19] Ibid., 110.

[20] Ibid., 110-111.

[21] *Life of Christ*, op. cit., 514–515.

[22] Alfred Wilson, C.P., *Pardon and Peace* (London: Sheed and Ward, 1947), 209.

[23] *Peace of Soul*, op. cit., 203.

[24] Cited in ibid., 195.

25 *Lift Up Your Heart* (Liguori, MO: Liguori/Triumph, 1997), 257.

26 *Your Life Is Worth Living*, op. cit., 235.

Chapter 6: The Mystery of Suffering

1 *Way to Inner Peace* (New York: Garden City Books, 1955; New York: ST PAULS/Alba House, 1995), 204-205.

2 *Life Is Worth Living* (San Francisco: Ignatius Press, 1999), 132.

3 Ibid., 133.

4 Ibid., 136.

5 *The Divine Romance* (Originally published in New York by The Century Company in 1930, this work was re-issued by Garden City Books in 1950 and is presently available from New York: ST PAULS/Alba House, 1982 and 1997), 84.

6 *St. Thérèse: A Treasured Love Story* (Irving, Texas: Basilica Press, 2007), 88.

7 Ibid., 90.

8 Ibid., 89.

9 *The Eternal Galilean* (Originally published in New York by D. Appleton-Century-Crofts, Inc., 1934; Garden City Books of New York re-issued it in 1950; New York: ST PAULS/Alba House, 1997), 245.

10 Ibid., 251.

11 *Life of Christ* (New York: Popular Library, 1960), 466.

12 *The World's First Love* (Garden City, NY: Image Books, 1956; San Francisco, CA: Ignatius Press, 1996), 188.

13 Ibid., 206.

14 Ibid., 206-207.

15 Ibid., 210.

16 Ibid..

17 Ibid., 212.

18 Ibid., 214.

19 Ibid., 217.

20 Ibid., 220.

21 Ibid., 227.

22 *The Eternal Galilean*, op. cit., 254-255.

23 *Life Is Worth Living*, op. cit., 133.

24 *Those Mysterious Priests* (Garden City, NY: Doubleday & Company, Inc., 1974; New York: ST PAULS/Alba House, 2005), 101-102.

25 Ibid., 101.

26 Ibid., 107.

27 Ibid., 110.

28 *Three to Get Married* (New York: Appleton-Century-Crofts, Inc., 1951; Princeton, NJ: Scepter Publishers, Inc., 1997, 2007), 200-201.

[29] Ibid., 202-203.
[30] Cited in ibid., 211.
[31] *Treasure in Clay* (New York: Doubleday & Company, Inc., 1980), 312-314.
[32] Cited in *St. Thérèse: A Treasured Love Story*, op. cit., 82.

Chapter 7: Prayer

[1] *The Divine Romance* (New York: The Century Co., 1930), 451.
[2] *Peace of Soul* (Originally published in 1949. Garden City, NY: Doubleday and Co., 1954; Liguori, MO: Liguori/Triumph, 1996), 51.
[3] Cited in ibid., 52.
[4] Ibid., 53.
[5] Ibid., 56.
[6] Ibid., 65.
[7] *Walk With God* (Originally published in New York by Maco Magazine Corporation, 1965; New York: ST PAULS/Alba House, 2008), 58.
[8] Ibid., 59.
[9] *Guide to Contentment* (New York: Simon and Schuster, 1967; New York: ST PAULS/Alba House, 1997), 75.
[10] Ibid.
[11] *Your Life Is Worth Living: A Christian Philosophy of Life* (Schnecksville, PA: St. Andrews Press, 2001), 336.
[12] *Life of Christ* (New York: Popular Library, 1960), 371.
[13] *Your Life Is Worth Living*, op. cit., 336.
[14] Ibid., 337.
[15] Ibid.
[16] *Lift Up Your Heart* (New York: Garden City Books, 1950, 1952; Liguori, MO: Liguori/Triumph, 1997), 185.
[17] *Your Life Is Worth Living*, op. cit., 338.
[18] *The Priest Is Not His Own* (Originally published in London by the Catholic Book Club, 1963; San Francisco, CA: Ignatius Press, 2005), 247.
[19] *Lift Up Your Heart*, op. cit., 188.
[20] Ibid., 188-189.
[21] Ibid., 199-200.
[22] Ibid., 203-204.
[23] *Those Mysterious Priests* (Garden City, NY: Doubleday & Company, Inc., 1974; New York: ST PAULS/Alba House, 2005), 169.
[18] *The Priest Is Not His Own*, op. cit., 230-237.
[25] *Malcolm Muggeridge: A Conversation* (New York: The National Committee of Catholic Laymen, Inc., undated), 35.
[26] *Treasure in Clay* (Garden City, New York: Doubleday & Company, Inc., 1980), 197.
[27] *Those Mysterious Priests*, op. cit., 185.

Footnotes

Chapter 8: The Blessed Virgin Mary

[1] *Treasure in Clay* (Garden City, New York: Doubleday & Company, Inc., 1980), 318.

[2] *Your Life Is Worth Living: A Christian Philosophy of Life* (Schnecksville, PA: St. Andrews Press, 2001), 328.

[3] *Three to Get Married* (Originally published in New York by Appleton-Century-Crofts, Inc., 1951; Princeton, NJ: Scepter Publishers, Inc., 1997), 163.

[4] Ibid., 164.

[5] Ibid., 165.

[6] Ibid., 166.

[7] Ibid., 169.

[8] *The Eternal Galilean* (Originally published in New York by D. Appleton-Century-Crofts, Inc., 1934; Garden City Books of New York re-issued it in 1950; New York: ST PAULS/Alba House, 1997), 261.

[9] *Your Life Is Worth Living*, op. cit., 330-331.

[10] *The Eternal Galilean*, op. cit., 271.

[11] *Life of Christ* (New York: Popular Library, 1958), 440.

[12] *Three to Get Married*, op. cit., 162-163.

[13] *The World's First Love* (Originally published in New York by McGraw-Hill Book Co., 1952; San Francisco, CA: Ignatius Press, 1996), 113.

[14] Ibid., 120.

[15] *Life Is Worth Living* (San Francisco: Ignatius Press, 1999), 205.

[16] Ibid., 206.

[17] *Those Mysterious Priests* (Garden City, NY: Doubleday & Company, Inc., 1974; New York: ST PAULS/Alba House, 2005), 317-318.

[18] Ibid., 320.

[19] Ibid., 321.

[20] *Three To Get Married*, op. cit., 170.

[21] *The Priest Is Not His Own* (Originally published in London by the Catholic Book Club, 1963; San Francisco, CA: Ignatius Press, 2005), 271-273.

[22] *The World's First Love*, op. cit., 178-179.

[23] Ibid., 184.

[24] *Misery of Soul and the Mother of Mercy* (Washington, DC: National Council of Catholic Men, 1951), 4.

[25] *Treasure in Clay,* op. cit., 188.

[26] *Misery of Soul and the Mother of Mercy*, op. cit., 5.

Chapter 9: Marriage

[1] *Old Errors And New Labels* (New York: The Century Company, 1931; New York: ST PAULS/Alba House, 2007), 109.

[2] *Peace of Soul* (Liguori, Missouri: Liguori/Triumph, 1996), 146.

3 Ibid., 147.

4 Ibid., 151.

5 Ibid., 158.

6 Ibid., 159.

7 *Your Life Is Worth Living: A Christian Philosophy of Life* (Schnecksville, PA: St. Andrews Press, 2001), 262.

8 Ibid., 263.

9 *Three to Get Married* (New York: Scepter Publishers, Inc., 1996), 60.

10 *Guide to Contentment* (New York: Maco Publishing Co., 1967; New York: ST PAULS/Alba House, 1997), 16.

11 *Three to Get Married* (Originally published in New York by Appleton-Century-Crofts, Inc., 1951; Princeton, NJ: Scepter Publishers, Inc., 1997), 43.

12 Ibid.

13 *Your Life Is Worth Living*, op. cit., 251.

14 Ibid., 252.

15 Ibid., 254-255.

16 Ibid., 254.

17 Ibid., 253.

18 *Guide to Contentment*, op. cit., 17.

19 Ibid., 20.

20 *Walk With God* (Originally published in New York by Maco Magazine Corporation, 1965; New York: ST PAULS/Alba House, 2008), 29.

21 *Way to Inner Peace* (New York: Alba House, 2005), 168.

22 *Life Is Worth Living* (San Francisco: Ignatius Press, 1999), 75.

23 Ibid., 76.

24 Ibid., 77.

25 Ibid., 78-79.

26 *Your Life Is Worth Living*, op. cit., 280.

27 *The World's First Love* (Originally published in New York by McGraw-Hill Book Co., 1952; San Francisco, CA: Ignatius Press, 1996), 126.

28 *Your Life Is Worth Living*, op. cit., 280.

29 Ibid., 267-268.

30 *Life Is Worth Living*, op. cit., 170.

31 Ibid., 173.

Chapter 10: Eucharist and Priesthood

1 *Your Life Is Worth Living: A Christian Philosophy Of Life* (Schnecksville, PA: St. Andrews Press, 2001), 197-198.

2 Ibid., 200.

3 Ibid., 201.

4 *Life of Christ* (New York: Popular Library, 1958), 146.

Footnotes

5   Ibid., 149.
6   Ibid., 320-321.
7   Ibid., 321.
8   Ibid., 322.
9   Ibid., 324.
10 *Calvary and the Mass: A Missal Companion* (Glenview, IL: Coalition in Support of Ecclesia Dei, 1996), 41.
11 Ibid., 42.
12 Ibid., 42-43.
13 *Your Life Is Worth Living*, op. cit., 203.
14 Ibid., 204.
15 Ibid., 205.
16 *Calvary and the Mass*, op. cit., 46.
17 *Your Life Is Worth Living*, op. cit., 207-208.
18 Ibid., 210.
19 Ibid., 208.
20 Ibid., 213.
21 Ibid., 244-245.
22 Ibid., 248.
23 *Treasure in Clay* (Garden City, New York: Doubleday & Company, Inc., 1980), 33.
24 Ibid., 34.
25 *The Priest Is Not His Own* (San Francisco: Ignatius Press, 2005), 25.
26 Ibid., 75.
27 Ibid., 78.
28 Ibid., 267.
29 *Those Mysterious Priests* (Garden City, NY: Doubleday & Company, Inc., 1974; New York: ST PAULS/Alba House, 2005), 67.
30 Ibid., 152-256.
31 *Treasure in Clay*, op. cit., 22.
32 Ibid., 38-39.

ST PAULS

This book was produced by ST PAULS/Alba House, the Society of St. Paul, an international religious congregation of priests and brothers dedicated to serving the Church through the communications media.

For information regarding this and associated ministries of the Pauline Family of Congregations, write to the Vocation Director, Society of St. Paul, 2187 Victory Blvd., Staten Island, New York 10314-6603. Phone (718) 982-5709; or E-mail: vocation@stpauls.us or check our internet site, www.vocationoffice.org